Curing Chronic Inflation

Arthur M. Okun and George L. Perry, Editors

Curing Chronic Inflation

THE BROOKINGS INSTITUTION
Washington, D.C.

Library of Congress Cataloging in Publication Data:

Main entry under title:

Curing chronic inflation.

   Papers and discussion from a special conference of
the Brookings Panel on Economic Activity held in the
Spring of 1978.
     1. Wage-price policy—United States—Congresses.
2. Inflation (Finance)—United States—Congresses.
I. Okun, Arthur M.   II. Perry, George L., 1934–
III. Brookings Panel on Economic Activity.
HC110.W24C87   332.4'1'0973   78-11859

ISBN 0-8157-6474-X
ISBN 0-8157-6473-1 pbk.

9 8 7 6 5 4 3 2 1

THE BROOKINGS INSTITUTION is an independent organization devoted to nonpartisan research, education, and publication in economics, government, foreign policy, and the social sciences generally. Its principal purposes are to aid in the development of sound public policies and to promote public understanding of issues of national importance.

The Institution was founded on December 8, 1927, to merge the activities of the Institute for Government Research, founded in 1916, the Institute of Economics, founded in 1922, and the Robert Brookings Graduate School of Economics and Government, founded in 1924.

The Board of Trustees is responsible for the general administration of the Institution, while the immediate direction of the policies, program, and staff is vested in the President, assisted by an advisory committee of the officers and staff. The bylaws of the Institution state: "It is the function of the Trustees to make possible the conduct of scientific research, and publication, under the most favorable conditions, and to safeguard the independence of the research staff in the pursuit of their studies and in the publication of the results of such studies. It is not a part of their function to determine, control, or influence the conduct of particular investigations or the conclusions reached."

The President bears final responsibility for the decision to publish a manuscript as a Brookings book. In reaching his judgment on the competence, accuracy, and objectivity of each study, the President is advised by the director of the appropriate research program and weighs the views of a panel of expert outside readers who report to him in confidence on the quality of the work. Publication of a work signifies that it is deemed a competent treatment worthy of public consideration but does not imply endorsement of conclusions or recommendations.

The Institution maintains its position of neutrality on issues of public policy in order to safeguard the intellectual freedom of the staff. Hence interpretations or conclusions in Brookings publications should be understood to be solely those of the authors and should not be attributed to the Institution, to its trustees, officers, or other staff members, or to the organizations that support its research.

Foreword

THE INFLATION that began when the American economy became over-heated during the Vietnam War has become a chronic malady in the 1970s. Public opinion polls show that citizens regard inflation as the most severe economic problem they face, and stopping inflation has become an increasingly important item on the nation's political agenda. But the cost in lost jobs and output of eliminating inflation by sole reliance on the conventional economic medicine of fiscal and monetary restraint appears to be high. The present inflation has continued despite two recessions in this decade, and there is little reason to expect that still another recession would restore price stability.

In the spring of 1978, the Brookings Institution held a special conference of the Brookings Panel on Economic Activity to evaluate innovative proposals for slowing inflation. The conference, under the chairmenship of Arthur M. Okun and George L. Perry, brought together economists representing a broad spectrum of views to assess the efficacy of various anti-inflation proposals. This volume presents the research papers prepared for that conference, together with the participants' critical discussion of them. The papers were published in June 1978 as a special issue of the journal, *Brookings Papers on Economic Activity,* and are presented here in book form in order to make them available to a broader audience.

The volume begins with an extensive introduction by the editors. The first major paper analyzes the macroeconomics of the current wage-price spiral and the macroeconomic implications of alternative policies for slowing it. Subsequent papers analyze tax-based incomes policies—a range of proposals for tax inducements to moderate wage and price increases—and the anti-inflationary potential of reforming particular federal policies that directly affect prices or costs. These papers evaluate the economic effects of alternative forms of tax-based incomes policies, the administrative feasibility of tax-based incomes policies, and the extent to which labor and business are likely to support or resist innovative anti-inflation policies. In a symposium that concludes the book, three distinguished economists present their overview of the current inflation and of alternative proposals for slowing it. Taken as a whole, the volume provides a critical and detailed examination of the various proposals. The conference yielded no consensus on what policies should be adopted, but it did produce the basis for a more informed discussion of alternatives.

Jesse M. Abraham, Nancy J. Delaney, Evelyn P. Fisher, and Jeffrey A. Goldstein assisted the editors in preparing the papers for publication by verifying data and sources. Robert Z. Lawrence helped edit the discussions. Karen Brown was responsible for editing the manuscript; Avima Ruder prepared the index.

To finance the special conference on which this book is based, the Brookings Institution was aided by grants from the Ford Foundation and from the Department of Labor, in addition to the continuing financial support of the Brookings Panel by the National Science Foundation. The views expressed in this volume are solely those of the contributors and should not be ascribed to the trustees, officers, or staff members of the Brookings Institution or to the foundations that contributed financially to the project.

BRUCE K. MAC LAURY
President

August 1978
Washington, D.C.

Conference Participants

Gardner Ackley *University of Michigan*
Martin Neil Baily *Yale University*
William C. Brainard *Yale University*
William H. Branson *Princeton University*
Robert W. Crandall *Brookings Institution*
Larry L. Dildine *Department of the Treasury*
Rudiger Dornbusch *Massachusetts Institute of Technology*
James S. Duesenberry *Harvard University*
David I. Fand *Wayne State University*
Martin Feldstein *National Bureau of Economic Research and Harvard University*
William J. Fellner *American Enterprise Institute*
Benjamin M. Friedman *Harvard University*
Stephen M. Goldfeld *Princeton University*
Robert J. Gordon *Northwestern University*
Edward M. Gramlich *University of Michigan*
Alan S. Greenspan *Townsend-Greenspan and Company, Inc.*
Robert E. Hall *Center for Advanced Study in the Behavioral Sciences*
Walter W. Heller *University of Minnesota*
Charles C. Holt *University of Texas at Austin*
E. Phillips Howrey *University of Michigan*
Saul H. Hymans *University of Michigan*
F. Thomas Juster *University of Michigan*
John H. Kareken *University of Minnesota*

Robert Z. Lawrence *Brookings Institution*
Abba P. Lerner *Florida State University*
Michael C. Lovell *Wesleyan University*
Bruce K. MacLaury *Brookings Institution*
Frederic S. Mishkin *University of Chicago*
Daniel J. B. Mitchell *Brookings Institution*
Franco Modigliani *Massachusetts Institute of Technology*
Donald Nichols *Department of Labor*
Arthur M. Okun *Brookings Institution*
Arnold H. Packer *Department of Labor*
Joseph A. Pechman *Brookings Institution*
George L. Perry *Brookings Institution*
Edmund S. Phelps *Columbia University*
William Poole *Brown University*
Albert Rees *Princeton University*
Laurence S. Seidman *University of Pennsylvania*
John B. Shoven *Stanford University*
Richard E. Slitor *Economic Consultant*
Emil M. Sunley *Department of the Treasury*
James Tobin *Yale University*
Lloyd Ulman *University of California, Berkeley*
George M. von Furstenberg *Indiana University*
Michael L. Wachter *University of Pennsylvania*
Henry C. Wallich *Federal Reserve Board*
Sidney Weintraub *University of Pennsylvania*

Contents

Tables

ARTHUR M. OKUN
Brookings Institution

GEORGE L. PERRY
Brookings Institution

Editors' Summary

THE INTEREST in new ways to curb inflation has grown along with the evidence that inflation has become deeply entrenched in the U.S. economic system. The inflationary era of recent history has now lasted more than a dozen years. It began in the mid-sixties when the economy became overheated by a combination of civilian and military demands, which were allowed to burgeon under a government policy that sought both guns and butter during the Vietnam War. That initial episode confirmed the widespread view of economists that inflation was basically a phenomenon of excess demand, reflected in overly tight labor and product markets. At that time, the overall unemployment rate was below 4 percent, and operating rates in industry were unusually high. Modern macroeconomic analysis thus accounted neatly for the major features of that experience.

A serious puzzle first emerged when the inflation rate scarcely budged in the recession of 1970. Indeed, price and wage inflation were both more rapid in 1970–71 than in any year of the 1960s. Against the background of that disappointment, the Nixon administration turned to wage and price controls in August 1971. Inflation slowed markedly in 1972, even

1

as output and employment rose dramatically. Both real wages and profits scored excellent gains. Despite these apparent successes, the controls program encountered growing opposition from business, labor, and the public, particularly when uncontrolled prices for food and fuel soared. It became an administrative monstrosity that required constant adjustment to minimize its distortive effects on economic decisions. And so it was phased out in stages during 1973 and 1974.

During the 1973–74 period, inflation surged as the result of several forces: the emergence of pockets of excess demand in the U.S. economy, the added pressures of a worldwide boom, some pent-up adjustments of prices and wages that followed decontrol and, most notably, the explosion of food prices in 1973 and of fuel prices in 1974. In that interval, prices accelerated much more than did wages. The relative moderation of wages helped to limit the severity of the inflation, but it also contributed to a squeeze on the real purchasing power of American families. The Federal Reserve kept firm control on the growth of money in the face of soaring prices and interest rates, and the federal budget was brought close to balance. As a result of the squeeze on real incomes and the restraint of monetary and fiscal policies, the economy fell into the most severe recession since the 1930s.

Double-digit inflation ended during the recession, but the rate remained near 6 percent as recovery began in the spring of 1975. During the three years of economic expansion since then, the inflation rate has varied over short intervals, reflecting erratic short-term movements in prices of food and energy; but it has averaged close to 6 percent throughout the period. The persistence of rapid inflation in a slack economy was a new experience: it was the first time in U.S. history that a severe recession had failed to stop inflation. And the inflation during the recovery has not resulted from special factors or particular sectors getting out of line. Prices of food, fuel, and imports have not significantly outrun the general inflation rate. Among major expenditure categories, only health care costs have risen exceptionally fast, and even so have played a small role in the overall price rise. The inflation of 1975–78 has been widespread and general; and in the aggregate it has been balanced as between wages and prices. Compensation per man-hour has advanced at a rate that exceeds consumer price inflation by more than 2 percentage points. Thus, real pay—compensation per man-hour, adjusted for inflation—has grown approximately in parallel with the trend growth of productivity.

There are no villains (or heroes) in the recent inflationary experience. All private groups have sought, understandably, to protect their own interests by passing on the higher costs of the items they buy in the form of higher prices of the goods or services they sell. With labor costs per man-hour rising faster than 8 percent, business is merely a transmission belt for inflation when its prices rise by 6 percent. And with consumer prices rising by 6 percent, workers who obtain pay increases above 8 percent are merely maintaining the long-run pattern of real gains that they have come to expect. But these normal patterns of behavior create a price-wage spiral and maintain the momentum of inflation.

Meanwhile, the American people express their antipathy toward inflation, pointing to it in opinion surveys as the nation's most serious economic problem. Because the problem has not been solved by prolonged treatment with the traditional remedy of weak demand, a number of economists have designed new and different remedies. A variety of proposals for innovative policies to slow inflation were subjected to a systematic professional evaluation in the papers and proceedings published in this volume.

In the first of the papers, George L. Perry discusses the workings of the aggregate economy that produce the observed inertia in inflation. He begins by describing a broad—although not unanimous—consensus among economists on how output, employment, and inflation respond to variations in total demand. According to his "mainline model," most prices (except those of raw materials and agricultural goods) are closely related to direct costs of production, of which by far the largest are labor costs. Thus, prices respond reliably and rather fully to wages; but the markup of prices over wages responds only slightly and sluggishly to overall demand conditions—whether the economy is in boom, recession, or somewhere in between. Wages do respond to the state of demand—tightness or slack in labor markets—but they also respond to "what has been happening to wages, prices, profit margins, or all three, or to what is expected to happen to them." These other factors in wage setting contribute significantly to the inertia of wage and price inflation.

Looking across industries, Perry finds that, while low-wage industries actually had slightly higher rates of pay increase during the 1960s than did high-wage industries, the reverse has held by a decisive margin in the 1970s. In general, the pay in low-wage industries is more responsive to unemployment, slowing down to a greater extent in the event of a recession, while pay in high-wage industries is more responsive to price inflation, translating a larger proportion of price increases into subsequent wage increases. A similar comparison emerges between union and nonunion wages. During the 1960s, the rate of increase of union wages, if anything, lagged a bit behind that of nonunion wages. But in the 1970s, union wages were held down much less by higher unemployment and were more successful in keeping up with the price increases of the period. On the whole, union members obtained real wage increases during the 1970s that matched their average rate of gain during the previous decade, whereas this was not true for nonunion workers as a group.

Analyzing statistically the track record of overall increases in wages during the past generation, Perry finds decisive evidence that the ongoing inflation rate strongly affects current rates of wage increase. Starting from a position of little or no inflation like that in the early 1960s, the economy can experience a large rise in demand and a reduction in unemployment with only a gradual rise in current inflation. Conversely, when the economy has been experiencing high rates of inflation, the current rate of wage inflation tends to stay high even though demand may be weak and labor markets slack. And that evidence of inflationary inertia is clear whether the past inflation record is summarized by past rates of wage inflation, past increases of the consumer price index (the market basket that workers buy), or past increases in the nonfarm private deflator (the market basket of goods that workers make and that are sold by their employers). Because certain types of policy would try to slow inflation by initially grabbing a handle on one or another of these variables, Perry is interested in disentangling their effects. But he points out that it is extremely difficult to do so. When he has to rely on any one of them, he finds past wage inflation seems to serve best in explaining current wage inflation. But in fact, he believes that all three probably play some significant role.

This aggregate statistical analysis also demonstrates that higher unemployment slows wage inflation to some extent. In this respect, Perry shows that the 1970s have not been a new departure for the U.S. economy. When he weights unemployment by demographic groups, a procedure that he first advanced in *Brookings Papers on Economic Activity* (3:1970), he finds that the effect of an extra percentage point of unemployment in slowing wages is little different when it is measured from evidence that includes the 1970s than when the estimates are confined to the 1954–69 period. Wages have not suddenly become much more immune to the effect of unemployment. On the other hand, there is evidence that wages today tend to perpetuate a given rate of inflation to a somewhat greater extent than they did in the past, perhaps responding more to that ongoing inflation simply because it has been higher and has remained high for so long.

Thus, the mainline model and its empirical findings reaffirm that there is a slow-growth, high-unemployment cure for inflation, but that it is an extremely expensive one. According to Perry's findings, any unemployment rate above 5½ percent, if maintained long enough, would lower wage inflation and, other things being equal, would translate into a reduction in price inflation. But using one of Perry's successful equations as an example, an extra percentage point of unemployment would lower the inflation rate by only about 0.3 percentage point after one year and by 0.7 percentage point if maintained for three years. That extra point of unemployment would cost over a million jobs and some $60 billion of real production each year. As Perry states, "the anti-inflation gains from restraining aggregate demand are disappointingly small." Furthermore, even modest upward shocks in inflation, such as those from rising food or import prices, could offset the small gains from demand restraint. Given the circumstances, it is understandable that the stabilization strategy pursued since 1975 has not succeeded in finding an output path that would gradually reduce unemployment and simultaneously slow inflation.

According to Perry's mainline model, budget deficits and monetary growth influence the inflation rate to the extent that they add to, or subtract from, the total demand for goods and services in the economy and thereby affect unemployment rates in the labor market and operating rates in industry. Thus, reduced fiscal stimulus and slower money growth could have prevented inflation from emerging in the late 1960s or from accelerating as much as it did after the 1972–73 boom period. They also could have produced more of a slowdown in inflation in the recent recovery, but only by prolonging the recession or making the recovery even slower in terms of the rebound of output and employment from recession lows. If that course had been pursued, the lost output and employment associated with a reduction in the inflation rate would have been enormous.

The paper discusses alternative views on the role of fiscal and monetary policy that lie outside the mainline model. Perry cites the widespread belief of noneconomists that government deficits are a major factor in any inflationary process and shows that the view is decisively rejected by a simple statistical test. He also cites empirical evidence which suggests that the growth of money has no "additional, special role" in causing inflation beyond its role as a determinant of total spending in the economy. Perry further discusses the importance some attribute to unemployment compensation and the minimum wage as sources of the stagflation of the 1970s. He notes that both of these social programs have potential effects on unemployment and wage inflation, but stresses that neither program has changed in the past decade in a way that could have affected overall economic performance significantly.

A view developed by William Fellner is taken more seriously by Perry as the principal challenge to his own pessimistic assessment of reliance on monetary and fiscal restraint to slow inflation. In Fellner's formulation, the inertia in inflation today reflects a self-fulfilling prophecy that inflation will continue at a high rate in the future; and this prophecy, in turn, is predicated on the belief that policymakers will not take the steps required to halt inflation. A sufficiently clear display by the government of its intention to restrain demand as much and as long as is necessary to stop inflation would thus have greater effects on inflation for any given costs in employment than the record of the past would suggest. According to this view, the estimates obtained from past experience reflect responses in the marketplace made by a public that had reason to doubt the government's determination to carry through an anti-inflationary strategy of demand restraint.

Perry recites his reasons for differing with Fellner's basic conclusion. He notes that the severity of the 1973–75 recession and the policies that permitted it to take place did not change inflation inertia. He also believes that much of the inertia is backward-looking rather than forward-looking, and so is not susceptible to even convincing demonstrations that demand will be restrained in the future. His own empirical evidence shows that wage developments are better explained in terms of the recent past history of prices and wages than on any assumption that people are predicting the future course of wages and prices in a way that differs from the past. And he notes that provisions such as escalator clauses are used precisely to avoid the need for predicting the future. Finally, to the extent that some decisions are forward-looking or expectational, he questions how much inflation expectations would be affected by even a convincing commitment to slow demand. Because actual unemployment has only a modest effect on inflation, he finds little reason to believe that people would drastically lower their estimates of future inflation because they expected unemployment to rise as a result of greater monetary and fiscal restraint. Thus, Perry sees room for only a "small gain" in the trade-off from Fellner's policy of announcing a maintained application of demand restraint and adhering to it.

In conclusion, Perry shows how the new anti-inflation proposals fit into his view of the wage-price spiral. Measures aimed at directly reducing costs and prices provide disinflationary "shocks," which have opposite effects from inflationary shocks of the past such as the increase in oil prices by the world cartel. To the extent that prices affect wages, such disinflationary shocks filter through into subsequent rounds of the price-wage spiral. A tax-based incomes policy breaks into the wage-price spiral both by influencing the decision process and by affecting the actual course of wages and prices to which the process responds. Such measures may find a shortcut to price stability without reducing real incomes. Because they permit the pursuit of the desired growth path of real output and employment with a lower inflation rate and hence with a lower growth of nominal GNP, they complement fiscal and monetary policies that are geared to slow inflation.

Laurence S. Seidman's paper analyzes the probable effects of tax-based incomes policies (TIPs). Seidman sees an analogy between private decisions to pollute and private decisions to make inflationary wage and price increases. In either case whether an action is taken to dirty the air or raise the price level, the decisionmaker may harm the welfare of others. Yet, the free market does not provide an adequate incentive for him to take these external consequences of his behavior into account. A tax on either polluting or inflating can correct this distortion by charging the decisionmaker for those social costs. Acting in his own self-interest, once the tax is in effect, he will make decisions that reflect the social interest in either clean air or a stable price level. In either case, the same shift toward socially desirable behavior can be accomplished by a subsidy— a negative tax—as by a penalty tax. This possibility of utilizing a carrot as well as a stick approach is reflected in the design of alternative tax-based incomes policies.

The ultimate objective of TIP is to bring down and control the rate of increase of *prices*. But Seidman argues that this objective is best accomplished indirectly by a TIP that curbs excessive increases in *wages*. While tax provisions could conceivably be devised that would directly penalize excessive price increases (or reward price moderation), he believes that they would be administratively unmanageable because of the enormous difficulties of measuring the average price behavior of individual firms. As evidence that controlling wage inflation will achieve a comparable control over price inflation, he cites the close historical relationship between the two—an understandable result because two-thirds of the price of output directly reflects labor costs.

A tax-based incomes policy to influence wages could, in principle, take a number of different forms. The tax provisions could apply directly either to employers or to employees; they could offer rewards or impose penalties. While Seidman believes that several variants of these programs could have desirable economic effects, he favors most strongly the imposition of a penalty tax on employers who grant excessive wage increases. That is the basic approach of the original Wallich-Weintraub proposal for TIP, and it is the focal point of Seidman's analysis and his policy recommendations.

The paper analyzes in detail how the penalty would operate to slow wage increases and thus price inflation. Suppose, for example, that a target of 6 percent were set for overall pay increases in the initial year of a TIP program. A firm might be confronted with a basic corporate income tax rate of 48 percent on its profits if its average pay increase came within the 6 percent target, but it might face a higher tax rate on profits if pay rose more than 6 percent. An illustrative schedule might call for a 52 percent tax rate if the firm's pay increase was 7 percent, 56 percent if pay rose 8 percent, and so forth. As a result, the firm would find that large pay increases had become more costly. In a nonunion situation, the firm would grant a lower wage increase to protect its profitability or market value; in a collective bargaining situation, the firm would resist demands for large wage increases more vigorously.

Unlike Henry Wallich and Sidney Weintraub, Seidman would reward firms whose pay increases were far below target, say, with a 44 percent tax rate for 5 percent pay increases, and so forth. He argues that a continuous system with penalties *and* rewards is most efficient because it encourages all firms to alter their behavior. But he would design the system so that most firms would be motivated by the threat of penalty rather than the promise of reward.

On the basis of evidence that high after-tax profits have stimulated large wage increases in the past, Seidman argues that the threat of reduced profits posed by the tax penalty is particularly effective in discouraging excessive pay increases—more effective than a reward to employees for moderation, along the lines proposed by Arthur Okun, would be. He also discusses another reason for preferring a tax imposed on employers to a tax reward for employees. Under the latter plan, the employee is granted a tax reduction if his firm's average increase in pay stays within the target during the year. Seidman believes that any tax reward would have to be large relative to the wage restraint it accomplished because workers would expect their wage level in subsequent years to be reduced by their current wage restraint.

The paper discusses in detail one common criticism of penalty plans, namely, the danger that firms will still award large pay increases and then pass through the higher taxes to their customers, thus actually exacerbating price inflation. He concedes that he cannot rule out such perverse results in all cases, but argues that they would be rare and transitory, especially if the tax penalty were set sufficiently high.

In Seidman's view, the penalty TIP on employers differs sharply from wage or price controls. It would not prohibit any wage increase and would thus permit employers and workers to respond to market forces and adjust relative wages when an industry faced a labor shortage. Of course, the smooth working of market forces requires that the tax penalty be kept in reasonable bounds. An extremely high penalty, which would have the greatest effect in discouraging inflationary wage increases, might seriously impede desirable adjustments in relative wages. Seidman believes that an effective compromise could be reached in setting the penalty to yield both an effective TIP and an efficient responsiveness of relative wages.

Like all proponents of TIP, Seidman believes that the program could remedy the current stagflation problem. But he espouses it mainly as a permanent device to permit the economy to operate at a lower unemployment rate without encountering intensified inflation. He attributes the inflationary tendencies of our economy to a variety of public and private institutions. Because of unemployment insurance, food stamps, and other government transfer programs, the unemployed can survive without leaping at job offers that provide mere subsistence wages. Through collective bargaining and personnel relationships between firms and workers, ethical norms develop that rule out the unbridled competition through which wages would be bid down during a slump. The paper stresses that these institutions are highly desirable. But they do have adverse side effects on the inflation-unemployment dilemma, which could be neutralized by long-term reliance on TIP.

Seidman also shows that the benefits of TIP are consistent with the view that, in the long run, inflation depends on the growth of the money supply. With or without TIP, the rate of money growth would have to be lowered markedly to bring about an ultimate noninflationary path; the contribution of TIP is to permit such a course of monetary restraint without recessions or persistently high unemployment.

In Seidman's view, TIP should not affect the distribution of income between wages and profits. He emphasizes that in the past, speedups and slowdowns in wages have been fully reflected in prices. Nonetheless, he believes that workers are entitled to reassurance and therefore proposes to supplement TIP with two special provisions. One would activate a special tax cut for workers if wage inflation slowed more than price inflation. The other would trigger a special added tax on corporate profits if they rose unusually relative to wages.

An alternative proposal, which has interesting similarities and contrasts to Seidman's recommendations, is advanced by Abba P. Lerner in a shorter report that follows the major articles. Lerner's plan would create incentives for employers to slow wage inflation through the issuance of wage permits (instead of the imposition of a penalty tax). Employers would be given permits that authorize them to increase pay by some target percentage of their payroll in the previous year. But they could grant larger raises by purchasing permits from other firms that were granting pay increases below the target. The costs of extra permits to the firm that bought them and the proceeds to the firm that sold them would serve as rewards and penalties, and hence provide incentives to slow inflation. The government would determine the volume of permits it issues and thus, in Lerner's view, would effectively control the total amount of wage inflation. The price of permits would be set in a free market, which, Lerner expects, would be self-regulating, without major administrative problems for the government.

The question of how TIP could be implemented by tax legislation and tax administration is tackled by Larry L. Dildine and Emil M. Sunley in the third article of this issue. The magnitude of the administrative problems depends on the particular design of the program. First, the authors see a distinct administrative advantage in a program that covers only large private corporations. A TIP that imposes extra taxes on firms making large pay (or price) increases can reasonably be restricted to that group; while one that grants a tax reduction—to workers or to firms —must, for equity reasons, be made universally available. Hence, they strongly prefer the penalty approach on administrative grounds.

Second, they see administrative advantages from a penalty that depends simply on whether the firm exceeds some particular threshold or hurdle, as opposed to a continuous one that is higher for each extra percentage point of wage (or price) increase. In the threshold approach, enforcement by auditing could focus merely on whether or not the firm was below the threshold, without a precise quantitative evaluation.

Third, because any program would introduce some special start-up problems in its initial year, Dildine and Sunley judge that a short-term program may impose a more serious administrative burden than would a longer-run venture.

Fourth, the authors suggest that the tax penalty (or reward) should be based on the overall performance of any group of related corporations that files a consolidated income tax return, and should be computed for the accounting period used for the payment of income taxes.

Finally, they list three ways that a TIP penalty could be levied on firms: by a special higher tax rate on corporate profits (as Seidman proposes), by an additional payroll tax, or by disallowing the deduction of excessive wages in the calculation of taxable income. They do not present a definite conclusion on this choice, viewing the higher corporate income tax as most logical, but noting its flaw of exempting firms that incur no corporate tax liability.

The measurement of pay increases is discussed in detail. To keep the program administratively manageable, Dildine and Sunley recommend against any exemptions or special treatment of overtime premiums, bonuses, or any other unusual forms of monetary compensation. They argue for a comprehensive concept of pay that includes not only monetary compensation but also all private fringe benefits, such as pension rights and group insurance. They note that the problems of measuring nonmonetary compensation are now encountered in administering the income tax, but they believe additional complications might be encountered in a TIP. With the threshold approach, a firm close to the threshold would have a strong incentive to substitute unmeasured increases in compensation for ones that are correctly measured. This incentive might add to existing pressures to provide on-the-job conveniences and company-paid luxuries in lieu of money wages. While general rules to close such loopholes are relatively easy to formulate, the authors report that they are difficult to administer in practice.

The easiest way to calculate the average pay of a firm (and then its percentage increase from one year to the next) is to divide its total payroll (including fringes) by a measure of total hours worked by its employees. This overall approach, however, could cause problems in the event of major changes in the distribution of employment within the firm among workers of different skills and seniority. For example, if, in a particular year, a company greatly increased its employment of high-salaried professional workers, that would appear in the aggregate calculation as a large increase in average pay, which might unfairly subject the firm to a penalty or disqualify it from a reward. As a result, firms might be encouraged to hire contractors for high-wage labor services or to discriminate against highly skilled workers in expanding employment. On the other hand, reliance on a classification system rather than on the simple total would complicate the auditing task and might encourage firms to make "paper promotions." While the authors prefer the overall approach on administrative grounds, they believe that the use of a few carefully specified, broad classifications might be viable.

Dildine and Sunley doubt the feasibility of applying tax penalties or tax rewards to price increases. Any equitable tax plan would have to be based on a value-added price index that would reflect increased costs of purchased materials and supplies, in effect allowing those increases to be passed through to customers. Thus, calculations would be needed for the prices of both the inputs and the products of the firm. Moreover, the task of defining a unit of product or unit of input seems far more difficult than that of defining a unit of employment. For example, each automobile manufacturer would have to specify how many types of cars it made in any given year and how each type could be compared with a corresponding model sold in the preceding year. If new products (or newly purchased inputs) emerged, special rules would be required.

Under the "term-limit price agreements" of the Nixon controls program, firms were subjected to a similar test based on a company price index. But few, if any, company reports were audited in that program, and the firms were essentially on an honor system. In general, Dildine and Sunley believe that a profit-margin limitation might be more administratively feasible than would a price-index test of the performance of a firm, but they note that such a limitation raises other problems and could have adverse effects on incentives for cost control.

The authors conclude: "TIP would entail significant administrative problems for the Internal Revenue Service and compliance problems for businesses. These problems could be reduced to a manageable size if TIP were applied only to business taxpayers, if it were limited to wages, if the hurdle approach were adopted, and if it did not apply to small companies."

In the fourth article in this issue, Robert W. Crandall describes some options through which the federal government could act to reduce the price level directly. Such opportunities exist because the government now imposes indirect taxes that enter into private costs of buying or producing goods and services, and also imposes, by regulation, implicit indirect taxes that raise private costs of production. A shift from these actual or implicit indirect taxes to direct taxes can clearly achieve a one-time reduction in the price level. As Perry points out in his paper, the extent to which such a reduction has favorable second-round and continuing effects on the inflation rate depends on how much a slowdown of consumer prices helps to slow wages.

The reduction of the federal payroll taxes that now finance social security is a major item on Crandall's list of options. On both empirical and analytical grounds, most economists conclude that payroll taxes levied on *employers* are passed on to the consumer in the form of higher product prices, just like other elements in the business costs of labor compensation. These payroll taxes, which are now scheduled for further increases beginning in 1979, could be rolled back by financing health and disability benefits with general revenues rather than trust funds. The resulting reduction in labor costs from the drop in the employer's payroll tax rate would potentially lower the price level by 0.7 percentage point.

A reduction in excise taxes could have even larger effects. Most federal excise taxes—like those on tobacco and alcohol—have a sumptuary justification. If the anti-inflation benefits of their repeal were regarded as more significant than the sumptuary benefits, federal excise taxes could be eliminated, thereby subtracting roughly a point from the price level.

At the state and local levels, indirect taxes are far more significant sources of revenue. All but five states have general sales taxes that yield revenues ranging from approximately 1 to 5 percent of personal income. A "buyback" grant from the federal government to states that lower their sales taxes by an amount up to 2 percent of their personal income could subtract about 1½ percentage points from the overall price level. The five states with no general sales tax could be given the grant at only trivial costs because they account for only 2½ percent of the nation's income. On the other hand, such a program would raise some problems of federal-state relationships. To cooperate, the states might want assurances that the grants would continue for a long time. Finally, the program would lose some effectiveness if the states raised specific excise taxes as they lowered general sales taxes.

A reform of 1977–78 agricultural programs could lower the overall price level by 0.2 percentage point, according to Crandall. Recently, farm policies have been shifted to greater reliance on acreage controls and output limitations. As compared with direct payments to farmers, these supply-cutting measures raise prices, and hence the burden on the consumer budget, while reducing the burden on the federal budget. Current federal farm programs (feed grains, wheat, and soybeans) could be confined to direct income payments with no resort to supply-cutting and price-raising, and the consumer budget could then be relieved of an estimated $3.5 billion a year.

Another option is the deregulation of transportation. According to Crandall, deregulation of airlines, trucking, and the coastal maritime trade would both improve efficiency and reduce annual costs to the purchasers of these services by between $5 billion and $10 billion, subtracting between 0.3 and 0.6 percentage point from the price level.

The various forms of social regulation (particularly those administered by the Environmental Protection Agency and the Occupational Safety and Health Administration) impose added costs of production that are sizable today and are mounting rapidly. Crandall emphasizes that this type of regulation "can and does bring substantial benefits to society," but also emphasizes the need for incentives to achieve the benefits at the lowest possible cost. He proposes the initiation of a "shadow budget" as the most practical way to supply these incentives. That annual budget, which would be separate from the budgetary provision of Treasury funds for the agency, would control the dollar costs that an agency could impose on private firms, and would thus limit the resources of the *private sector* that it could command and consume. That budget would be published along with the federal budget, would become subject to debate and discussion, and could be monitored by the Congress and the Office of Management and Budget. The regulatory agency would then have the clear assignment to achieve the greatest possible social gains in its area, subject to the ceiling on the costs it could impose on private producers.

The minimum wage is another government-mandated cost on business that is generally passed on to the consumer in the form of higher prices. As an alternative way of aiding low-income workers, an effective employment subsidy that substituted for the 1978 increase in the minimum wage would reduce business payroll costs by about $3 billion a year, or about 0.2 percentage point of the price level.

Crandall finds cost-reducing possibilities wherever he looks: the introduction of incremental costing for imported natural gas, increased allowances for cutting timber on federal lands, a reversal of some recent actions to restrain imports, and the implementation of the Carter administration's program to control hospital costs. As he concludes, none of these proposals would solve the inflation problem, but a combination of them might contribute significantly to a gradual slowdown of inflation, and, in many cases, also improve economic efficiency.

The skeptical reactions of business and labor to proposed new anti-inflationary policies are discussed and explained by Albert Rees in the fifth and final article. Corporate and union executives alike have reacted adversely to proposals for tax-based incomes policy, without a detailed explanation of their concerns. Rees rationalizes their position, elaborating on the problems that business and labor would confront under a program such as the Wallich-Weintraub plan. In general, the price and wage decisionmakers see important similarities between such a plan and controls, to which they are now united in opposition. The basic attitude on TIP versus controls reminds Rees of the cartoon in which a little girl, when urged to eat her broccoli, snaps at her mother: "I say it's spinach and I say to hell with it."

In particular, union leaders interpret the focused effort to influence wages as an implied diagnosis that inflation is primarily of the wage-push nature, and they strongly disagree with that diagnosis. Nor are they convinced of the close linkage between wages and prices that is claimed by the proponents of TIP. The 1973–74 experience of inflation erupting from sharp increases in food and fuel prices has intensified their opposition to any incomes policy that concentrates on wages. Moreover, TIP depends on an explicit and basically uniform wage guideline, which conflicts with the conviction of union leaders that rates of wage increase among occupations and industries should vary to correct inequities and to respond to changing market conditions. Rees suggests that, in this respect, TIP might be even worse than wage controls, which can be operated without an explicit guideline for pay increases.

A program with a pair of guidelines for wage and price inflation that leaves room for a growth of real wages equal to the trend growth of productivity implicitly seeks to hold constant the shares of income obtained by labor and property. Thus, such a program can be viewed as an attempt to freeze the distribution of income. Over the long run, labor's share of income has tended to rise gradually; Rees suggests that, understandably, labor leaders would not accept any moratorium on the operation of this trend. Finally, Rees summarizes the dissatisfaction of unions with past incomes policies: from their standpoint, the Kennedy-Johnson wage guidelines became unfair to labor during the mid-sixties, and the Nixon controls program should not have maintained unchanged wage targets after prices accelerated in 1973.

Rees is less certain about the intensity of opposition of union leaders to the reward form of TIP, but he sees a number of grounds for reservations on their part. Even if they could be convinced that the tax reward would enhance the individual worker's real take-home pay, the leaders would be concerned that the gains would not be attributable to the union as an organization, nor to the efforts of the leaders themselves. Hence, Rees believes that many unions would not participate in a voluntary reward program.

The paper also discusses the sources of concern to business leaders from a penalty TIP. First, all large corporations would be subject to the tax penalties, while some of their competitors that are smaller or unincorporated might be exempt. Beyond that, such a program would complicate personnel management and wage negotiations. In an effort to avert strikes and at the same time avoid tax penalties, firms might react to TIP by holding down the wages of nonunion workers and the salaries of managers. But such a course would risk lowering morale and inviting a spread of unionization, as well as affecting adversely the pay of the managers themselves. Similar problems might arise if a single company bargained with two unions of unequal strength: the large raises required for the powerful group could leave the cupboard bare for the weak one.

Businessmen might also expect a penalty TIP to increase and lengthen strikes, which they and labor leaders prefer to avoid. This is another way in which TIP may be inferior to wage controls, Rees argues, because controls deter a union from pressing the employer for wage concessions that the government will not permit to take effect. Finally, the administrative problems that Dildine and Sunley describe from the government's point of view are seen by business as potentially significant costs of compliance with the program. The costs from a price-restraint TIP could be enormous, Rees suggests. On the wage side, multiyear agreements negotiated before the inauguration of a TIP would bring special problems. If these were not exempted, employers would become liable for tax penalties that were unanticipated when they entered into the agreement; if special exemptions were granted, TIP would need three years to become fully effective.

The attitudes of business and labor toward some of the proposals discussed by Crandall might be more sympathetic, insofar as those policies do not trespass on the domain of price and wage determination. In particular, Rees would expect many private leaders to support reductions in excise, sales, and payroll taxes. In the field of deregulation, he observes that attitudes of businessmen differ on a case-by-case basis, depending on how any particular proposal affects their enterprise. For example, in the transportation area, many shippers favor deregulation while many common carriers (and their employees) are fearful of its consequences. With respect to pollution and hazards to health and safety, business generally wants less regulation while labor supports tighter enforcement.

Rees concludes by discussing business and labor attitudes toward old-style anti-inflationary policies. He suspects that labor would see renewed wage and price controls as a greater evil than TIP, because under TIP they might expect to win large wage increases through militant strikes and impose the consequences largely on management. For management, while this consideration alone might make wage and price controls the lesser evil, the disruptive aspects of controls point in the opposite direction.

Rees notes that business generally supports reliance on monetary and fiscal restraint to fight inflation, and still seems devoted to "the old-time religion." Although the labor movement opposes such restrictive policies, they impinge less directly than does TIP on the central function of the trade union, namely, winning wage gains. Furthermore, legislation is not required to apply restrictive macroeconomic policies; hence, labor's opposition can be overridden more easily.

As was expected, a broad spectrum of views about the various innovative policies was expressed in the discussions of the papers and in the symposium at the conclusion of the conference. In large part, differences of opinion reflected varying assessments of how serious the economy's current problems are and how adequate conventional policies are for solving them. As Henry Wallich said: "Of course, nobody likes TIP per se. It is really a question of the alternatives."

To some, the alternative of maintaining the present stance of policy seemed acceptable. Robert Hall, for example, questioned whether the kind of chronic inflation the United States has been experiencing is an overwhelming social evil. Alan Greenspan thought that the unwinding of inflation resulting from the 1974–75 recession might not necessarily be over. And Franco Modigliani was even more optimistic that inflation would continue to slow with present unemployment targets.

Most participants who explored the probable consequences of fiscal and monetary restraint as a cure for inflation shared Perry's grim assessment. Some who conceded that demand restraint might require prolonged slack or recurrent recessions believed nonetheless that it should be pursued. For example, William Poole stated that, to establish its commitment to fight inflation, "it may well be necessary for the government consciously and deliberately to avoid following expansionary policies in the next recession."

A few participants expressed hopes that a consistent, reasonable pursuit of traditional anti-inflationary policies might impose smaller costs than Perry had implied. The point of view was succinctly summarized by

Greenspan: "I think it is much too soon to throw in the sponge on macro-policy, especially if TIP is being considered as the alternative."

The alternative of statutory price-wage controls received no support from anyone. Indeed, as Modigliani observed: "Almost everyone participating in the discussion seems to agree that TIP . . . is better than controls." While Rees stressed similarities between controls and TIP in his paper, Daniel Mitchell and Lloyd Ulman added to Seidman's list of the contrasts that favor TIP. Mitchell suggested that TIP would avoid the confrontations between unions and government authorities over new labor contracts that can disrupt controls or jawboning programs. And he agreed with Seidman that TIP can provide enough built-in flexibility to minimize distortions and shortages. Ulman added that the flexibility also preserved the wage-bargaining function of unions and, more generally, avoided an abridgment of economic freedom.

To some, the administrative problems of TIP seemed overwhelming, not merely "significant [but] manageable," as Dildine and Sunley had suggested. Joseph Pechman expressed his serious concerns vigorously in his detailed comments on their paper. He emphasized that major problems would arise because the reporting unit for tax purposes often bears little relationship to the units that enter into wage bargains with their employees. Gardner Ackley saw the principal problem, not in evasion or cheating, but rather in the enormous difficulty of coping with legitimate objections about the workability or fairness of any general rules in specific situations. Both Pechman and Ackley feared that, in the process of enactment, any proposed program might be encumbered with additional legislative provisions that would create an administrative monstrosity. Ackley nonetheless concluded that, if a TIP limited to wages were politically feasible, he would find it clearly preferable to both the usual "jawboning model" of incomes policy and price and wage controls. But he thought it best to develop a new type of incomes policy, independent of the tax system, which would be basically voluntary but more formalized than previous jawboning efforts, and would have a well-defined, selective coverage of wages and prices and effective representation from labor, business, and the public. As he saw the key issue, it was "not whether to use an incomes policy but only what kind to use."

James Duesenberry stressed that any incomes policy—whether tax-based or not—had to be built on a broad social consensus in favor of reducing inflation through cooperative efforts. Some participants in the discussion saw little chance of developing that consensus politically in the foreseeable future, in light of the attitudes of business and labor that Rees described. But Mitchell noted that these attitudes sometimes change rapidly. In particular, he thought that "the prospect of another recession [might] . . . be a powerful factor in stimulating a rethinking concerning some sort of social compact on the part of organized labor."

Several issues about the best design of a tax-based incomes policy were aired thoroughly. In the discussion of Seidman's paper, some commentators differed sharply on whether TIP should be conceived basically as a temporary or a permanent program. For policy purposes, however, there seemed to be a viable compromise—enacting a provisional program for a few years, subject to renewal if that should prove to be desirable.

Many participants rejected the direct application of TIP to price increases as unworkable, seconding Dildine and Sunley's concerns about the complexity of measuring the average price increase of a firm. Okun, who had advocated a tax reward to firms displaying price restraint, conceded that these criticisms were persuasive.

It was generally agreed that small firms could be safely exempted from a penalty TIP on wages imposed on employers, while all employers and their workers had to be given the opportunity to qualify for any reward TIP. Richard Slitor, Modigliani, and others agreed with Dildine and Sunley that limited coverage was an important administrative advantage of the penalty approach. Modigliani and Wallich thought that the coverage might be confined to perhaps the 2,000 largest private employers, but Rees and Ulman emphasized the importance of the exempted areas in such a narrow program. Greenspan suggested that the conference had produced something approaching a consensus that the penalty TIP on employers was the form most likely to work in practice. Perry and Okun disagreed with that view. They suggested that both compliance and effectiveness would be enhanced by a reward approach in which firms qualified their workers for tax cuts. And they stressed that the administrative burdens of universal coverage are now shouldered in the many special features of our income tax, which are reasonably well enforced by random audits.

Several participants grappled with the problem of how fairness to workers could be ensured under a TIP that, like the Wallich-Weintraub plan, imposed penalties for excessive wage increases. No one expressed any doubt that a wage slowdown would lead to a corresponding price slowdown. But Robert Gordon cited statistical evidence that the full response of prices would take some time; hence, some squeeze on real wages would be likely during the initial year of such a plan. Weintraub and Wallich countered that the danger of a shift in income distribution could be obviated along lines suggested by Seidman—especially by a contingent tax surcharge on corporations that would take effect automatically if profits rose excessively.

In contrast to the wide-ranging disagreements about TIP, there was no major controversy over Crandall's list of government options to reduce the price level directly. One specific dissent was expressed by Michael Lovell and Martin Baily, who saw a much more promising role for antitrust policies. The only significant reservation about the basic price-reducing strategy was registered by Hall, who saw the proposals for a pure shift from indirect to direct taxes as mere gimmicks to influence the consumer price index. Other participants differed in their best estimate of the size and the duration of the anti-inflationary benefits from the price-reducing strategy, but generally supported many of the proposals. Indeed, some of the measures discussed by Crandall have long been favored by a majority of professional economists as a means of improving economic efficiency, quite apart from their anti-inflationary benefits. At the same time, unlike TIP, the price-reducing strategy was not espoused by anyone as the principal remedy for the stagflation problem.

The participants recognized and lamented the political difficulties of implementing proposals to lower the price level in the face of various interest groups that benefit from current cost-raising programs. Walter Heller counseled against despair. He cited the current deregulation of airlines as evidence that the crusades of the professional community sometimes pay off after a long time.

GEORGE L. PERRY
Brookings Institution

Slowing the Wage-Price Spiral: The Macroeconomic View

OVER A DECADE has passed since the standard remedy of demand restraint was first urged to combat inflation. By the mid-1960s, many economists, including those at the Council of Economic Advisers, believed war expenditures were pushing the economy into the inflationary, excess-demand zone and recommended tax increases to help restrain aggregate demand. We cannot know how different subsequent economic performance would have been if that advice had been heeded. But it was not. Unemployment continued to decline into 1969, and the inflation rate in consumer prices rose above 5 percent. Inflation, by then, had become firmly entrenched in economic decisionmaking. When demand finally fell and unemployment rose in the recession of 1970, the inflation rate scarcely budged. Both average hourly earnings and the private nonfarm price deflator rose faster during 1970–71 than in any year of the 1960s.

Many observers concluded that a recession deeper than that of 1970 would be needed to stop inflation. In summer 1971, the Nixon administration tried a different cure, imposing wage and price controls that lasted in modified form until April 1974. These controls slowed the inflation rate for most wages and prices. But by the time the controls expired, higher prices for food and fuel, which were largely unrelated to the state of demand, and for industrial raw materials, which reflected strong world demand and speculative buying, had created double-digit rates of overall

Note: I am grateful to Jesse M. Abraham for his extensive research assistance.

23

Table 1. Wage and Price Inflation in the United States, Selected Periods, 1954–78
Average annual percent change

	Private nonfarm economy			
Period	Compensation per hour	Hourly earnings index	Price deflator	Consumer price index
Post-Korean War (1954–59)	4.6	4.1	2.4	1.4
Early 1960s (1960–65)	4.0	3.1	1.1	1.3
Late 1960s (1966–69)	6.4	5.6	3.7	3.8
Precontrol 1970s (1970–71)	6.7	6.8	4.7	5.1
Controls (1972–73)	6.8	6.5	3.6	4.8
Food-fuel explosion (1974–75)	9.5	8.5	10.7	10.1
1976	8.7	7.2	5.2	5.8
1977	8.8	7.3	5.4	6.5
1978:1[a]	9.1[b]	8.0[b]	6.3	6.6

Source: U.S. Bureau of Labor Statistics.
a. Percent change from the first quarter of 1977 to first quarter of 1978.
b. Without the large increase in the minimum wage in January 1978, the increases would have been an estimated 8.9 percent for compensation and 7.6 percent for hourly earnings.

inflation. Together with a nonaccommodating aggregate-demand policy, this price explosion also started a recession that was double the size of the average previous postwar recession and that lasted until spring 1975.

It is now three years since the trough of this deepest postwar recession. By the end of that recession, inflation had slowed sharply from its 1974 pace, but further improvement was slight once recovery began. From 1975 through 1977, all available measures of tightness in either labor markets or product markets registered ample slack. And no large upward movements have occurred in particular components of the price level since the Organization of Petroleum Exporting Countries increased oil prices in 1974. Yet despite all these disinflationary developments, the rate of inflation, by any broad measure, has continued at a historically high rate and now shows signs of creeping still further upward.

Table 1 summarizes the inflation in the economy since the Korean War as measured by four alternative indexes: compensation per hour, the hourly earnings index, and the price deflator, all of which are averages for the private nonfarm economy; and the consumer price index. Except in 1974 and 1975, when controls ended and oil prices soared, the three measures for the private nonfarm economy have moved closely together, with compensation per hour and the price deflator differing by approximately the trend rate of growth in labor productivity. The consumer price index is more volatile than the deflator. They have differed noticeably when the relative prices of food or imports changed a great deal, although the inclusion of these prices is not the only difference between the indexes. By any of these measures, inflation has been noticeably faster in the 1970s than in previous periods. It has been faster since 1975 than in the early 1970s. And it has been faster over the most recent four quarters than in previous years of the present recovery.

Inflation is unpopular. It hampers policymaking and inhibits the pursuit of high employment. This paper provides a basis for evaluating alternative approaches to slowing it.

The Mainline Model

In this section I briefly outline what I perceive to be the important characteristics of the U.S. economy that have led to the present stubborn inflation. Unlike many journalists describing the stagflation period, I do not conclude that economists fail to understand the economy. And unlike some professional writers of this period, I do not conclude that the Keynesian revolution got everything wrong. However, we have learned during the past ten years that the Keynesian analysis stops short of adequately modeling the inflation process.

Let me begin by describing the essential features of what I call the mainline model of the U.S. macroeconomy. It offers a description of macroeconomic behavior that is compatible with a broad range of more specific models that would have similar policy implications. I later discuss some alternative views of the economy and of the current stagflation that are not consistent with this mainline model and that have policy implications that I believe are basically misleading.

In the mainline model, wage and price behavior are closely linked, and there is at least some mutual causality between them. Because the effect of wages on prices is more predictable and better established, it is useful to begin analyzing the inflation problem by describing the macroeconomics of labor markets.

Wages respond to the tightness of labor markets but not enough to avoid fluctuations in employment brought about by corresponding fluctuations in demand. Thus, something like a Phillips curve exists, at least for periods that are relevant to policymakers and to the conduct of economic affairs, and for the range of unemployment actually experienced. Within this framework, average wages begin to rise at an inflationary rate while unemployment is still well above frictional levels.

Wages also respond to what has been happening to wages, prices, profit margins, or all three, or to what is expected to happen to them. All these alternatives are accommodated in the mainline model and are discussed further below. What is important is that they all predict considerable inertia in wage inflation. The response of wages to variations in demand is characteristically sluggish.

Some prices are sensitive to demand, particularly prices of industrial raw materials and goods whose costs include a large component of costs for raw materials. Agricultural prices are sensitive to world crop conditions, and prices of tradable goods respond to competition from goods produced abroad. But prices in most of the private sector are closely related to variable costs, the most important of which are labor costs. Given wages, these prices are only slightly affected by demand, and consequently their movement in response to demand variations is also sluggish.

With the possible exception of situations in which unemployment is exceptionally low or industrial operating rates are exceptionally high, variations in aggregate demand lead primarily to variations in output, employment, and unemployment. There can be sustained unemployment arising from inadequate demand. At the aggregate level, the response to variations in demand is similar whether the variation comes from fiscal policy, monetary policy, an unexplained change in velocity, or from some shift in demand from the private sector or from foreign demand for exports.

Within this general description, a number of issues that are important to the design of anti-inflation policy remain open. What is the response of inflation to alternative paths of real activity? Are wages affected by past wages, past living costs, past price margins or profitability, or all three? Is the inertia of inflation essentially backward looking or forward looking; and to the extent that expectations matter, how can they be affected? These are difficult questions that are not easily settled by empirical evidence. But that is a place to begin.

The Empirical Mainline Model

The empirical counterpart to the model of the inflation process that I have sketched has been presented before with many variations. Although the level of aggregation may differ, the essentials are an equation relating a price deflator for the private sector to wage costs, to materials costs, and possibly to some additional effects from demand and the prices of competing imports; and an equation relating wages to the tightness of the labor market and to past or expected future inflation.

I do not present any new results on the price equations. Robert Gordon has recently reviewed the aggregate evidence and reaffirmed that prices change in proportion to wage changes.[1] Other factors also have an effect, including the costs of raw materials, competing imports, and to a small extent, variations in demand. However, including them in the explanation does not diminish the importance of labor costs.

The principal unsettled issues are concerned with the causes of inertia in wage inflation. I turn first to some disaggregated evidence from the 1960s and 1970s.

DISAGGREGATED WAGE CHANGES

The first evidence of the stubbornness of inflation came when average wages and prices failed to decelerate much despite rising unemployment after 1969. The behavior of wages in particular sectors is noteworthy during this period. Some wages are set under collective bargaining agreements, frequently with three-year contracts. Many factors can enter into union wage demands in such bargaining situations, including wage levels elsewhere and living costs. There is no well-established model of what unions can successfully bargain for and, especially when contracts are negotiated infrequently and prices and other wages have changed between contracts, new settlements can bear little relation to current unemployment rates. While wages set under collective bargaining may represent an especially obvious departure from short-run market clearing in wage setting, virtually no wages are set in auction markets. Long-term attachments between firms and workers are useful to both sides and characterize a large portion of the job market. In such situations, equity, which may embrace relative wages or inflation, becomes an important consideration in wage setting. Both unionization and long-term attachments characterize some industries more than others. As a consequence, wages in different industries do not move in parallel under changing economic conditions.

High- and Low-Wage Industries. A random sample of 39 industries at the three-digit level of aggregation was divided into groups with high, medium, and low wages according to the average of their hourly earnings

1. Robert J. Gordon, "Can the Inflation of the 1970s be Explained?" *Brookings Papers on Economic Activity, 1:1977,* pp. 253–77. (Hereafter *BPEA*).

over the 1959–76 period. For each group, the following table shows the
average wage increases during the 1960s and 1970s and the difference
between the averages for the two periods.

Industry classification	Average annual percent increase in hourly earnings		Acceleration
	1959–69	*1970–76*	
Low wage	3.8	6.5	2.8
Medium wage	3.7	6.9	3.3
High wage	3.5	7.8	4.3

After rising slightly more slowly than wages in the low-wage group during the 1960s, wages in the high-wage group accelerated 4.3 percentage
points in the 1970s, compared with an acceleration of 2.8 points for the
low-wage group. The consumer price index accelerated by 4.0 points over
the same interval. The acceleration of wages in the high-wage industries
kept pace over the 1970–76 interval with the acceleration in the consumer
price index.

The coefficient of variation of wage levels among the industries sam-
pled declined gradually from 0.20 in 1959 to 0.18 in 1968.[2] It then rose
gradually to 0.21 in 1974 and then to 0.23 in 1975 and 0.24 in 1976.
Over the period from 1959 to 1976, an equation of the form developed
by Wachter to explain the coefficient of variation (CV) among industry
wages produced the following estimates:[3]

$$(1) \qquad CV = 0.20 - 0.10\, u^{*-1} + 0.26\, \Delta \ln CP,$$
$$ (12.0)\ (-3.2) \qquad (2.7)$$
$$\text{Durbin-Watson} = 1.1;\ \text{standard error} = 0.11,$$

where u^{*-1} is the inverse of the weighted unemployment rate and CP is
the consumer price index. The numbers in parentheses in all equations are
t statistics.

Wachter reasoned that wage dispersion was cyclical. He found that the
variation was reduced by inflation, which was closely correlated with unemployment in his sample period. Equation 1 supports Wachter's cyclical
conclusion that lower unemployment reduces wage dispersion; but it im-

---

2. Only 38 of the 39 industries were included in the coefficient of variation because wage data for industry 421–3 were available only for 1964–76.

3. Michael L. Wachter, "The Wage Process: An Analysis of the Early 1970s,"
BPEA, 2:1974, pp. 507–24.

plies that inflation independently increases it. Stagflation increases it on both counts.

Equations for annual wage increases in individual industries also reveal the relatively stronger effect of inflation and the weaker effect of unemployment in the high-wage industries. Tables 2a and 2b show simple Phillips curves for each of the 26 industries in the low-wage and high-wage groups. In each case, the change in hourly earnings adjusted for overtime was regressed on the average increase in the CPI over the two previous years and on the inverse of weighted unemployment.[4] A dummy variable equal to 1 in 1974 and 1975 was included in each equation to avoid giving undue weight to the observations for those two years. Using annual data, wages in both years were strongly affected by the combination of food and fuel inflation and the end of controls. This situation is examined more carefully below using aggregate wage equations.

Although the individual industry equations are often unsatisfactory, the average coefficient in each group fits the expected pattern. The average coefficient on unemployment is 11.5 for the low-wage industries and 6.8 for the high-wage industries; the average coefficients on the CPI are 0.6 and 0.8, respectively. Similar results are also obtained when the CPI is replaced by average hourly earnings as the lagged inflation variable. The change in the minimum wage makes no contribution as an additional explanatory variable, even in the low-wage industries. I assume this negative result reflects the poor quality of equations for individual industries. In Gramlich's careful analysis of minimum wages, a 1 percent change in the minimum adds 0.03 percent to average wages.[5] The impact on wages in low-wage industries should be many times larger than this estimate for the aggregate.

Union Wages. For the past two years, data from the employment cost index have been available for wage and salary increases in occupations both covered and not covered by collective bargaining agreements. Covered wages rose 8.1 and 7.6 percent during 1976 and 1977, respectively (fourth quarter to fourth quarter). These increases are 1.3 and 1.0 percentage points more than the rise in uncovered wages in the two years.

For years before 1976, effective union wage changes can be compared

4. The overtime adjustment could not be made for nonmanufacturing industries. Those equations refer to hourly earnings.

5. Edward M. Gramlich, "Impact of Minimum Wages on Other Wages, Employment, and Family Incomes," *BPEA, 2:1976*, pp. 409–51.

Table 2a. Disaggregated Wage Change Equations: Low-Wage Industries[a]
Percent

Standard industrial classification code	Independent variable			Standard error	Durbin-Watson statistic
	Unemployment	Lagged CPI	1974–75 dummy		
23	12.60 (2.4)	0.46 (2.4)	1.79 (1.2)	1.74	1.7
22	13.40 (3.9)	0.54 (4.3)	1.87 (2.0)	1.13	1.6
203	8.90 (2.8)	0.73 (6.2)	3.51 (4.0)	1.05	1.4
25	16.02 (7.0)	0.53 (6.3)	2.39 (3.8)	0.76	1.8
39	14.31 (6.7)	0.53 (6.8)	2.51 (4.3)	0.70	2.4
367	10.18 (2.7)	0.41 (3.0)	4.67 (4.5)	1.25	2.4
365	13.12 (2.9)	0.64 (3.9)	3.86 (3.1)	1.47	0.9
209	7.00 (2.5)	0.67 (6.6)	1.21 (1.6)	0.92	1.3
243	14.35 (6.8)	0.88 (11.4)	1.85 (3.2)	0.70	2.7
FIRE[b]	7.82 (3.5)	0.38 (4.6)	1.81 (2.9)	0.75	2.2
364	7.77 (2.5)	0.61 (5.5)	2.58 (3.1)	1.01	1.4
52–59	10.77 (5.6)	0.39 (5.5)	1.87 (3.5)	0.63	2.6
375–9	13.83 (2.7)	0.54 (2.8)	1.48 (1.0)	1.72	2.5
Mean	11.5	0.56	2.4	...	...

See sources and footnotes for table 2b.

with changes in the average hourly earnings index, which includes both union and nonunion workers. During most of the 1960s, effective median union wage increases lagged slightly behind the increases in average hourly earnings. Beginning in 1968, data on mean increases are available that show union increases equaling average increases outside the union sector in 1968–69 and then outpacing them in subsequent years.

Table 3 compares the percentage increase in union wages with the increases in the index of average hourly earnings for 1970–77. Union

Table 2b. Disaggregated Wage Change Equations: High-Wage Industries[a]
Percent

Standard industrial classification code	Independent variable			Standard error	Durbin-Watson statistic
	Unemployment	Lagged CPI	1974–75 dummy		
366	6.39	0.71	2.28	1.00	2.2
	(2.1)	(6.3)	(2.7)		
357	6.49	0.47	2.70	1.20	1.7
	(1.8)	(3.5)	(2.7)		
481	c	1.18	1.25	2.58	1.7
		(4.2)	(0.6)		
356	6.96	0.68	2.45	0.75	1.6
	(3.1)	(8.2)	(3.9)		
335	5.41	0.81	2.34	1.23	1.2
	(1.5)	(6.0)	(2.3)		
352	2.79	0.57	4.80	1.27	2.3
	(0.7)	(4.0)	(4.5)		
353	5.76	0.77	3.41	0.93	1.2
	(2.0)	(7.4)	(4.4)		
354	11.94	0.66	1.88	0.58	2.0
	(6.8)	(10.3)	(3.9)		
331	2.72	1.01	5.31	2.21	1.7
	(0.4)	(4.1)	(2.9)		
12	11.54	1.17	3.16	2.36	1.8
	(1.6)	(4.4)	(1.6)		
421–3	c	0.56	−0.86	3.03	0.8
		(1.4)	(−0.3)		
332	7.72	1.12	−0.25	1.04	2.5
	(2.5)	(9.7)	(−0.3)		
371	7.31	0.64	3.37	1.65	2.2
	(1.5)	(3.5)	(2.4)		
Mean	6.8	0.80	2.5	...	...

Sources: Data from U.S. Bureau of Labor Statistics, with wages in manufacturing industries adjusted for overtime by the author. See text for definitions of the variables.

a. All equations are estimated for the period 1959–76, with a constant term that is not reported. The dependent variable is the percent change in overtime-adjusted hourly earnings. The numbers in parentheses are t statistics. The regression for industry 421-3 is for the period 1964–76.

b. FIRE is the fire insurance and real estate industries.

c. The unemployment coefficient was negative, so the equation was reestimated without it.

wages rose much faster in 1970 and 1971 when union increases were unaffected by the recession and when unions negotiated to catch up for their small real gains during the late 1960s. During the control years, union wages moved in step with the average. And both accelerated sharply in the two subsequent years of price explosion. For the eight years

Table 3. Union and Total Private Wage Increases, 1970-77

Percent per year

Year/ Period	Effective union wage-rate change[a]	Increase in index of average hourly earnings	Difference	Real union wage-rate change[b]
1970	8.8	6.6	2.2	2.9
1971	9.2	7.0	2.2	4.9
1972	6.6	6.6	0.0	3.3
1973	7.0	6.4	0.6	0.8
1974	9.4	8.2	1.2	−1.6
1975	8.7	8.8	−0.1	−0.4
1976	8.1	7.2	0.9	2.3
1977	8.0	7.3	0.7	1.5
1970-77 average	8.2	7.3	0.9	1.7

Source: U.S. Bureau of Labor Statistics.

a. Average effective union wage-rate changes in agreements covering 1,000 or more workers.

b. Effective union wage increases less the increase in the CPI.

as a whole (1970–77), union wages have risen an average of 1 percent a year faster. But while they have outpaced average wages over this period, the 1.7 percent average annual increase in real wages in the union sector during the 1970s just maintained the average rate of real wage increase of the previous decade.

Looking Forward or Backward? The data on union wage increases during the inflationary period of the past decade can help distinguish between forward-looking and backward-looking views of the inflation process. Purely expectational models can have different implications from those that relate current wage and price developments to actual developments of the past. If the inertia in inflation arose from a purely backward-looking process, current wage setting would be influenced by wage changes that have already occurred elsewhere or by price changes that have occurred since wages currently being set were last changed. The prospect that inflation would accelerate or decelerate in the future would not enter because wage changes would be simply catching up with past events. If the process were purely forward looking, only expectations of future inflation would matter. Bygones are presumably bygones and past changes in wages or prices enter only as people form expectations from them. Unfortunately, analysis with statistical time series is unsuccessful in distinguishing between forward-looking and backward-looking processes when "expectations" are not directly observable and are modeled as

Table 4. Real and Relative Wage Gains in Major Union Contracts, 1968–75

Percentage points over three years

Contract year	Average wage gain (1)	Relative wage gain[a]		Real wage gain[a]	
		Forward looking[b] (2)	Backward looking[b] (3)	Forward looking[b] (4)	Backward looking[b] (5)
1968	19.5	0.1	3.9	4.0	9.5
1969	23.4	3.2	5.7	7.8	10.9
1970	25.9	5.7	6.5	12.4	10.4
1971	26.1	6.1	5.9	12.3	10.5
1972	24.9	3.7	4.7	4.4	11.4
1973	23.5	0.1	3.5	−2.8	9.7
1974	25.2	1.0	4.0	−0.7	4.7
1975	25.7	2.4	2.3	4.3	−0.6
Standard deviation		2.3	1.4	5.1	4.2

Sources: Union wage changes are calculated as described in notes to this table using data from U.S. Bureau of Labor Statistics on effective wage rate changes. Adjusted average hourly earnings and consumer price indexes are from BLS.

a. Relative wage gain is union wage change (defined in the next note) relative to the change in the average hourly earnings index. Real wage gain is union wage change relative to the change in the consumer price index.

b. The union wage change each year is the increase from current settlements plus average gains in the next two years from prior settlements and escalator provisions. Forward-looking gain is this change less the increase over the same time interval in average hourly earnings or the consumer price index. Backward-looking gain is this change less the increase in average hourly earnings from three years earlier or the CPI.

lagged values of past inflation. In order to distinguish between the two, it is necessary to turn to other types of evidence.

Various institutional or political arrangements whose purpose is to neutralize, at least partly, the effects of inflation on wages are based on a backward-looking approach. Adjustments in labor contracts to account for increases in the cost of living modify wages according to past changes in the CPI. Such arrangements make it possible to avoid forecasts of future inflation. The minimum wage law has typically been adjusted to take account of past changes in average wages. And the comparability rule for government wages relates them to past changes in wages of workers in the private sector in similar occupations.

Major union wage contracts are the clearest instance of wage commitments made well into the future. If the forward-looking hypothesis works anywhere, it should work in explaining these settlements. Table 4 analyzes wage gains in major union contracts for the period 1968–75. Column 1 shows the estimated average wage gain from settlements over

Table 5. Phillips Curve Equations for Wages in the Private Nonfarm Sector, Selected Periods, 1954–77[a]

Period and equation number	Constant	$u*^{-1}$	Independent variable[b]							Sum of lagged effects	Standard error	Durbin-Watson statistic
			$\Delta \ln E_{-1}$	$\Delta \ln E_{-2}$	$\Delta \ln CP_{-1}$	$\Delta \ln CP_{-2}$	$\Delta \ln DP_{-1}$	$\Delta \ln DP_{-2}$	$DNIX$			
1954–69												
5.1	−0.37 (−0.4)	8.55 (4.5)	0.54 (2.9)	−0.05 (−0.2)	...	...	...	...	...	0.49	0.56	1.6
5.2	1.04 (1.5)	9.06 (3.8)	...	...	0.29 (1.5)	−0.05 (−0.2)	...	...	...	0.24	0.72	1.1
5.3	0.42 (0.9)	7.53 (5.0)	...	...	...	...	0.55 (3.5)	0.19 (1.2)	...	0.74	0.42	2.1
1954–71												
5.4	−1.36 (−1.4)	7.75 (3.4)	0.70 (3.3)	0.13 (0.5)	...	...	...	...	...	0.83	0.67	1.5
5.5	1.01 (1.4)	7.45 (3.0)	...	...	0.47 (2.6)	0.11 (0.5)	...	...	...	0.58	0.79	1.1
5.6	0.33 (0.7)	6.54 (4.2)	...	...	...	...	0.68 (4.4)	0.27 (1.6)	...	0.95	0.46	1.9
1954–77												
5.7	−1.88 (−2.2)	7.44 (3.5)	0.79 (4.6)	0.21 (1.1)	...	...	...	...	1.07 (2.9)	1.00	0.70	1.5
5.8	1.03 (1.3)	7.39 (2.9)	...	...	0.55 (3.8)	0.09 (0.6)	...	...	−0.02 (−0.0)	0.64	0.85	1.3
5.9	0.55 (0.6)	7.88 (3.0)	...	...	...	...	0.52 (3.7)	0.24 (1.7)	0.68 (1.3)	0.76	0.88	1.2

Sources: *Economic Report of the President, January 1978*; U.S. Bureau of Labor Statistics; and author's estimates.

a. The dependent variable is adjusted average hourly earnings (100 × Δ ln E). The numbers in parentheses are t statistics.

b. All change variables are multiplied by 100; $u*^{-1}$ = inverse of weighted unemployment rate; E = adjusted average hourly earnings; CP = consumer price index; DP = private nonfarm deflator with a fuel correction for 1974 and 1975 of −1.5 and −0.8 percent, respectively; DNIX = dummy to account for wage and price controls with values of −1 in 1972 and 1973, +1 in 1974 and 1975.

the life of the contract, including gains from escalator provisions.[6] Columns 2 to 5 compare these settlement increases with both past and future changes in the CPI and in adjusted average hourly earnings for the private nonfarm economy. The hypothesis that settlements are forward looking is expressed in columns 2 and 4, where the percentage increases in average earnings throughout the economy and in the CPI over the three-year duration of union settlements are subtracted from the increases under the settlements. Columns 3 and 5 express the hypothesis that settlements are backward looking. There the increase in average earnings for the economy as a whole and in the CPI over the three years ending in the year of the settlement are subtracted from the increases under the settlements. Data are available for these calculations only for the years shown.

Because these major settlements are concentrated in situations that are comparatively insensitive to unemployment rates and presumably sensitive to living costs and relative wages, the hypothesis that yields the less erratic series for wage gains should be preferred. In this case, the backward-looking hypothesis is a more satisfactory one, even though the forward-looking hypothesis is given an advantage in the contest through comparing CPI gains with settlement gains that include escalator adjustments for the same years.

AGGREGATE WAGE EQUATIONS

I turn now to some aggregate wage equations to observe how well the Phillips curve and alternative specifications of lagged inflation effects predicted wages during the 1970s. Table 5 presents Phillips curve equations for the annual change in adjusted hourly earnings in the private nonfarm sector ($100 \times \Delta \ln E$), using three alternative lagged inflation variables: the dependent variable, the CPI ($100 \times \Delta \ln CP$), and the private nonfarm deflator after the effects of the rise in fuel prices in 1974–75 have been removed ($100 \times \Delta \ln DP$). Two years of lagged inflation are shown in each case, although the second year is frequently insignificant. A third-year lag invariably was insignificant and small or wrong-signed. Esti-

6. The average gain from settlements made in year t is estimated by adding the average deferred increases in years $t + 1$ and $t + 2$ to the average first-year increase in t. The deferred increases in each year are averaged over the number of workers who did not receive first-year increases in that year. This procedure is not precise and can only approximate the actual increases that occur over the life of contracts newly negotiated in any given year.

mates are shown for periods beginning in 1954 and ending in 1969, 1971, and 1977.

The quarterly pattern of wage and price changes during 1973–74 clearly points to a discontinuity with the end of controls in the second quarter of 1974. It is difficult to model this situation. Controls were ended when the CPI was already soaring as a consequence of increases in uncontrolled prices of food and fuel and, to a lesser extent, raw materials and imports. Without these price shocks, wages might have behaved differently when controls ended. Nonetheless, in the equation estimated through 1977, I allowed for an amount of wage catch-up in 1974–75 equal to the amount wages were held down in 1972–73 by adding a dummy variable ($DNIX$) equal to -1 in 1972 and 1973 and $+1$ in 1974 and 1975. If one believes that little or no postcontrol "make-up" in wages would have occurred if it had not been for the rapid inflation caused by food and fuel prices, this procedure underestimates the response of wages to that price explosion by attributing a part of actual wage changes in 1974 and 1975 to a reversal of the wage moderation accomplished by controls.

Labor Market Effects. The labor market variable is the weighted unemployment rate, holding constant the 1966 demographic proportions of the labor force. The weighting produces a wage-bill concept of unemployed labor resources; maintaining fixed labor force proportions provides a measure that will not show a change in the tightness of the labor market if the unemployment rate of each group is constant while its relative proportions vary. This measure of weighted unemployment will not capture the possibility that some groups are on flatter or steeper portions of their "own" Phillips curves than other groups. However, it is difficult to model that possibility from available data.

A striking feature of table 5 is that the estimated short-run effect of changing labor market tightness on wages is nearly the same for any of the three periods and for any of the three measures of lagged inflation. They all indicate only a modest first-year effect on inflation from a change in unemployment. For instance, using equation 5.1, an unemployment rate 1 percentage point lower than present levels would add about 0.43 percentage point to the rate of wage inflation, while an increase of 1 percentage point of unemployment would subtract about 0.28 point. Using equation 5.7, the estimates are 0.37 point and -0.25 point, respectively. The lagged effects would continue to enlarge these impacts, but only gradually. In the third year, equation 5.1 predicts that wages would be rising 0.5 percentage point slower if unemployment were sustained at a level 1 point higher, and 0.8 point faster with unemployment sustained 1 point lower. The corresponding third-year estimates from equation 5.7 are 0.7 point slower and 1.0 point faster.

Another way to compare the estimates for different periods is to observe their characterizations of high employment. Equation 5.7, whose lagged wage effects sum to 1.0, implies that 4.0 percent weighted unemployment—corresponding today to about 5.5 percent conventional unemployment—is consistent with a steady long-run inflation rate. At this weighted unemployment rate, equations 5.1 and 5.4 predict an eventual steady rate of wage increase of 3.5 percent and 3.4 percent. Such wage increases would yield about a 1.5 percent rate of price inflation, which is about as close as the economy ever comes to price stability.

Lagged Effects. Lagged values of the unemployment measure did not enter the wage equation significantly for any period of estimation. Whatever effect there is on average wages from the state of labor markets apparently occurs promptly. However, the influence of lagged inflation is strong and the estimated size of this influence is substantially greater when the 1970s are included in the estimation period.

The straightforward interpretation of this drift in the estimated size of lagged inflation effects is that the significance of ongoing inflation has risen together with the rising rate of inflation. According to this interpretation, so long as rapid inflation was not sustained for an extended period, it was less important in setting wages. Alternatively, it may be that the importance of lagged effects are misestimated in the equations for some periods, and there exists a "true" set of lagged inflation coefficients that is unchanged.

Whether the lagged effects actually sum to 1.0 or to a little less than 1.0 is not important for understanding the current inflation predicament. There will be considerable inertia to inflation with any large value of these lagged effects. When the lagged effects sum to 1.0, the model has only one unemployment rate at which inflation is predicted to remain unchanged in the long run. For relevant time horizons, the predictions from that model are little different from the predictions of a model that has a long-run trade-off with coefficients on recent inflation summing to 0.8 or so.

The errors for the 1970s from the equations of table 5 are shown in table 6. Even the equations estimated through 1977 show persistent un-

Table 6. Prediction Errors from Wage Equations for 1970–77

Actual less predicted value in percentage points

Estimation period and equation	Errors								Sum of errors	Average error		
	1970	1971	1972	1973	1974	1975	1976	1977		1970–77	1972–75	1976–77
1954–69												
5.1	1.2	2.0	1.2	0.9	3.0	3.5	1.1	2.3	15.2	1.9	2.2	1.7
5.2	1.5	2.3	2.1	1.7	2.9	3.3	2.4	3.0	19.2	2.4	2.5	2.7
5.3	0.7	1.2	0.7	1.0	2.8	1.4	−1.6	0.6	6.8	0.9	1.5	−0.5
1954–71												
5.4	0.4	1.1	0.2	−0.1	2.1	2.3	0.1	0.9	7.0	0.9	1.1	0.5
5.5	0.4	0.8	0.9	0.9	1.7	0.7	−0.6	1.0	5.8	0.7	1.1	0.2
5.6	0.2	0.6	0.1	0.6	2.3	0.2	−3.3	−0.5	0.2	0.0	0.8	−1.9
1954–77												
5.7	−0.1	0.6	0.7	0.5	0.6	0.6	−0.7	0.2	2.4	0.3	0.6	−0.3
5.8	0.1	0.4	0.6	0.8	1.4	a	−1.1	0.7	2.9	0.4	0.7	−0.2
5.9	0.4	0.9	1.1	1.3	1.8	0.6	−2.0	0.1	4.2	0.5	1.2	−0.9

Sources: Table 5 equations.
a. Positive but less than 0.05.

derpredictions through 1975; and in the equations estimated through 1969, with their smaller lagged effects, the underpredictions are large. The catching up of union wages in 1970–71 and the price explosion of 1974–75 are two events of the period that would not be predictable from aggregate wage equations, and that may help explain the underpredictions of this period.

Lagged CPI. There is no clear preferable alternative among the measures of lagged inflation, although based on the standard errors for all three sample periods, the CPI is unsatisfactory as a single explanatory variable for inertia. The Durbin-Watson statistics for the CPI equations are also consistently low, and when the equations are reestimated with a rho correction, the sum of the lagged CPI coefficients falls to 0.2 in the 1977 regressions. Thus, the estimates give no support to the hypothesis that wages vary in order to attain some real wage level. However, the evidence in favor of *some* CPI effects on wages is considerably stronger. During the 1976–77 period when inflation slowed substantially, the CPI equations clearly outperformed the equations using the nonfarm deflator. And residuals from any of the equations show that the food-fuel price explosion did affect wage behavior in 1974–75.

Lagged Deflator. The nonfarm deflator provided the best overall fit in the equations estimated through 1969 and 1971, but also provided the worst fit when the sample period was extended to 1977.

The deflator might be expected to work in wage equations for one of two reasons: either because it represents past wage changes that affect current wages, or because changes in the price margins or profitability of firms affect wages. If it is only a proxy for the former effect, then a wage-wage model should be used directly. But occasional observations of rapid wage gains in suddenly prosperous industries—such as coal and oil after 1973 —suggest that profitability may influence wage setting.

Generalized effects of profitability are difficult to find in time-series data. Although early work on Phillips curves found an important role for profits, time-series studies that include the latest decade generally do not. A secular decline in average profitability that coincides with the acceleration of inflation may be masking a causal relation between variations around that secular decline and wage changes. Laurence Seidman, in his paper in this volume, makes such an adjustment and finds that profitability is an important explanatory variable for wages.

Attempts to use both past wages and past deflator prices in the wage equation have been unsuccessful. The effect of wage costs on prices makes them highly collinear, and one or the other dominates depending on the sample period. Competition among tradable goods makes the price of imports one source of influence on deflator prices that is independent of wage costs. When the change in the import price of manufactured goods is added to the wage-wage equations of table 5, that price is significant. However, the equation coefficients are somewhat unstable over the different sample periods. The equations could only be estimated beginning with 1960 because the import price series is not available before 1959. The equation estimated for 1960–71, the period before flexible exchange rates, is:

(2) $\Delta \ln E = -1.05 + 7.40\, u^{*-1} + 0.41\, \Delta \ln E_{-1}$
         $(-2.4)\quad (4.6)\qquad\quad (1.8)$

$\qquad\qquad\qquad\qquad + 0.42\, \Delta \ln E_{-2} + 0.11\, \Delta \ln MP_{-1},$
$\qquad\qquad\qquad\qquad\ \ (1.5)\qquad\qquad (2.3)$

Durbin-Watson = 2.6; standard error = 0.28.

where all $\Delta \ln$ terms are multiplied by 100 and MP is the price index for finished manufactured imports. For the same equation estimated through 1977, the sum of the coefficients on the lagged wage term is 0.88; and the coefficient on import prices, 0.07. These equations indicate that beyond the effects of unemployment and a lagged wage elasticity of about 0.85, a 10 percent change in the price of manufactured import goods alters the price of competing tradable goods by enough to change average wages by about 1 percent. This estimate seems high and should probably not be taken at face value. It does provide some evidence that profit margins have an independent effect on wages, although it is hardly conclusive or successfully quantified.

Lagged Wages. The most robust simple specification of the inertia process seems to be the wage-wage view modeled in equations 5.1, 5.4, and 5.7. Their errors for the two latest years are relatively small, and the two years are tracked rather well without a huge change in the error such as that produced by the deflator equations. The equations fitted through 1969 or 1971, however, greatly underpredict wage changes in subsequent years. The equation estimated through 1977 reduces these overestimates by raising the sum of the lagged wage coefficients to about 1.0.

A close look at the errors in the 1972–75 period shows some direct effect of price inflation on wages. In table 6 the errors from equations 5.1

or 5.4 declined by about 1 percentage point in 1972–73. This may be interpreted as the direct effect of controls. The errors then jump by over 2 percentage points in 1974–75. There is no wage-wage view of the inflation process that predicts this. The earlier disaggregated results show that the acceleration in 1974–75 was the same in both high-wage and low-wage industries, so the possibility can be ruled out that a distortion of relative wages in the control period led to this acceleration in the average. Even the assumption that controls suppressed a stubborn rate of wage inflation would only account for a return to 1 percent underpredictions. Something between this and no change from the 1972–73 residuals should have been expected if the actual wage experience of 1972–73 affected the wage-wage process and, therefore, wage changes in 1974–75. The actual behavior of wages indicates they responded to the actual behavior of prices.

When the lagged CPI and lagged wages are used together as explanatory variables, the coefficients on unemployment and on wage changes that lag by one year are quite uniform for the three sample periods. The estimated coefficient on the lagged CPI rises from near zero when the equation is estimated through 1969 to about 0.2 in equations estimated through 1971 or 1977. Wage changes lagged two years only become important when the estimation period is extended to 1977, raising the sum of all lagged inflation coefficients to 0.93. The equation fitted to the 1954–71 period (all logs × 100) is:

$$(3) \quad \Delta \ln E = -0.69 + 7.34u^{*-1} + 0.52 \, \Delta \ln E_{-1}$$
$$ (-0.7) \quad (3.3) \qquad (2.1)$$
$$+ 0.07 \, \Delta \ln E_{-2} + 0.21 \, \Delta \ln CP_{-1}.$$
$$(0.3) \qquad\qquad (1.3)$$

Durbin-Watson = 1.8; standard error = 0.66.

The prediction errors are:

1970	1971	1972	1973	1974	1975	1976	1977	Sum
0.2	0.8	0.3	0.2	1.7	1.3	−0.4	0.9	5.0

WAGE BEHAVIOR: CONCLUSIONS

Once changes in demographics have been allowed for (by measuring tightness in the labor market with the weighted unemployment rate used here), the major change in the inflation-unemployment relation between the 1960s and 1970s is associated with the effects of lagged inflation on current wage changes. The existence of large lagged effects created inertia in inflation that transmitted past inflation to current wage changes even when current unemployment rose. In addition, the importance of these lagged effects apparently grew as inflation itself became more entrenched. Today inertia is a more important characteristic of the inflation process than it was in the 1950s and 1960s.

The disappointing experience with inflation during the 1970s can be understood as a consequence of this strong and growing inertia together with some one-time developments that added to inflation during this period. These include, in particular, the catch-up in union wages at the start of the decade and the international explosion of prices for food and fuel before the great recession.

The source of this inertia is not easily identified. Wages in high-wage industries and those set under collective bargaining are relatively insensitive to unemployment and relatively responsive to the ongoing rate of inflation. They may have been particularly important in the failure of average wages to decelerate after 1969. However, for aggregate wages to rise as fast as they have in the 1970s, the ongoing inflation rate must be an important factor in wage determination more generally, possibly as a consequence of patterning other wage changes on those in the high-wage sectors or occupations.

No single explanatory variable adequately describes the effect of past inflation on current wage changes. In general, wages responding to past wages offer a better description of the process than wages responding simply to the CPI. But to explain the developments of the mid-1970s, one needs to believe there was a substantial direct influence of prices on wages as well. This period may have been unusual, but some direct effect of past prices on wages is also estimated in equations such as 3, which are fitted to long periods that do not include the mid-1970s. In summary, to explain current wage behavior, the importance of ongoing inflation is well established, but the particular importance of ongoing price (as opposed to wage) inflation remains unsettled.

Although it is difficult to disprove the hypothesis that the inertia in aggregate wages represents expected inflation, the estimates favor the more direct hypothesis that inertia is a backward-looking phenomenon. That view is supported directly by the analysis of changes in union wages. In the aggregate equations, it is supported by the fact that inertia appears through large coefficients on recent inflation rather than through modest coefficients on inflation rates over a long past period: expectations models generally assert that expectations are adjusted gradually and therefore depend on a long past history of actual inflation. A large coefficient on recent wage changes is most naturally interpreted as a process in which wages are adjusted to keep up continuously with other wages. If these results are taken to mean that expectations are simply formed by the most recent observation of inflation, the expectations hypothesis loses any distinctive significance, for then any change in actual inflation will have a full impact on inflation in the next period, just as the backward-looking hypothesis would predict. Finally, the failure of any lagged values of unemployment to enter the wage equation argues against expected unemployment rates as an important determinant of wage changes.

Alternative Views

The mainline model that I described at the outset of this paper and the empirical evidence just presented provide a fairly general description of the macroeconomy and the inflation process. Although they leave room for alternative views about the microeconomic underpinnings of inertia and for further research on quantitative questions, they do provide a basis for discussing anti-inflation policies. The blame for inflation or the remedies for it, however, are often argued along lines that are not predicted by the mainline model or from views of the economy that are incompatible with it. Before examining what there is to learn from the mainline model about strategies for slowing inflation, I review some of these dissenting views.

BUDGET DEFICITS

If a poll were taken to sample opinions on the causes of inflation, most votes would probably go to government deficits. An economist would grant the effects of deficits on aggregate demand and would be hard pressed to find causal links between deficits and inflation over and above their effects on demand. He would also be aware that historically most deficits have come from the operation of automatic stabilizers during periods of underemployment.

Although to my knowledge no serious model predicts that actual deficits will explain inflation, equations 4 and 5 were estimated in response to the opinion polls, as follows:

(4) $\Delta \ln GP = -0.0 + 1.04 \, L\Delta \ln GP - 0.19 \, LRDG.$
              (-0.3) (5.5) (-1.4)
Period, 1954:1 to 1973:4; Durbin-Watson = 1.7; standard error = 0.004.

(5) $\Delta \ln GP = 0.00 + 1.11 \, L\Delta \ln GP + 0.00 \, LRDG + 0.003 \; DNIX.$
              (0.1) (6.5) (0.04) (1.9)
Period, 1954:1 to 1977:2; Durbin-Watson = 1.8; standard error = 0.004.

Four-quarter percentage changes in the GNP deflator ($\Delta \ln GP$) are explained with Almon lagged values of the deflator itself ($L \, \Delta \ln GP$) and of the ratio of the federal deficit to the GNP ($LRDG$). The lags extend 16 quarters. The equations fitted through 1977 include the dummy variable ($DNIX$) for the control and postcontrol period of the Nixon years that sums to zero. The qualitative results are unaffected by this dummy or by a dummy for the wage-price guideposts of the 1960s. Equation 4, fitted through the end of 1973, reveals the negative effect associated with deficits, which is predicted from the fact that variations in the deficit result primarily from variations in the degree of slack in the economy. When the period is extended to 1977 in equation 5, the coincidence of the price explosion of 1974–75 and the deep recession and consequent large budget deficit raise the coefficient estimated for the deficit to zero.

The actual relationship between budget deficits and economic performance is complicated, and the equations above are not intended to summarize that relationship in any meaningful way. At a minimum, variations in the deficit would have to be decomposed into those that are induced by economic activity and those that represent changes in fiscal policy at a fixed level of utilization. Equations 4 and 5 are intended simply to dispel the view that the present inflation is caused by deficits or that cutting the deficit would help eliminate inflation without causing recession.

The lack of a causal connection between budget deficits and inflation does not deny possibly important linkages between government programs and the current inflation. One important message in Robert Crandall's paper in this volume is that government programs have contributed to inflation by pursuing goals through means that raise the price level rather than through means that show up in the budget deficit. If the costs took the form of federal expenditures or tax credits and thus appeared in the deficit, they would not affect the price level, providing that the level of aggregate demand remained the same. Paradoxically, excessive anxiety about deficits can itself be inflationary.

EXCESSIVE GROWTH OF MONEY

Besides deficits, a close contender in public opinion polls on the causes of inflation would be excessive growth of money. Unlike the deficit explanation, a positive connection between money growth and inflation is acknowledged widely by the professional community. What divides economists is the issue of whether or not a causal role can be assigned to money in addition to its role as a determinant of aggregate demand. The mainline view acknowledges the role of aggregate demand in inflation and the role of money in aggregate demand. It denies any additional, special role of money in causing inflation.

Franco Modigliani and Lucas Papademos have reported on attempts to put money into mainline inflation equations.[7] Like many other authors, they found a long mean lag for the effect of money on prices when money was used alone in a reduced-form equation. This result is entirely in accord with the view that money affects aggregate demand, thereby promptly influencing real activity and employment, and eventually the inflation rate. But they found that money was insignificant when added to equations that explain prices with the unemployment rate, import prices, and lagged inflation.

Modigliani and Papademos estimated their equations through 1971. By extending the data period, it is possible to modify these results. I explained the annual change in the GNP deflator using the current unemployment rate and three years of lagged values of the change in money and of the dependent variable. When the equation was run from 1954 to 1971, the sum of the coefficients on lagged money was only 0.13, with successive t statistics of only 0.6, 0.1, and 0.2. When the same equation was rerun for the 1954–77 period, the sum of the money coefficients rose to 0.71 with successive t statistics of 1.7, 1.2, and 0.6. Adding a dummy for the control and postcontrol period raised the sum of coefficients to 0.77. Apparently the recent interest in this type of explanation of inflation arises from the general inability of demand variables to explain the inflation of the mid-1970s and the coincidental acceleration of money growth. All the

7. Franco Modigliani and Lucas Papademos, "Targets for Monetary Policy in the Coming Year," *BPEA, 1:1975,* pp. 141–63.

independent explanatory power of money comes from this one episode. To believe that money has this independent role in causing inflation, one has to believe that the relatively rapid money growth of 1972–73 caused the subsequent explosion of prices in 1974–75, creating inflation directly rather than through demand variables for perhaps the first time in history. This interpretation not only strains the imagination, but is inconsistent with the historical evidence of long lags in reduced-form equations explaining prices with money.

SOCIAL WELFARE PROGRAMS

Government programs of income maintenance would also be high on a list of popular explanations of inflation. Unemployment compensation and the minimum wage are the two programs that are most clearly related to wage behavior. Both have been studied carefully by economists and have at least potentially significant effects on labor markets.

Table 7 shows the percentage of after-tax earnings that was replaced by unemployment benefits and the minimum wage as a percentage of average earnings during recent periods. Both measures rose gradually during the postwar period until the last half of the 1960s. Between 1966–70 and the present, the net replacement ratio under unemployment compensation increased slightly, while the relative minimum wage declined sharply.

As was noted earlier, Gramlich estimated that average wages rise by about 0.03 percent for each 1 percent change in the minimum.[8] A substantial rise in the minimum, such as the 15 percent increase of January 1978, will have a noticeable effect on aggregate wages. However, during the period that inflation was worsening, the relative minimum wage was falling. And as the disaggregated results showed, wages in low-wage industries (where increases in the minimum wage have their principal effect) were falling behind other wages. The coverage of the minimum wage was substantially expanded in the mid-1960s, adding to its impact on average wages at that time. But that episode is too remote to have any relevance to the inflation of the 1970s. Finally, by reducing the employment prospects of young workers, the minimum wage may add to their unemployment and thus have a modest effect in shifting the Phillips

8. Gramlich, "Impact of Minimum Wages."

Table 7. Unemployment Benefits and Minimum Wage Relative to Average Earnings, Selected Periods, 1951-77

Percent

Description	1951-55	1956-60	1961-65	1966-70	1971-75	1976-77
Unemployment compensation replacement ratio (net)[a]	39.4	42.9	44.4	46.0	47.3	47.1
Relative minimum wage[b]	45.4	47.6	48.3	51.1	47.2	44.3

Sources: Average weekly unemployment compensation benefits, *Economic Report of the President, January 1978*, table B-33, and updates from U.S. Department of Labor, Employment and Training Administration; spendable earnings (worker with 3 dependents), U.S. Bureau of Economic Analysis, *Business Statistics, 1975* (Government Printing Office, 1976) and *Survey of Current Business*, various issues; straight-time earnings in manufacturing, U.S. Bureau of Labor Statistics, *Employment and Earnings, United States, 1909-75*, Bulletin 1312-10 (GPO, 1975), and *Employment and Earnings*, various issues.

a. Unemployment compensation benefits as a percentage of spendable weekly earnings.

b. Minimum wage as a percentage of straight-time hourly earnings in manufacturing.

curve. Any such effect—and I would expect it to be quite small—is captured in using the weighted unemployment rate in the wage equation.

Unemployment compensation has a potential effect on wage inflation by reducing the willingness of recipients to accept available job offers. Together with other programs of income maintenance, it provides a disincentive to work compared with a situation in which no support is provided or one in which support does not depend on unemployment. However, such programs are not new to the recent years of rapid inflation. And as table 7 shows, the benefits have not become much more generous during the period when inflation has worsened.[9]

In the majority of cases, workers receiving unemployment compensation benefits have been laid off from jobs to which they expect to return. Wages in those jobs are inflexible because of the formal and informal relations binding employers and employees, not because workers who have been laid off are holding back their services waiting for better wages. While unemployment compensation may have some effect on the response of wages to unemployment, it is doubtful that the effect is large.

9. In a series of articles providing many constructive suggestions for reforming the unemployment compensation system, Martin Feldstein has pointed out that replacement ratios for certain workers can rise above the averages shown in table 7. See Martin Feldstein, "Unemployment Compensation: Adverse Incentives and Distributional Anomalies," *National Tax Journal*, vol. 27 (June 1974), pp. 231-44. However, I doubt that such calculations could alter the verdict that there has been little change in the last decade in the relative benefits of the program.

The outcome might be different if most of unemployment among those who receive benefits were well described by simple search models and if wage offers were varied by firms in response to short-run variations in labor market tightness. But this is not the case.

MISPERCEPTION, PERFECT MARKETS, AND RATIONAL EXPECTATIONS

The most serious conceptual challenge to the mainline model I have outlined comes from a view that attributes all of inflation and unemployment to misperceptions on the part of workers and firms: workers are led into more or less employment than they would normally want by their incorrect reading of wage or price trends. In a related set of models, "rational" expectations and extreme price and wage flexibility are assumed to characterize the macroeconomy. Workers are assumed to make market-clearing wage and price changes continuously, based on the best information available and constrained only by existing contracts. Except for information lags and delays until existing contracts expire, wages and prices are always adjusted to provide equilibrium levels of output and employment. Both these models have an important common feature: in contrast to the mainline model, they have variations in inflation causing variations in unemployment rather than the reverse. Without inflation surprises, unemployment would always be at a "natural rate."

The search models fail to explain the widespread phenomenon of layoffs or the cyclical pattern of quits. To the extent they predict that wages must accelerate if unemployment is to be maintained below its natural rate—their central implication—they predict wages must decelerate if unemployment is to stay above the natural rate for any sustained period. Alternatively, they may assume that misperceptions about available wage offers take a long time to be corrected. On the basis of this argument, the persistence of unemployment and inflation since the mid-1970s is understood as a continued overoptimism about available wage offers. Because most periods of unemployment have a duration measured in days or at most several weeks, it seems unrealistic to assume years of misperception to explain unemployment.

Models that combine wage and price flexibility with assumptions embodied in rational expectations about behavior have similar problems explaining persistence. Any deviation of unemployment from the natural

rate can persist only until people become aware of the situation or re-negotiate existing contracts. Except for three-year wage agreements negotiated with some large unions—agreements that cover only a small fraction of the work force—it is difficult to imagine price or wage arrangements in any important area of the economy that are bound by long-term contracts. Thus, when unemployment has deviated from past levels for any sustained period, the new unemployment level must be interpreted as a new natural rate. By contrast, the mainstream model that I have described recognizes sustained periods of underemployment and leaves open the possibility of changing unemployment through demand management.

Slowing Inflation: Aggregate Demand

The inflation of the 1970s does not change the conclusion that slowing the economy and raising unemployment can slow and eventually eliminate inflation. The evidence is, however, that inflation would slow only gradually in response to holding back aggregate demand, and that the cost in lost employment and output per point of disinflation would be large. The equations of table 5 generally predict inflation will be less than one point slower in the third year of a policy that holds the unemployment rate one point higher. And the additional unemployment implies a loss of $50 billion to $60 billion a year in output in today's economy.

A different specification might alter the numerical estimates, but it could not reverse the verdict that the anti-inflation gains from restraining aggregate demand are disappointingly small. Arthur Okun recently summarized the estimates from six different econometric models and came to a similarly pessimistic conclusion.[10] Whatever view is held on the urgency of slowing inflation today, it is unrealistic to believe that the public or its representatives would permit the extended period of high unemployment required to slow inflation in this manner.

Stabilization strategy since 1975 may be interpreted as an attempt to find an output path that would gradually reduce unemployment and at the same time slow inflation. The evidence of the past few years provides little hope for such a possibility. After the hourly earnings index slowed in the early quarters of recovery, it began to accelerate gradually in 1977.

10. Arthur M. Okun, "Efficient Disinflationary Policies," *American Economic Review*, vol. 68 (May 1978), pp. 348–52.

Equations based on the level of tightness in the labor market predicted a continuing deceleration given the slack labor markets of 1976–77. But the predicted unwinding of inflation in response to unemployment is so gradual that it is easily offset by other inflationary developments. Food and import prices rose faster in 1977 than in 1976, although the effect on wages of their speedup in 1977 should have been slight. Unemployment declined noticeably during 1977, and this could help explain the wage speedup if the change in unemployment as well as its level has an effect on wage inflation that is not captured in estimates using annual data.[11] But whatever the explanation is for recent wage changes, such developments further dramatize the difficulty of slowing the present inflation with demand management alone.

Slowing Inflation: Expectations

William Fellner has articulated the principal challenge to the pessimistic verdict on using aggregate demand to slow inflation.[12] He views the inertia of inflation as a consequence of generalized expectations of inflation. According to Fellner, in recent years contracts governing wages and prices have been formulated with the expectation that inflation will continue into the future.[13] So long as these expectations are maintained, they become a self-fulfilling prophecy. To stop inflation, policy must change these expectations. In Fellner's view, the only way to change them is through a convincing demonstration that monetary and fiscal policies will not accommodate the expected inflation rate.

An example will serve to illustrate this point. Assume that 4 percent

11. An effect from such changes appears in equations estimated with quarterly data. The insignificance of lagged unemployment when added to the wage equations reported in table 5 argues against any important effects from a change in unemployment over a period as long as a year. I regard the correct specification as an open question in light of the differing results with quarterly and annual data.

12. William J. Fellner, *Towards a Reconstruction of Macroeconomics: Problems of Theory and Policy* (American Enterprise Institute, 1976).

13. Martin Neil Baily, in "Stabilization Policy and Private Economic Behavior," *BPEA, 1:1978,* pp. 11–50, has recently explored the idea that the generalized expectation of prosperity has influenced the behavior of firms in a stabilizing way. Believing that the government will avoid the deep slumps of the past, firms themselves respond with hiring, stocking, and investment decisions that are more stabilizing than in the past. I interpret Fellner's views on inflationary expectations as analogous to this model of changing real behavior.

real growth is the desired path for output and that 6 percent is the expected inflation rate. A 10 percent growth rate of aggregate demand would be accommodating. If aggregate-demand growth were held to 8 percent, the econometric evidence predicts that real growth the first year would slow by nearly 2 percent while inflation would slow only slightly. After two years, real output would be more than 3 percent below the 4 percent growth path, and prices would be about 1 percent below that path. Fellner reasons that, by making the decision to slow aggregate demand convincing, expectations would change and the division between real growth and inflation would improve. The coefficients of the model that yield pessimistic projections today would be changed by the clear determination of the authorities to adopt a nonaccommodating policy.

How plausible is this remedy for inflation? The 1973–75 recession apparently did not change the coefficients. It could be argued, however, that this period did not demonstrate nonaccommodation convincingly because policies promptly turned to aiding recovery once unemployment increased. Let me bring together the scattered evidence presented earlier for questioning Fellner's optimism.

First, the evidence is that the inertia process is expectational but to only a limited extent. That does not mean that people do not have expectations about inflation, but simply that current wage and price decisions, as opposed to decisions in other spheres such as lending or investing, are not governed by those expectations. Even in the area of long-term labor contracts, in which expectations could be important, the analysis presented above shows that wage developments are better explained as backward looking and that escalators are used to avoid predicting the future. For most questions regarding inflation it is not crucial to know whether the inertia process is forward looking or backward looking. It does matter here.

Second, even if the econometric coefficients from Phillips curves are interpreted as expectational rather than backward looking, how much will an announced policy of demand restraint affect those expectations? If a nonaccommodating aggregate-demand policy is totally convincing, it will lead people to expect that unemployment will rise. But why should this affect their expectations about inflation by more than the short-run Phillips curve predicts? If inflation responds weakly to actual unemployment, why should expected inflation respond so strongly to expected unemployment?

This leaves room for a small gain in Fellner's scheme. If there are some wage contracts made with a view to the unemployment rate anticipated in the future, expecting more unemployment should modify such contracts by the amount predicted by the Phillips curve. If a restrictive nominal GNP path is to be pursued, there is thus some gain from announcing it ahead of time. My only question is whether there is reason to expect more than the improvement predicted by the Phillips curve as applied to the expected *future* course of unemployment. And if even that effect is confined to a small subset of contracts that are actually forward looking, the total benefits would be limited. On the price side, there are depletable resources whose price depends on expectations of prospective demand, but these are not important in the overall price level.

If wage and price setting were sufficiently concentrated in this economy, the possibilities for affecting inflation through Fellner's route would be greatly enhanced. A roomful of private decisionmakers who recognized that their inflationary behavior would directly affect their level of output and employment would be expected to respond favorably to a government policy of nonaccommodation. That is not what occurs in the U.S. economy.

Linking an incomes policy to an announced nonaccommodating policy on aggregate demand would help achieve Fellner's result. As discussed below, an effective incomes policy would produce a more favorable prospective split between real growth and inflation for any given path of nominal demand growth. Thus, expectations of inflation would change by more than the Phillips curve predicts. And to the extent that expectations do affect current wage decisions—which is still an open question—they would complement an incomes policy. Although it is an incomes policy that changes the immediate trade-off, the nonaccommodating demand policy is a necessary complement. Without it, the reduced inflation promised by the improved trade-off could be dissipated by a movement along the new trade-off curve.

Slowing Inflation: Tax-Based Incomes Policies

Although there are several variations of tax-based incomes policies (TIPs), their differences are primarily important in determining their acceptability, the ease of their implementation, and their effectiveness in altering individual wage and price decisions. These matters are discussed in other papers in this volume. At the macroeconomic level, the main impact of alternative TIPs affecting wages will be similar. And TIPs that act on prices primarily ensure that price restraint parallels wage restraint, which is what the macroeconomic model predicts without such policies.

It is simplest to integrate TIP effects into the macroeconomic model by assuming that the same path of real output is pursued with and without the program. Starting from the present state of the economy, a TIP that causes individual wages to rise more slowly than they otherwise would can be represented simply as a reduction in the constant term of the wage equation. Whether TIP will alter the slope of the short-run Phillips curve or whether it will reduce permanently the unemployment rate that represents full employment are separate issues that are briefly considered below. With a downward shift in the constant term of the wage equation, nominal aggregate demand must be reduced by an amount that is proportional to the shift in order to maintain the desired output path. This necessitates an appropriate combined adjustment in fiscal and monetary policies. This relatively simple procedure is all that is needed to integrate TIP and aggregate demand policies in the first year; a similar adjustment is required in subsequent years if the shift caused by TIP each year could be specified. But the macroeconomic analysis does raise some questions about the size of that shift in subsequent years and the difficulty of attaining it.

LAGGED EFFECTS

In most views of the inflation process, the slower average wage increases resulting from TIP in the first year will reduce wage pressures in the second year. If prices slow correspondingly, as would be expected, this favorable lagged effect would be predicted by any of the aggregate equations discussed earlier. Because the estimated lags are short, a major fraction of the first year's improvement in inflation will be perpetuated into the second year. In actual experience, however, some of the complications introduced by TIPs might lead to lagged effects that are different from these estimates.

Any TIP program may alter slightly the distribution of wages. The possibilities are numerous and the likely outcomes differ according to whether a penalty or reward TIP is employed. The main possibility for obtaining lagged effects that are noticeably smaller than the macromodel predicts probably arises in the case of a reward TIP that is employed for only one year. On the one hand, without a reward in the second year, workers whose wages had been restrained would tend to increase their wage demands to catch up with those that had not. On the other hand, firms that had not participated would be at a competitive cost disadvantage relative to firms that had, and that would put downward pressure on their wage offers. If these two influences cancel each other, the lagged effects from the economic equations should hold.

If the lagged wage effects in the macroeconomic model represent generalized expectations, the TIP program can be viewed in two ways. First, expectations that are based on actual experience should be favorably influenced by the initial slowdown in average wages and prices under TIP. This influence can be expected to grow if TIP effects are present over successive years. Second, expectations should be influenced by the existence of TIP as a specific and acceptable anti-inflation program. It should enhance the effects on inflationary expectations that Fellner looks for through policies of nonaccommodating aggregate demand. I have argued that these policies may be weak because their primary effect would be to change expectations of unemployment. Together with TIP, a greater part of any change in nominal demand expectations would be changes in expectations of the price level.

CHANGING THE STRUCTURE

TIPs are sometimes espoused as a means of shifting the Phillips curve in a favorable direction. This is one interpretation of shifting the constant term in the aggregate-wage equation. There is little basis, however, for judging whether such a favorable shift would be maintained in a period of substantially tighter labor markets. Because excess demand in the labor market now appears to develop gradually, TIP might make the Phillips curve more nearly L-shaped. In moderately tight markets, wages might be restrained, producing an improved trade-off; but in extremely tight labor markets, TIP might be relatively ineffective and the short-term trade-off might be the same as before.

TIPs do not have to reduce the unemployment rate that represents full employment in order to be useful. They would be a valuable tool if they were simply a shortcut to price stability and slowed the present wage-price spiral without a period of sustained high unemployment. If they were also an indirect remedy for structural problems in the labor market that produce inflation while involuntary unemployment still exists, that would be a bonus.

Measures to Cut Costs and Prices

What effect can we expect on the ongoing inflation rate from one-time increases or reductions in prices or costs? We can rely on cost changes to be reflected in prices. Beyond that, the empirical evidence is unfailingly ambiguous. The price shocks of the mid-1970s affected wages, but not proportionately. Consumer prices appear to have some persistent effect on wages, but it is modest once the effects of lagged wages themselves are allowed for. On the basis of the evidence, it appears that only a minor fraction of any shock to prices would filter through into average wage changes and thus have some multiplied effect. That still makes measures to cut prices and costs worth pursuing and their opposites worth avoiding. Even if only one-quarter of any price change influences wages, 1 percent removed from the CPI reduces wage inflation by about as much as 1 percentage point more unemployment for one year.

Measures to cut prices and costs can be effectively included as part of a larger anti-inflation strategy. In any such strategy, success will be self-perpetuating. Failure in the aggregate will almost surely cause the pieces to come apart. If the government can point to direct price-cutting measures of its own, it would stand a better chance of obtaining support from the private sector, either for voluntary restraint or for TIP. And if the government could accomplish that, it could change the inertia equations in a favorable way.

Comments and Discussion

Martin Neil Baily: George Perry presents and discusses in an interesting and provocative way several hypotheses relevant to anti-inflationary policy. Perry describes convincingly the tremendous inertia in wage behavior during inflation and also brings out some new and informative aspects of the Phillips curve. I have a few doubts to raise, however, about his conclusions.

First, Perry shows the relatively greater inflexibility of wages in the high-wage and union sectors. The low-wage and nonunion sectors appear to be more responsive to short-run economic conditions. This result is plausible and can be rationalized, for example, on the grounds that wage contracts are more important in the high-wage and union sectors. The disaggregated wage equations that Perry estimates, however, contain no variables that will hold the wage distribution together. In *BPEA, 2:1977*, James Tobin and I developed some results suggesting the importance of the relative sectoral wage level as a determinant of the rate of change of a sector's wage. Perry does not have to accept our formulation, but one would expect some variable to be included that prevents relative wages from diverging indefinitely. In the past few years union wages have increased relative to nonunion wages. This fact is interesting in itself and relevant for wage policy. But if union wages continue to grow faster than nonunion wages, there will surely be increasing stress in the wage structure that will eventually affect the rates of change of wages in both sectors.

Second, Perry argues that the true wage equation is characterized by a "catch-up" augmented Phillips curve, rather than by an expectations-augmented Phillips curve. The arguments for this view seemed to me unconvincing. To demonstrate this would require an analysis of how expectations are formed and how the catch-up is computed, realizing that these two are different in principle and that they have in fact behaved differently enough over some historical period that the data can test the two alternatives. To be more specific, given all the shocks that have hit the economy recently and the tremendous inertia evident in wage behavior, it may have been true that the best estimate of one year's wage increase was the previous year's wage increase. If even half-true, this would make the two hypotheses difficult to distinguish.

Third, I was puzzled by two aspects of Perry's procedure and so I reran his aggregate equation. I was surprised that his wage-wage equation did not allow for serial correlation of the errors, but I discovered that this was because the correction made only a minor difference. Perry himself notes that the price feedbacks do seem to decline in importance with a serial correlation correction. However, I came to a different conclusion than Perry did regarding the stability of the equation. His predictions are made using *actual* values of the feedback variables rather than the predicted values from previous periods. This is a great help in keeping the equation on track through the 1970s. My version of Perry's equation 5.4 (the unemployment rate for adult males used in place of the weighted aggregate rate) underpredicted the rate of wage inflation in every year from 1971 through 1977 and gave a cumulative underprediction of over 16 percent by 1977.

In fairness to Perry, I should point out that he does say that the wage-wage spiral alone cannot explain the behavior of the 1970s. This is a crucial point for both theory and policy, however, and requires more emphasis. It is difficult to avoid the conclusion that the rapid price inflation and slow growth of real wages in the 1970s caused an upward pressure on wage settlements, particularly in the union and high-wage sectors, as Perry's earlier results suggested. The only other alternative is to argue that Perry has sharply underestimated the true nonaccelerating-inflation rate of unemployment (NAIRU) or natural rate. Wage acceleration has occurred, in this alternative view, because the actual unemployment rate for 1971–77, which averaged 6.5 percent, was below the NAIRU.

As a final check on the stability of the Phillips curve, I ran an F-test to see if the coefficients of the wage-wage or wage-price equations had shifted significantly. The null hypothesis was that the coefficients had remained constant across the 1956–69 and 1970–77 periods. These dates were selected because the lack of responsiveness of wages to the 1970–71 downturn was seen by many observers as an important break in wage behavior. The null hypothesis was rejected at the 5 percent level for my calculations of Perry's wage-wage and wage-price equations.

In short, therefore, I am less confident than Perry that we really do have a stable structural relation in current Phillips curve specifications. However, there are two lessons that Perry wants us to learn from the 1960s and 1970s. If the economy is wound up too much, wages and prices begin to accelerate. If unemployment is raised to slow things down again, it is a painful process. I have no quarrel with either of these lessons.

The regressions on inflation against the deficit and on inflation against money growth are fun. I hope the myth about the deficit is diminished by these findings. The improved performance of money growth as an explanation of the 1972–77 inflation does not give greater support to the monetarist than to the structuralist view of inflation. The Federal Reserve Board is not immune from political forces, nor should it be. It cannot tolerate prolonged, excessive unemployment. If structural factors push out the inflation/unemployment trade-off—resulting in inflationary price pressure even at high unemployment—the Federal Reserve Board is forced to accommodate at least some of this pressure. Consequently, high inflation and high money growth will tend to go together, even with a structuralist perspective.

Perry presents a brief discussion of the misperception theories. I think these theories can accommodate layoffs better than Perry indicates, but I share his general skepticism that expectational errors can plausibly explain the persistence of unemployment movements. And this also leads me to agree with his mistrust of the use of policy announcements to reduce inflationary pressure directly.

In conclusion, I commend Perry for his interesting and stimulating paper. If it did not convince me on all points, this merely reflects the difficulty of the issues being tackled.

William Poole: The basic message of George Perry's paper is that the Phillips curve is alive and well and that the evidence continues to support the proposition that higher unemployment buys a distressingly small rate of deceleration in inflation. I do not have any major quarrels with Perry on the matters analyzed in his paper.

For the purposes at hand it is not necessary to say much about the theory behind the Phillips curve. Perry is clearly writing within what may be called the original Phillips curve tradition, as distinguished from the more recent view of the curve developed by Milton Friedman, Edmund Phelps, and Robert Lucas. Under the traditional view, wage and price behavior—supported by contractual, collective bargaining, and other institutional considerations—reflects a substantial degree of inertia, whereas according to the view held by Friedman, Phelps, and Lucas, inertia is not inherent in behavior but reflects correctly perceived inertia in inflation caused by the monetary policies of the government. The importance of distinguishing between these two views is that according to the traditional view, demand management can reduce inflation only slowly and painfully, while under the alternative view, expectations could in principle be altered relatively quickly and, therefore, at little unemployment cost.

Perry attempts to provide evidence on this issue by examining what he calls forward-looking and backward-looking Phillips curve specifications. I find his evidence supporting the backward-looking specifications unconvincing. Consider, for example, the implications of the forward-looking theory for the apparently backward-looking wage-wage specification. Suppose wages are set on the basis of a price forecast for the next several years. Clearly, in trying to explain the wage behavior of the current year, last year's wages could be a more accurate measure of current expectations of future inflation than any proxy constructed from past or future price changes. I believe that it is simply not possible to obtain convincing evidence on this issue from the approach Perry follows.

From other evidence there can be no question that forward-looking behavior is important. The increasing use of cost-of-living clauses reflects a structural modification to contracts in anticipation of continuing inflation. In nonunion situations many companies have apparently replaced annual salary reviews with semiannual reviews so that wages can be linked more closely to changes in price level. And evidence from episodes of hyperinflation in other countries makes it clear that institutional practices seemingly anchored in bedrock are adjusted amazingly rapidly when inflation reaches triple-digit and higher rates.

If Perry underestimates the importance of forward-looking behavior, as I think he does, the near-term policy significance of this issue is nevertheless limited. Even the most ardent believer in the importance of expectations has a difficult time finding policy proposals that promise to generate a quick and lasting change in inflationary expectations. Suppose, for example, that the Federal Reserve announced that money growth would be reduced to a 4 percent annual rate immediately and then held at that rate indefinitely. It would be unlikely that this announcement would change inflationary expectations. The Federal Reserve has not always achieved its announced money growth targets; moreover, there is a possibility that the President, the Congress, or both would force a change in Federal Reserve policy if a recession occurred. From this viewpoint, the problem is not an economic policy problem at all, but rather one of constructing a political consensus for a noninflationary monetary policy.

It is unlikely that long-run inflationary expectations can be reduced without an actual decline in inflation *and* clear evidence of a commitment to less inflationary policies. For the evidence to be clear, it may well be necessary for the government consciously and deliberately to avoid following expansionary policies in the next recession.

If Perry's estimates are taken at face value, a monetary policy that kept the unemployment rate 1 percentage point above the natural rate would be consistent with a decline in the inflation rate by 0.3 percentage point each year. That policy would then call for a deceleration of money growth sufficient to slow nominal GNP growth by 0.3 percentage point a year. With this policy it would take at least twenty years of unemployment at 1 percentage point above the natural rate to reduce the inflation rate to zero. (Indeed, with Perry's two-year lag structure, it would take nearly thirty years.) It is difficult for me to believe that prediction of the results of such a monetary policy; surely in time the policy would change expectations and lead to adaptations consistent with full employment on the average. Nevertheless, Perry's estimates may well be reasonable for the time required for changed policies to become credible and to affect expectations. This period could easily be three to five years.

A number of policy proposals, including tax-based incomes policies, should be viewed in the light of their prospects for reducing the unemployment costs of the more basic anti-inflationary policy of slowing money growth. Perry mentions, but insufficiently emphasizes, the importance of reducing nominal income growth. Without monetary deceleration, other policies to reduce inflation are absolutely guaranteed to fail; with monetary deceleration, these other policies may reduce the employment costs of slowing inflation.

Perry does not discuss this possibility in detail, but I think that the importance of nonmonetary policies for the inflation issue is primarily political and expectational. The economics of these policies should be judged on efficiency and public finance considerations.

General Discussion

William Fellner amplified his views on anti-inflationary policy. He agreed with Perry that reasonably optimistic views about the output and employment consequences of his demand policy implied changes in specific regression coefficients in response to a consistent and credible policy line. He suggested that the coefficient that would change could be identified, for example, in a model of the type developed in Phillip Cagan's current work. For a slack of given size, this is the coefficient by which it is necessary to multiply the difference between the expected long-run inflation rate and the currently observed rate to obtain the current downward revision of the expected long-run rate. This revision causes current price deceleration, which either is added to the deceleration resulting from any increase in the slack or is deducted from the price acceleration resulting from any decrease. Fellner suggested that, under a credible policy of gradually reducing the rate of increase of money GNP until inflation is eliminated, the numerical value of the coefficient determining the adjustment of price-trend expectations would increase significantly. This, he argued, is because the erratic policies of the past must have made the public hesitant to lower its long-run inflation expectations during the brief periods of nondiminishing slack. Fellner also said that the alternative to the course he is advocating would be an uncomfortably controlled system, rather than the kind of economy envisaged by the advocates of incomes policy.

Michael Wachter agreed with Fellner on the importance of the changing responsiveness of inflation to government policy actions and pronouncements. Wachter said that the government had actually reduced the effectiveness of its anti-inflation policy and increased confusion during the most recent recession by frequently stating that policy was much less contractionary than it actually was.

James Tobin noted that if a TIP scheme were successful, the nominal money stock should grow less rapidly than if such a scheme were not in effect. He cautioned against accompanying a TIP scheme with aggregate demand policies that are contractionary in real terms.

Robert Gordon said that it was clear from the evidence of the 1960s and early 1970s that wages do not adjust fully to accelerations in the consumer price index; but he considered current knowledge about the effects of other wage determinants uncertain. In particular, he stated that it would be difficult to distinguish between the influence of product prices and the influence of other wages because of the high collinearity in these variables. Franco Modigliani reported that the coefficient on wages had been inappropriately negative in wage regressions with both past wages and past prices as independent variables. Perry responded that this result came from using hourly compensation as a wage variable; such compensation is currently poorly measured and is influenced by many nonmarket events such as payroll tax changes. Edward Gramlich argued that wages tend to be considerably more inflexible than prices in the U.S. economy. Thus, the use of longer lags might lend support to a price-wage hypothesis. Wachter voiced the opinion that the lagged money supply would perform as well as lagged prices or wages in explaining wage inflation. But Modigliani agreed with Perry that money supply or fiscal policy have no effect above that already captured by the excess demand variable.

Other participants at the conference discussed whether expected or past prices were more important in determining wages. Frederic Mishkin suggested that the presence in wage equations of only short lags on price inflation did not provide evidence supporting backward- rather than forward-looking wage behavior. If the inflation rate followed a random walk, for example, the most recent inflation rate would be the best predictor of future inflation rates. Therefore, even if wage behavior was forward looking, the most recent inflation rate would contain all the relevant information about expected inflation. Mishkin emphasized, however, that the relationship between past and expected price inflation need not be a stable one and might depend on the exact nature of the inflationary process. Thomas Juster said that short-run inflationary expectations were more volatile than long-run expectations and that long-run rather than short-run expectations were relevant for wage determination. This suggested the need to use longer lags.

Gardner Ackley and James Duesenberry questioned the usefulness of searching for a single determinant of wages. Duesenberry noted that there were good microeconomic reasons for product prices, consumer prices, and other wages to enter the process in both a retrospective and a prospective form. Greater disaggregation would be required to distinguish their relative importance. This uncertainty suggested that policies should not be adopted that depend too heavily on any single explanation. Ackley reasoned that each of these variables might be important to different sectors at various times. As inflation increased, institutional innovations, such as cost-of-living allowances, might well lead to changes in the relative importance of different variables.

The discussion turned to the behavior of relative wages. John Shoven suggested that the larger recent increases in wages in the high-wage industries might be explained either by the greater use of cost-of-living allowances in the high-wage unionized sector, or by the fact that as skilled wages moved into higher marginal tax brackets a larger before-tax dispersion was required to maintain the same after-tax differentials. Duesenberry mentioned Perry's evidence that wages in the high-wage sector were more sensitive to inflation and less sensitive to unemployment than those in the low-wage sectors. If the Phillips curve in the high-wage sector were flatter than that in the low-wage sector, it was likely they would intersect; if they did not, it would not lead to the cumulative divergence in wages that concerned Martin Baily in his discussion.

Modigliani and Robert Hall said that Perry had treated the rational expectations school too casually. Hall stated that Perry should have discussed the new view of this school—that recent changes in the inflation rate have been caused by changes in the natural rate because of supply shifts. Despite this omission, he agreed with Perry's Keynesian conclusion that changes in aggregate demand influence output far more than prices. Perry replied that he had not tried to present a comprehensive discussion of the rational expectations view but simply discussed where it differed from the mainline model. The principal difference is that the mainline model recognizes the possibility of extended periods of cyclical unemployment, while the rational expectations model treats such occurrences as changes in the natural rate.

LAURENCE S. SEIDMAN
University of Pennsylvania

Tax-Based Incomes Policies

GIVEN the institutional features and ethical norms of modern labor markets and the income-maintenance programs of the welfare state, it appears that substantial macroeconomic slack is required to keep the rate of wage inflation and therefore the rate of price inflation from accelerating. Because of these deviations from a purely atomistic, competitive labor market, the unemployment rate required to prevent a rise in wage inflation is economically inefficient. The central policy problem, therefore, is to reduce this nonaccelerating-inflation rate of unemployment (NAIRU) of the economy.

The aim of an incomes policy is to introduce a direct restraint on the growth rate of money wages and salaries, so that less macroeconomic slack is required to keep the inflation rate from accelerating. Traditionally there have been two methods of implementing an incomes policy: persuasion and controls. Each has serious shortcomings as a permanent policy.

A microeconomic perspective, however, leads naturally to tax incentives, a new method of implementing an incomes policy. A comparison with the environmental pollution problem is instructive.[1] Few economists seriously advocate persuasion because in the microeconomic sphere it is taken as an axiom that each economic agent will pursue his own self-

Note: For comments and discussions on this paper I am grateful to Douglas H. Blair, Philip J. Cook, Adrian M. G. Darby, Wilfred J. Ethier, Robert H. Frank, Robert P. Inman, Eitan Muller, Jeffrey M. Perloff, Robert A. Pollak, Sidney Weintraub, and participants in the Brookings Panel.

1. This analogy is developed in Laurence S. Seidman, "A New Approach to the Control of Inflation," *Challenge*, vol. 19 (July/August 1976), pp. 39–43, and Abba P. Lerner, "Stagflation—Its Cause and Cure," *Challenge*, vol. 20 (September/October 1977), pp. 14–19.

interest. At the same time, most economists reject controls—the use of regulatory quotas for each polluter—as economically and administratively inefficient. Instead, economists generally advocate effluent taxes to "internalize the externality" of pollution.

Similarly, the excessive NAIRU can also be viewed as a microeconomic problem. Suppose that the institutional features and ethical norms of modern labor markets and the income-maintenance programs of the welfare state cause the average individual firm to raise its rate of wage increase (relative to that of the last period) at an unemployment rate at which the marginal unemployed worker would prefer work (for a wage equal to his marginal product) to leisure or job search. Then the wage behavior of the firm imposes an external cost on society in either of two forms. If monetary and fiscal policy attempt to maintain this unemployment rate, the public "bad" called accelerating inflation is generated. If monetary and fiscal policy accept a higher unemployment rate to control inflation, the result is above-optimal unemployment and lost output, the value of which exceeds the value of leisure or job search to the marginal unemployed workers.

It should therefore be natural for economists to prescribe a tax to internalize the externality, so that each firm must weigh the social cost of raising the NAIRU when it sets its wage increase. This is exactly the strategy embodied in the tax-based incomes policy (TIP) suggested several years ago by Sidney Weintraub and Henry Wallich. They proposed "to levy a surcharge on the corporate profits tax for firms granting wage increases in excess of some guidepost figure. If the wage guidepost were 5.5 per cent, and a wage increase of 7 per cent were granted, the corporate profits tax for the firm would rise above the present 48 per cent by some multiple of the 1.5 per cent excess."[2]

The proposal implies a tax rate t for the ith firm, as follows:

$$(1) \qquad\qquad t_i = b + m(w_i - n), \qquad m > 0,$$

where

b = the base tax rate

w_i = the average wage increase (percent) at firm i, including executive compensation and fringe benefits

n = the interim TIP target for wage increases (percent)

m = the TIP "multiplier" (policy parameter).

2. Henry C. Wallich and Sidney Weintraub, "A Tax-Based Incomes Policy," *Journal of Economic Issues,* vol. 5 (June 1971), p. 2.

Alternative tax-based incomes policies are possible.[3] In this paper the acronym TIP will refer to any of these variants. A TIP can provide a penalty for a w_i above a target, a reward for a w_i below a threshold, or both (if the threshold equals the target). It can be continuous, so that the size of the penalty or reward varies directly with the divergence from the target or threshold; or it can be discontinuous (all or none), so that the firm either does or does not reach the target, thereby avoiding a fixed penalty or earning a fixed reward. The incentive can be aimed at employees, either in addition to or in place of the employer incentive. A central objective of this paper will be to compare alternative TIPs.

After several years of dormancy, the tax-incentive approach to incomes policy is emerging as a major policy option. It has recently received attention in the press and is a topic of concern among policymakers.[4] A growing number of economists have shown their support.[5] Despite this new

3. A proposal receiving serious attention is described by Arthur M. Okun in "The Great Stagflation Swamp," *Challenge*, vol. 20 (November/December 1977), p. 13, as follows: *"Tax relief for price-wage restraint . . . a tax-relief incentive* should be offered to workers and businessmen who enlist in a cooperative anti-inflationary effort. To qualify for participation, a firm would have to pledge, at the beginning of 1978, to hold the average rate of wage increase of its employees below 6 percent and its average rate of price increase below 4 percent (apart from a dollar-and-cents pass-through of any increases in costs of materials and supplies) during the course of the year. In return for participation, employees of the firm would receive a tax rebate (generally through withholding) equal to 1.5 percent of their wage or salary incomes with a ceiling of $225 per person; and the firm would receive a 5 percent rebate on its income tax liabilities on domestic operating profits."

An employee incentive, intended as a complement to the Weintraub-Wallich incentive, is analyzed in Laurence S. Seidman, "A Payroll Tax-Credit to Restrain Inflation," *National Tax Journal*, vol. 29 (December 1976), pp. 398–412. Modifications to TIP are suggested in Lerner, "Stagflation—Its Cause and Cure," pp. 14–19. An excellent survey of alternative incentives is given by Michael P. Fogarty, "Fiscal Measures and Wage Settlements," *British Journal of Industrial Relations*, vol. 11 (March 1973), pp. 29–65.

4. "Another Weapon against Inflation: Tax Policy," *Business Week*, no. 2503 (October 3, 1977), pp. 94, 96; "Some New Ideas for Release," *New York Times*, October 17, 1977; Michael Ruby and others, "Carter's New Option Play," *Newsweek*, vol. 90 (November 28, 1977), pp. 91–92; U.S. Congressional Budget Office, *Recovery with Inflation* (Government Printing Office, July 1977), pp. 39–41; *The 1977 Midyear Review of the Economy*, Report of the U.S. Joint Economic Committee, 95:1 (GPO, 1977), pp. 76–77.

5. William D. Nordhaus reflected this sentiment in "Inflation Theory and Policy," *American Economic Review*, vol. 66 (May 1976), p. 64: "There is probably no . . . ideal anti-inflation policy, but economists have shown little inventiveness in designing durable antidotes to inflation other than recessions. One serious suggestion

attention, only a few serious analyses have been attempted within the economics profession.[6] There is currently a large disparity between the public interest devoted to TIP, and the analysis provided by economists. This paper seeks to contribute to closing this gap.

Several previous analyses have focused primarily on the microeconomic response of the firm or its employees (or union).[7] A distinctive feature of this paper is that it tries to integrate the microeconomic analysis of firm response with the macroeconomic impact on inflation and unemployment.

Such integration is crucial. TIP is designed to have a direct effect on the wage decision of the firm. The logic may appear to imply that TIP depends crucially on an exogenous wage theory of inflation. Clearly, a satisfactory analysis must address the apparent conflict between that wage view of inflation that seems to underlie TIP and the monetary view of inflation held by many economists, in which, over the longer run, the average growth rate of the money supply is a primary determinant of the inflation rate. The microeconomic analysis of the impact of TIP on the firm must be consistent with the process by which inflation and unemployment are determined in the macroeconomy.

In fact, TIP, the wage view, and the flexible monetary view of inflation are all fully compatible. If the growth rate of the money supply influences the average inflation rate in the long run, the impact of TIP should be

---

is an inflation tax which would penalize firms or workers to the extent that they deviated from a national norm."

James Tobin also expressed his concern in "How Dead Is Keynes?" *Economic Inquiry,* vol. 15 (October 1977), p. 467: "The way out, the only way out, is incomes policy. In 1961 the same dilemma . . . inspired the 'guideposts for noninflationary price and wage behavior'. . . . Those guideposts were advisory. But similar standards could be given, if not teeth, at least some carrots and sticks. Use corporate, personal income, and payroll taxes to reward and insure compliant employers and workers, and possibly—as Wallich and Weintraub independently proposed—to penalize violators."

6. An in-depth analysis of the theory and implementation of TIP is provided by Sidney Weintraub, *Capitalism's Inflation and Unemployment Crisis: Beyond Monetarism and Keynesianism* (Addison-Wesley, 1978).

7. Peter Isard, "The Effectiveness of Using the Tax System to Curb Inflationary Collective Bargains: An Analysis of the Wallich-Weintraub Plan," *Journal of Political Economy,* vol. 81 (May/June 1973), pp. 729–40; Yehuda Kotowitz and Richard Portes, "The 'Tax on Wage Increases': A Theoretical Analysis," *Journal of Public Economics,* vol. 3 (May 1974), pp. 113–32; R. W. Latham and D. A. Peel, "The 'Tax on Wage Increases' When the Firm is a Monopsonist," *Journal of Public Economics,* vol. 8 (October 1977), pp. 247–53.

to lower the NAIRU—enabling the economy to function at a lower unemployment rate without causing the inflation rate to accelerate. Proper monetary growth would then be required to achieve an average inflation rate near zero over the longer run. From this perspective, contrary to some popular discussion, TIP should not be regarded as a policy that tries to reduce the inflation rate permanently, even in the presence of excessive monetary growth. Instead, it should be considered a policy to reduce the NAIRU permanently.

Nevertheless, TIP deserves its description as an anti-inflation policy. At the NAIRU prior to TIP—apparently in the 6 percent range for the United States currently—TIP should cause wage and price inflation to decelerate gradually, rather than remain constant. It is true that the deceleration of inflation will only be permanent if the growth rate of the money supply is simultaneously reduced, and that a deceleration of monetary growth, even without TIP, would eventually bring down the inflation rate, but only at the cost of a prolonged, deep recession. TIP, however, enables monetary policy to reduce the inflation rate without imposing that cost.

TIP also deserves to be called an anti-inflation policy in light of the political economy of inflation and unemployment. Without TIP, the economy is characterized by an excessive NAIRU that entails significant hardship for particular social groups in the labor market. Political pressure will therefore be exerted on policymakers to reduce the unemployment rate below the excessive NAIRU in order to reduce that hardship. The result, however, is gradually accelerating inflation. If TIP succeeds in bringing down the NAIRU, hardship can be reduced without causing inflation to accelerate. With TIP and the lower NAIRU, the economy is likely to generate less inflation, given political concern for the unemployed.

In this paper I outline a classification scheme for alternative TIPs. I analyze the impact of a TIP imposed on the employer (an employer TIP) in a value-maximization model and also in a collective bargaining model. The difference between a penalty TIP and a reward TIP is illuminated. I link this microanalysis to a macromodel of wage and price inflation and analyze the impact of TIP on the NAIRU of the economy. I then compare an employee TIP to an employer TIP. Next, the welfare economics of TIP is examined—its impact on allocative efficiency and income distribution. Finally, conclusions and recommendations are presented.

A Taxonomy of Alternative TIPs

A TIP can provide an incentive for the employer, the employees, or both at a firm. It is useful to distinguish a penalty TIP from a reward TIP. Under a penalty-only TIP, the employer, or employees, are subject to a higher tax rate if w_i is greater than the interim target; but if w_i is less, the tax rate remains at the base. The target is assumed to be less than what the average firm would have granted without TIP. Thus, under a penalty-only TIP, t_i is given by equation 1 if w_i is greater than or equal to n, but equal to b if w_i is less than n. Under a reward-only TIP, the tax rate would be given by 2 below if w_i is less than or equal to g, but would equal b if w_i is greater than g:

$$(2) \qquad\qquad t_i = b - m(g - w_i), \qquad m > 0,$$

where g is the "threshold" percentage wage increase.

Under a penalty-only TIP in 1, for w_i greater than or equal to n, a 1 percentage point increase in w_i raises t_i by m. Similarly, under a reward-only TIP in 2, when w_i is less than g, an increase of 1 percentage point in w_i raises t_i by m. For a penalty-only TIP, a 1 point increase in w_i raises the penalty by m. For a reward-only TIP, a 1 point increase in w_i reduces the reward by m. In both cases, the marginal tax penalty $\partial t_i / \partial w_i$ is identical (equal to m). Thus, a given marginal tax penalty m can be provided by either a penalty-only TIP or a reward-only TIP.

An example will illustrate. Suppose that b is 48 percent and m is 4. Under a penalty-only TIP, assume n is 6 percent. If the firm raises w_i from 6 percent to 7 percent, its tax rate will increase from 48 percent to 52 percent, or by 4 percentage points. Under a reward-only TIP, assume g is 8 percent. If the firm raises w_i from 6 percent to 7 percent, its tax rate will increase from 40 percent to 44 percent, or by 4 percentage points.

Without TIP, a 1 point increase in w_i causes a given decline in gross (before-tax) profit π^G and therefore, for a fixed tax rate, a given decline in net (after-tax) profit π^N. If an employer TIP were introduced (either a penalty-only or a reward-only TIP), a 1 point increase in w_i would cause the same decline in gross profit that would occur without TIP; but because it also would raise the tax rate, it would cause a greater decline in net profit than would occur without TIP. This change in the value of

$\partial\pi^N/\partial w_i$ is called the TIP incentive effect. A comparable TIP incentive can be provided by either a penalty-only TIP or a reward-only TIP because it depends primarily on m. This can be shown as follows:

(3) $$\pi^N = (1 - t_i)\pi^G.$$

Without TIP, because t_i is not a function of w_i,

(4) $$\frac{\partial\pi^N}{\partial w_i} = (1 - b)\frac{\partial\pi^G}{\partial w_i}.$$

With either a penalty-only TIP (t_i given by 1) or a reward-only TIP (t_i given by 2):

(4a) $$\frac{\partial\pi^N}{\partial w_i} = (1 - t_i)\frac{\partial\pi^G}{\partial w_i} - \pi^G \cdot m.$$

The change in $\partial\pi^N/\partial w_i$ due to TIP is obtained by subtracting 4 from 4a:

(5) $$\left(\frac{\partial\pi^N}{\partial w_i}\right)_{TIP} - \left(\frac{\partial\pi^N}{\partial w_i}\right)_{No\ TIP} = (b - t_i)\frac{\partial\pi^G}{\partial w_i} - \bar{\pi}^G \cdot m.$$

At the w_i' for which $\partial\pi^G/\partial w_i$ is zero, the TIP incentive effect would equal $(-\pi^G \cdot m)$ for both a penalty-only TIP and a reward-only TIP. At other w_i, the TIP incentive effect would still depend primarily on m, whether TIP was penalty or reward, as long as the magnitude of the second term dominated the magnitude of the first term. It will be a convenient simplification to regard the TIP incentive effect as primarily determined by m, the marginal tax penalty. The above can be applied to an employee TIP by simply substituting employee gross income for gross profit, and net income for net profit.

Consider a TIP for which 1 holds for w_i less than n as well as w_i greater than or equal to n and a TIP for which 2 holds for w_i greater than g as well as w_i less than or equal to g. Then for both these TIPs, t_i is given by:

(6) $$t_i = B + mw_i, \qquad m > 0,$$

where

$B = b - mn$ for t_i given by 1, and
$B = b - mg$ for t_i given by 2.

Under both, $\partial t_i / \partial w_i$ equals m for all w_i. For the TIP given by 1, the dividing line between penalty and reward (relative to the base tax rate b) is w_i equal to n. For the TIP given by 2, the dividing line is w_i equal to g. Although a TIP given by 6 for all w_i has both a penalty range and a reward range, it will be shown later that it is essential to make the following distinction. Let w^* be the wage increase that the average firm would have granted in this period without TIP. Then if $t_i(w^*)$ is greater than b in 6, it will be called penalty-reward TIP, in that order; if $t_i(w^*)$ is less than or equal to b, it will be called reward-penalty TIP. Because it is a hypothetical wage increase, w^* cannot be known with certainty either before or after TIP is enacted. If it is assumed that w^* equals w_0 (where w_0 is the wage increase in the period preceding the introduction of TIP), then TIP can be identified as a penalty-reward TIP depending on whether $t_i(w_0)$ is greater than b.

An example will illustrate. Suppose an employer TIP is introduced with t_i given by equation 1 for all w_i, and n is 6 percent, so that the dividing line between penalty and reward is 6 percent. The current U.S. w_0 is 8 percent. If w^* is also 8 percent, this would be a penalty-reward TIP. On the other hand, suppose that t_i is given by 2 for all w_i and g is 8 percent, so that the dividing line between penalty and reward is 8 percent. Then this would be a reward-penalty TIP. The key issue is this: if the firm grants 8 percent—the average wage increase projected to occur without TIP—would the tax rate increase relative to the base, or would it remain the same or decrease? I indicate below why this distinction is of great importance.

If t_i were given by 6 for all w_i, then TIP would be fully continuous. At each w_i, $\partial t_i / \partial w_i$ equals m. Under a penalty-only TIP, the incentive is only partly continuous. For w_i greater than n, $\partial t_i / \partial w_i$ equals m; but for w_i less than n, $\partial t_i / \partial w_i$ equals 0. Similarly, a reward-only TIP is only partly continuous. Under an all-or-none TIP, the incentive is completely discontinuous. Under an all-or-none, penalty TIP, t_i is greater than b by a fixed amount for all w_i greater than n; but t_i equals b for all w_i less than or equal to n. Under an all-or-none, reward TIP, t_i is less than b by a fixed amount for all w_i less than or equal to g; but t_i equals b for all w_i greater than g.

In summary, two points deserve emphasis. First, any partly or fully continuous TIP can provide the same incentive effect, whether it is penalty (penalty-only or penalty-reward) or reward (reward-only or reward-penalty) because the TIP incentive effect depends primarily on the TIP multiplier m. Either a penalty or a reward TIP can increase the loss to the employer or reduce the gain to employees, from a given increase in w_i.

Second, any penalty TIP (penalty-reward, penalty-only or all-or-none) differs from any reward TIP (reward-penalty, reward-only, or all-or-none) as follows. For any penalty TIP, $t_i(w^*)$ is greater than b; for any reward TIP, $t_i(w^*)$ is less than or equal to b. Any penalty TIP would raise the tax rate above the base rate if the average firm granted the same w^* it would have granted without TIP. Any reward TIP would not raise the tax rate if the same w^* were granted.

The employer TIP proposed by Weintraub and Wallich is implemented through the income tax of the firm. The incentive could be attempted on another tax, such as payroll or sales. It has been suggested that the wage bill in excess of the guidepost be disallowed as a deduction for the computation of income tax liability by the firm. The analysis below of the employer TIP will focus on the income tax, but a brief comparison with other taxes will also be given. The employee TIP can be implemented by adjusting withholding rates.

I limit the analysis to tax incentives to reduce wage and salary increases (including executive compensation and fringe benefits). Tax incentives to reduce price increases are not examined, for a number of reasons.

First, the crucial practical problem for the tax incentive is defining and measuring the wage or price increase of the firm. For wage increases this is likely to be difficult, but appears feasible. For this purpose "wages" under TIP mean all types of employee compensation, including fringe benefits. It seems doubtful, however, that the average price increase of a firm could be satisfactorily measured for tax purposes. Most firms make products with a variety of qualities. It is extremely difficult to distinguish a price increase from a quality increase. Because the quality problem seems much more serious for prices than for wages, it seems sensible to concentrate on wage incentives. Second, as will be shown, theory and empirical evidence strongly suggest that price inflation will decline automatically when wage inflation declines. Third, as will be explained below, there are other more practical ways to protect labor, even if no direct attempt were made to restrain prices. And fourth, a price target for individual firms is less defensible than a wage target. The variance of wage increases among firms appears to be smaller than that of price increases because the former is limited by labor mobility across firms, and perhaps by conceptions of equity. Different growth rates of productivity across firms cause a larger variance in unit cost increases, and therefore in price increases.

Finally, a nontax permit form of wage incentive such as Lerner suggests should be noted.[8] According to this plan, the government would fix the number of wage permits and let employers bid for permits, with price set by supply and demand. While appealing in theory, the practical aspects of the permit proposal would require careful scrutiny. For example, the impact of precautionary and speculative motives on the permit market would have to be assessed. Even if these practical difficulties prove decisive, the wage permit proposal is a close intellectual cousin of the tax incentive, and helps illuminate the underlying logic of the incentive approach.

The Impact of TIP in a Value-Maximization Model

I now turn to an analysis of the impact of an employer TIP on the optimum wage increase of the firm. The firm is assumed to be a monopsonistic competitor in its labor market, confronting an upward-sloping labor supply curve; and a monopolistic competitor in its product market, facing a downward-sloping demand curve. Initially, nonunion wages are considered (collective bargaining will be discussed below).

In this model, the objective of management at firm i is to choose the wage that maximizes the present value of the firm. Given the wage of the last period, the choice of the optimum wage is equivalent to the choice of the optimum percentage wage _increase_ for this period. Throughout this paper the choice variable will be w_i, the percentage wage increase.

The value-maximization model is presented in detail in the appendix. Here, its main features will be summarized. The model has two objectives: to contrast a penalty TIP with a reward TIP and to explain why a penalty TIP should be able to reduce the firm's wage increase without causing an actual rise in its tax rate or an actual squeeze in its after-tax profit.

The key features of the value-maximization model, in which management considers future as well as current net profit, can best be appre-

8. In "Stagflation—Its Cause and Cure" and in his report in this volume.

ciated by first considering a myopic profit-maximization model, in which management considers only current net profit. The main implication of the myopic model is that the incentive to reduce w_i under a penalty TIP and a reward TIP with the same TIP multiplier would be identical.

For a monopsonistic-monopolistic firm there is a w_i' that maximizes current gross profit; if the firm granted a lower w_i, the reduction in labor supply and output would outweigh the lower wage per man-hour, thereby reducing current gross profit. If the tax rate of the firm were independent of w_i, the same w_i' would also maximize current net profit (according to 4). In the myopic model, management chooses this w_i'—so that both $\partial \pi^G / \partial w_i$ and $\partial \pi^N / \partial w_i$ are zero.

If either a penalty TIP or a reward TIP were introduced with a given m, $\partial \pi^G / \partial w_i$ would still be zero at w_i'; but $\partial \pi^N / \partial w_i$ would now be negative and equal to $(-\pi^G \cdot m)$, as shown in 4a. A reduction in w_i still would not raise gross profit at w_i'; but it would now raise net profit by reducing the tax rate t_i, which TIP makes a function of w_i. The magnitude of the incentive to reduce w_i, measured by $(-\pi^G \cdot m)$, depends on m and is the same whether TIP has a penalty or a reward. Moreover, the new optimum under TIP, w_i'', would also depend primarily on m. According to 4a, w_i'' would occur where the loss in gross profit from a further decrement in w_i exactly offsets the reduction in t_i, so that there would be no further increase in net profit.

The myopic model therefore implies that TIP would reduce w_i. But it would also reduce employment because a lower wage corresponds to a lower supply of labor. Furthermore, the myopic model implies that a penalty TIP that would severely squeeze net profit if the firm remained at w_i' would provide no stronger incentive to reduce w_i than a reward TIP. The reason is that there is no slack with respect to current net profit in the myopic model. Without TIP, the w_i' is chosen that would maximize current gross profit, and therefore net profit. If a profit squeeze threatened, management might not be able to reduce w_i in order to raise gross profit. Without TIP, if a decline in product demand threatened to squeeze net profit, management might still choose the same w_i' because that choice might still maximize net profit.

This feature of the myopic model is counter to intuition, which would lead the analyst to believe that, in response to a potential squeeze in current net profit, management would choose a smaller w_i and this would, in turn, succeed in partly mitigating the decline in net profit. A value-maximization model is presented below that embodies the above intuition, and predicts that a penalty TIP probably will provide a stronger incentive to reduce w_i than a reward TIP with the same m.

In the myopic model, management chooses the w_i that maximizes current net profit. In contrast, management in the value-maximization model finds it optimal to grant a w_i above the level that would maximize current net profit because a larger wage increase is regarded as an investment in personnel policy: it contributes to employee satisfaction with the firm, and this is expected to reduce future quit rates, recruitment and training costs, and therefore to increase future net profits. The firm operates to the left of its labor supply curve at the wage increase it grants. To maximize present value, it is optimal for management to sacrifice some current profit in order to raise future net profit through an investment in personnel policy.

This means that, beginning at the optimum wage increase, the firm has the ability to raise current net profit by reducing its wage increase; there is slack with respect to current net profit. Moreover, the firm can accomplish this without reducing employment.

The second key assumption of the value-maximization model is that if the level of current net profit declines, an increment of net profit will become more valuable relative to an increment of investment in personnel policy. In response to a threatened squeeze in the level of net profit, management will therefore find it optimal to reduce w_i and therefore its investment in personnel policy in order to raise current net profit.

This change in the marginal rate of substitution between current net profit and personnel investment when current net profit declines seems intuitively plausible. It would occur, by definition of the marginal rate of substitution, if the impact of an increment of net profit on the value of the firm increases proportionally more than the impact of an increment of personnel investment on the value of the firm when current net profit declines. This is likely to be the case through effects on the cost of capital.

The firm's cost of capital from retained earnings is generally viewed as less than the cost from external borrowing (which, in turn, is less than the cost from new equity). Consider a firm with current net profit larger than planned investment, so that it can finance its investment from retained earnings. If its current net profit declined, at first there would be no change in its cost of capital. If its net profit declined sufficiently, however, it would be forced to finance its investment partly from external borrowing, thereby raising its cost of capital.

Moreover, it seems plausible that each decrement of current net profit will cause a larger increment in the cost of external borrowing. Beyond some point, a decrement of net profit will probably raise the risk premium imputed by creditors and included in the cost of external borrowing; and each successive decrement may cause a larger increment in the risk premium as the prospect of loan default becomes greater.

Thus, once current net profit declines beyond some point, each successive decrement in current net profit will cause a larger increment in the cost of capital. Conversely, if the firm is at a low, rather than a high, level of current net profit (relative to its investment options), an increment of current net profit should cause a larger decrement in the cost of capital and thus yield a greater increment in firm value.

The personal incentives of management may also change the marginal rate of substitution in favor of current net profit when the level of current net profit declines. Suppose management believed that the board of directors (and perhaps also the stockholders) regarded current net profit as a tangible indicator of the competence of management. Thus, current net profit may serve as a signal when there is a disparity in information between management and the board (and perhaps stockholders). As long as the firm's current net profit rate is "normal," it will be optimal for management to undertake any investment—such as one in personnel policy—that is expected to raise the value of the firm. If the level of net profit declines significantly below normal, however, it may be optimal for management to sacrifice some investment in personnel policy to raise current net profit in order to protect its own position.

If the two key assumptions of the value-maximization model are correct, a penalty TIP would almost certainly provide a stronger incentive to reduce w_i than a reward TIP with the same TIP multiplier m. Both a penalty TIP and a reward TIP raise the absolute value of $\partial \pi^N / \partial w_i$ by an amount that depends primarily on m. But according to the value-maximization model, there is also an income effect. This means that if a current net profit squeeze were threatened by a penalty TIP, in contrast to a reward TIP, management would have the ability, and find it optimal, to reduce w_i in an attempt to mitigate the decline in current net profit. At w_i^*, the optimum wage increase without TIP, a penalty TIP would

use both the substitution and the income effects to provide an incentive
to reduce w_i; in contrast, a reward TIP would rely solely on the substitution effect.

The central feature of the value-maximization model—that the level
of current net profit influences the size of the wage increase—is supported by econometric evidence. Table 1 presents econometric estimates
for a wage equation from a time series of U.S. manufacturing. By abstract-
ing from the distributed lags in that fitted equation, its basic form can be
represented as:

$$(7) \quad w_t = r\left(\frac{\bar{U} - U_t}{U_t}\right) + z\left(\frac{\pi_t^N - \bar{\pi}^N}{\bar{\pi}^N}\right) + w_{t-1}, \quad r > 0, \quad z > 0,$$

where

w = growth rate of money wages
U = unemployment rate
π^N = net profit rate
$\bar{U}, \bar{\pi}^N$ = parameters of the economy.

The equations in table 1 differ solely according to the adjusted unemployment rate variable used. The t statistic for the profit variable exceeds four in all three equations. A special test suggested by J. Durbin
for equations with lagged right-hand dependent variables indicates that
the probability of autocorrelation, with its serious econometric implications when w_{t-i} is on the right, fortunately is low in these equations. More
detailed analysis of these and related wage equations is presented elsewhere.[9] The result for the profit variable is important for choosing between a penalty and a reward TIP, and further econometric research on
it should receive high priority.

The second important conclusion provided by the value-maximization
model is that, although a penalty TIP threatens a net profit squeeze if
the firm fails to reduce w_i, it *need not* cause an actual net profit squeeze
if the TIP multiplier m is set at the proper magnitude. That result is
demonstrated in the appendix; here, the argument will be summarized.

At each w_i, TIP causes a larger decrement in net profit as a result of a
given increment in wages because the TIP incentive effect makes the tax
rate vary directly with w_i. Let w_i* be the optimum without TIP, and

9. Laurence S. Seidman, "The Return of the Profit Rate to the Wage Equation,"
Review of Economics and Statistics (forthcoming).

Table 1. Wage Equations for U.S. Manufacturing, Quarterly, 1955:2–1975:2[a]

		Independent variable[b]				Regression statistic		
Equation	*Constant*	*Profit measure*	*Unemployment measure*[c]	w_{t-i}		$\bar{R}^2$	*Standard error*	*Durbin-Watson*
1.1	−5.58	5.58	2.00	0.94		0.73	1.21	2.03
	(−4.08)	(4.19)	(1.45)	(8.58)				
1.2	−6.26	6.10	3.24	0.94		0.73	1.20	2.08
	(−4.43)	(4.26)	(1.23)	(8.82)				
1.3	−6.60	6.12	6.07	0.88		0.74	1.18	2.11
	(−4.71)	(4.43)	(2.00)	(8.06)				

Sources: The dependent variable, the rate of change in the hourly earnings index, and data on unemployment rates were provided by the U.S. Bureau of Labor Statistics. The profit variable, π_{t-i}, is the ratio of the actual after-tax profit rate on equity to the normal profit rate for that quarter, estimated as a linear trend, and is from U.S. Federal Trade Commission, *Quarterly Financial Report for Manufacturing, Mining and Trade Corporations*, various issues.

a. All regressions were estimated using the technique of ordinary least squares. The numbers in parentheses are t statistics.

b. Each variable is a polynomial-distributed lag of second degree; π_{t-i} and U_{t-i} are lagged four quarters, beginning in $t - 1$ (constrained to zero in the fifth quarter), while w_{t-i} is lagged twelve quarters (constrained to zero in the thirteenth). The coefficient shown for each variable is the sum of the individual lag coefficients, and the t statistic applies to the sum.

c. Equation 1.1 uses the inverse of the unemployment rate for prime-age males; 1.2 uses the inverse of the weighted unemployment rate described in George L. Perry, "Changing Labor Markets and Inflation," *Brookings Papers on Economic Activity, 3:1970*, pp. 415–16; and 1.3 uses UGAP, described in Michael L. Wachter, "The Changing Cyclical Responsiveness of Wage Inflation," *BPEA, 1:1976*, pp. 125–33.

w_i^{**} be the optimum under a penalty TIP (w_i^* greater than w_i^{**}). At w_i^*, the penalty TIP threatens a net profit squeeze because $t_i(w_i^*)$ is greater than b. For some appropriate value of m, the new optimum w_i^{**} will equal the TIP target n; and $t_i(w_i^{**})$ will equal b, so that no actual net profit squeeze occurs. Thus, it may be optimal for management to choose a wage increase at which the tax rate is unaltered, solely because $\partial \pi^N / \partial w_i$ has been raised in absolute value by TIP.

It is instructive to contrast a penalty TIP with an increase in b, the ordinary income tax rate. At w_i^*, both threaten a net profit squeeze, and both would cause the firm to reduce w_i. In the case of an increase in the ordinary tax rate, however, the final equilibrium w_i^{**} must involve a higher tax rate, and therefore a lower level of net profit because t_i equals b for all w_i.

Thus, the impact of TIP at w_i^* and w_i^{**} must be carefully distinguished. Both a penalty TIP and a reward TIP sustain the new optimum, w_i^{**}, primarily through the TIP incentive effect. The difference between a penalty TIP and a reward TIP is important at w_i^*, the wage increase that would have been chosen without TIP. A reward TIP would not decrease the level of current net profit at w_i*; in contrast, a penalty TIP would squeeze net profit at w_i*. Thus, it is almost certain that a penalty TIP will provide a stronger incentive to reduce w_i below w_i*.

The Impact of TIP in a Collective Bargaining Model

Perhaps the most important and difficult test for TIP is whether it can reduce the wage increase in an oligopolistic industry, in which large corporations engage in industry-wide (explicit or implicit) collective bargaining with a "strong" union.

The basic assumption of the collective bargaining model is that the actual wage increase in a given industry can be regarded as the result of the interaction of union "push" (P) and management "resistance" (R). The interaction of union push and management resistance, prior to the introduction of TIP, is shown in the diagram, which seeks to explain why the wage increase was 8 percent. As the diagram shows, if a 6 percent increase had been tentatively considered at the bargaining table, the union's push for a larger raise would have exceeded management's resistance to it. Similarly, if a 10 percent increase had been considered, management's determination to achieve a lower settlement would evidently have exceeded the union's determination to prevent such a reduction. At 8 percent, labor's push and management's resistance are balanced.

Push and resistance should be regarded as bargaining postures or attitudes that imply particular concrete actions. For example, union push at 8 percent would increase if workers were willing to endure a longer strike in order to achieve some extra raise. Similarly, management resistance at 8 percent would increase if it were willing to endure a longer strike in order to prevent a given increment.

What determines the shape and position of the two curves? The union's push for an additional increment is positive at all tentative w_i. But the larger the tentative w_i, the smaller the push. Workers are willing to endure a strike of only X days to raise w_i from 10 to 11 percent, while they would be willing to endure a strike of Y days (with Y greater than X) to raise w_i from 4 to 5 percent. The position of the union-push curve at each w_i will be higher: (1) the greater the rate of wage increase that other workers have recently achieved, (2) the greater the expected rate of price

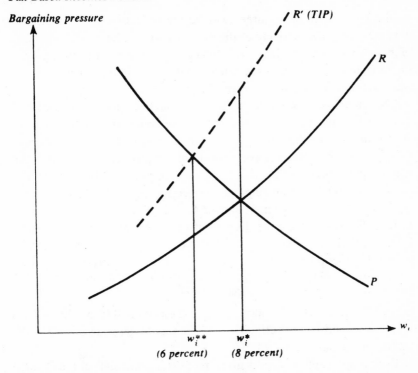

inflation, (3) the lower the unemployment rate, and (4) the larger the net profit rate expected to result from a given wage. Factors (1) and (2) are based on the assumption that workers are concerned about relative and real wage increases rather than absolute nominal wage increases. Factor (3) is plausible in part because workers might be more willing to risk a prolonged strike and layoffs after the settlement if the prospects of finding a new job were greater. Factors (1) and (3) are consistent with the wage equations presented in table 1. And factor (4) may be plausible because the larger the net profit expected to result from a given w_i, the larger is the apparent ability of management to "afford" higher wages, thereby inducing workers to risk a longer strike to achieve a given increment.

The resistance of management is based on the objective of maximizing the value of the firm (or perhaps the value of its own income stream). In the range relevant for bargaining, the resistance of management to any addition is positive because a larger wage increase would reduce the value of the firm. The larger the tentative w_i, the lower will be the level of net profit, and therefore the larger will be the resistance to an additional amount, using the reasoning of the previous section. Thus, the resistance of management to a still larger raise at a given w_i is greater (1) the greater the reduction in net profit that would result from the increment, and (2) the lower the level of current net profit at w_i.

This model is consistent with the wage equations presented in table 1. The level of net profit is assumed to affect both push and resistance curves, and should therefore affect the wage increase that results. Factors (1) and (3) that influence the position of the push curve are consistent with the performance of the w_{t-i} and U_t variables, respectively, in table 1.

The introduction of an employer TIP results in an upward shift of the R curve shown in the diagram above. At each w_i, TIP (whether penalty or reward) will increase the decrement in current net profit that results from a given increase in w_i. This is the TIP incentive effect, and its magnitude depends primarily on m. A penalty TIP, in contrast to a reward TIP, however, will also influence the position of the R curve because it will reduce the level of net profit w_i^*. This is the penalty TIP income, or profit squeeze, effect at w_i^*. Because the penalty TIP combines both substitution and income effects at w_i^*, it should generate greater resistance at w_i^* than a reward TIP.

Even if the union P curve is unaltered, the upward shift of the R curve should reduce the resulting wage. Under a penalty TIP, however, it is plausible that the P curve will shift down at w_i^* because it would reduce the expected net profit rate at w_i^* (the fourth influence on the position of the P curve). The shift in the P curve is not shown in the diagram. If the TIP multiplier is properly set, then w_i^{**} will equal n; and the tax rate will equal b, so there would be no actual profit squeeze. As in the value-maximization model, the new optimum w_i^{**} does not require an actual net profit squeeze. At w_i^{**}, the R curve is higher, although the tax rate and level of net profit are unaltered, because an increment in w_i would cause a greater decrement in net profit.

It has thus far been assumed that an increase in the tax rate would in fact reduce current net profit. In an oligopolistic industry, however, the same wage increase often is set for all firms. Is it possible that, in response to a penalty TIP, firms will grant the same w_i^*, and then raise price sufficiently so that gross profit increases, offsetting the higher tax rate, and thereby preventing a decline in current net profit at w_i^*? In this extreme case in which firms shift the penalty fully in the short run, a penalty TIP would actually temporarily worsen inflation.

I have examined this possibility.[10] The main points of that analysis are summarized below. First, if m is sufficiently large, the tax surcharge must outweigh any rise in gross profit, thereby squeezing net profit at w_i^*. In the extreme, suppose that $t_i(w_i^*)$ equals 100 percent. No matter how much the firm raises gross profits at w_i^*, its net profit will be zero. A key feature of a tax penalty on the income tax of the firm is that, in effect, the Internal Revenue Service "goes last." First the firm raises price in an attempt to raise gross profit; then the Internal Revenue Service taxes a larger portion of the gross profit. For a sufficiently large m, full short-run shifting of the TIP penalty so that net profit is not squeezed at w_i^* is literally impossible. Even with realistic, modest values of m, however, large increases in gross profit would be required to keep net profit from declining. For example, if m were 6 percent and n were 6 percent in equation 1, the tax rate would rise from 48 percent to 60 percent if the firm granted a wage increase of 8 percent. The firm must then be able to raise gross profit by 30 percent to avoid a reduction in net profit.

Moreover, it is far from certain that firms will be able to raise gross profit significantly. Even with industry-wide bargaining, import competition may limit the ability of oligopolists to raise gross profit by increasing prices. Because wages are set separately for different industries, one industry cannot assume that its own wage increase will be matched by others; thus, an industry that significantly exceeds the TIP target may find sales growing more slowly as demand shifts to other industries.

Although partial shifting is certainly possible, it would involve a net profit decline at w_i^*, so that both income and substitution effects would provide an incentive to hold down wages. Despite the reduction in w_i, might the partial shifting worsen price inflation? Briefly stated, in an oligopolistic industry with reserve market power, it is possible, though very unlikely, that shifting would cause a temporary rise in the inflation rate. Even under this worst scenario, the temporary rise would soon be permanently reversed after a transition period when firms raised their markup to cover the higher tax rate. Thereafter, the price inflation rate would follow the decline in the wage inflation rate. A permanent rise in the inflation rate could occur only if there were a permanently rising tax rate—not merely a new, higher tax rate.

If a penalty TIP were only a temporary policy, even the small chance of an initial rise in the inflation rate would be a serious liability. As the

10. Laurence S. Seidman, "Would Tax-Shifting Undermine the Tax-Based Incomes Policy?" *Journal of Economic Issues* (forthcoming, September 1978).

next section will show, however, a penalty TIP should be viewed as a permanent policy with a permanent impact; hence, the small risk of a temporary adverse effect is less serious.

When the penalty tax is levied on the income of the firm—revenue minus cost—in effect, the Internal Revenue Service "goes last." If the penalty tax were levied on either cost or revenue, the shifting problem would be much more serious: in effect, the Internal Revenue Service would "go first," and the firm would "go last." For example, suppose the penalty were levied on the payroll (wage bill) of the firm. The firm might then be able to raise price and revenue sufficiently to maintain net profit. One version of employer TIP—that the wage bill in excess of the guidepost be disallowed as a deduction in the computation of income tax—is in effect a payroll tax surcharge, and would therefore be more vulnerable to shifting than the income tax surcharge.[11]

The Impact of TIP on the NAIRU

The microanalysis thus far has established that, given the recent rate of wage increase throughout the economy, the product demand of the firm, and the unemployment rate, TIP would cause the average firm to grant a smaller wage increase than it otherwise would. However, the final impact of TIP on the macroeconomy can be determined only when the micromodel is linked to a macromodel that relates wage inflation, price inflation, unemployment rate, and money supply. This section will provide such a macromodel.

PRICE BEHAVIOR

Consider the following price equation:

$$(8) \qquad\qquad p_t = w_t - a,$$

where a is the trend growth rate of average labor productivity (output per man-hour). Here, p refers to increases in the *value-added* price, which nets out the unit cost of purchases from other sectors.

11. Wallich and Weintraub, "Tax-Based Incomes Policy," p. 4.

The derivation of 8 is as follows.[12] First, define the markup $\bar{M}$ of value-added price P over standard unit factor cost UC, where UC excludes intermediate product cost, but includes a minimum rate of return on capital per unit of trend output:

$$(9) \qquad \bar{M} \equiv \frac{P}{UC}.$$

Next, consider the markup of price over standard unit labor cost ULC; ULC equals the ratio of wages per man-hour W to trend output per man-hour A. Let F be the ratio of standard unit labor cost to standard unit cost:

$$(10) \qquad F \equiv \frac{ULC}{UC}.$$

The markup K of price over standard unit labor cost is defined as:

$$(11) \qquad K \equiv \frac{P}{ULC}.$$

From equations 9, 10, and 11:

$$(12) \qquad K \equiv \frac{\bar{M}}{F}.$$

If two industries have the same F, then the one with the greater market power will have the larger K. From 11 the following relationship among growth rates must hold approximately:

$$(13) \qquad p = k + ulc = k + w - a.$$

The secular trend of k is close to zero, so that 13 is approximated by 8. In 1977, the annual growth rate of wages in the United States was approximately 8 percent; the trend growth rate of productivity, 2 percent; and the inflation rate, 6 percent.

The near-zero trend value of k reflects the behavior over the long run of $\bar{M}$ and F. According to standard microeconomics, the markup of a

---

12. An early exposition is given in Sidney Weintraub, *A General Theory of the Price Level, Output, Income Distribution, and Economic Growth* (Chilton, 1959). Econometric price equations similar to 8 are presented in Otto Eckstein, ed., *The Econometrics of Price Determination*, A Conference sponsored by the Board of Governors of the Federal Reserve System and Social Science Research Center (Board of Governors, 1972).

firm is determined by the degree of competition in its industry. Whatever the level of $\bar{M}$, its secular trend (ignoring fluctuations over the business cycle) is close to horizontal; the average degree of market power in the economy generally changes only slowly, if at all, over time. Unit factor cost UC equals the sum of unit labor cost and unit nonlabor cost, including unit depreciation cost, unit net capital cost, and unit indirect business tax cost. It is possible that the ratio of unit labor cost to unit nonlabor cost changes only slowly over time.

The fact that the trend value of k is close to zero is crucial for the trend in the distribution of income between labor and capital, as can be seen from 11. However, the main conclusion of this section—that TIP can lower the NAIRU—would hold for any constant k, as will be shown below.

INTEGRATING MONEY INTO THE SYSTEM

Equations 7 and 8 imply a relationship between inflation and unemployment. To focus on this relationship, the following (simplified) inverse correlation between the unemployment rate and the net profit rate will be assumed:

$$(14) \qquad \frac{\pi_t^N - \bar{\pi}^N}{\bar{\pi}^N} = c\left(\frac{\bar{U} - U_t}{U_t}\right), \qquad c > 0.$$

When U_t equals $\bar{U}$, π_t^N equals $\bar{\pi}^N$. Substituting 14 into 7 yields:

$$(7a) \qquad w_t - w_{t-1} = h\left(\frac{\bar{U} - U_t}{U_t}\right), \qquad h = r + zc > 0.$$

If U_t equals $\bar{U}$, the wage inflation rate remains constant; if U_t is less (greater) than $\bar{U}$, the wage inflation rate rises (falls). To simplify matters, h will be regarded as constant in the relevant range. If 8 is substituted into 7a:

$$(15) \qquad p_t - p_{t-1} = h\left(\frac{\bar{U} - U_t}{U_t}\right).$$

It should be noted that if 13 rather than 8 had been substituted into 7a, 15 would still follow, as long as k_t equals k_{t-1}. A constant growth rate of the markup, which may or may not be zero, is sufficient to yield 15.

The system is accelerationist in the following sense. If the monetary and fiscal authorities try to peg U_t below $\bar{U}$, the inflation rate will rise without limit, rather than converging to any stable rate. This follows from the assumption, supported in table 1, that the coefficient of w_{t-1} in 7a is 1. The system has a NAIRU, defined as the unemployment rate at which the inflation rate would remain constant (not necessarily zero) at its initial value. Prior to the introduction of TIP, the NAIRU is $\bar{U}$, according to 15.

The price equation 8 embodies the wage view of inflation. According to the wage equation 7a, however, w_t is endogenous and depends on U_t, another endogenous variable. This wage-price system is, in fact, consistent with a monetary view of inflation.[13] Given the monetarist assumption that in the long run the growth rate of the money supply s determines the growth rate of nominal income, then if s is held constant, U_t will converge to the NAIRU; p_t and w_t will converge to equilibrium values that depend on s.

The impact of TIP on the wage-price system will now be shown. In the earlier microanalysis, TIP causes a smaller w_t in a particular period than would have occurred in its absence, other things held constant. An important consequence of TIP as a permanent policy is that this effect would occur each period. Suppose that in the first year U_t is at $\bar{U}$, the NAIRU without TIP, so that if w_{t-1} were 8 percent, the average firm would grant 8 percent this year without TIP; and if a were 2 percent, p_t would be 6 percent. Suppose that a penalty TIP with an interim target n of 7 percent would threaten a higher tax rate at 8 percent, and therefore cause the firm to cut w_t by 1 percentage point below w_{t-1}. Thus, w_t would be 7 percent; and p_t, 5 percent. Then in the following year, w_{t-1} would be 7 percent. The labor supply function implied by the value-maximization model and the union push curve in the collective bargaining model would shift to reflect the fact that w_{t-1} equal to 7 percent is the new norm. (And p_{t-1} would be 5 percent.) If n is now cut to 6 percent while m is held constant, a penalty TIP would threaten the same higher tax rate if 7 percent were granted. Once again, this should cause the firm to cut w_t perhaps 1 point below w_{t-1}, to 6 percent.

Let w_t^* be the wage inflation rate that would occur without TIP in period t according to 7, given the values of the right-hand variables U_t, π_t^N, and w_{t-1}. Suppose that in each period, under a permanent penalty

13. Laurence S. Seidman, "The Tax-Based Incomes Policy and the Monetary View of Inflation: A Reconciliation" (University of Pennsylvania, Department of Economics, November 1977; processed).

TIP, n_t were set so that $(w_t* - n_t)$ were equal to θ, where θ is some constant percentage (1 point in the example just given). Then in each period, with m held constant, a penalty TIP would threaten the same higher tax rate at w_t* and exert the same downward pressure on w_t at w_t*. In each period, therefore, a penalty TIP should cause w_t to be less than w_t*. Thus, a penalty TIP should permanently shift down the wage equation by θ:

(7b) $$w_t - w_{t-1} = r\left(\frac{\bar{U} - U_t}{U_t}\right) + z\left(\frac{\pi^N - \bar{\pi}^N}{\bar{\pi}^N}\right) - \theta, \qquad \theta > 0.$$

Then 7a and 15 become:

(7c) $$w_t - w_{t-1} = h\left(\frac{\bar{U} - U_t}{U_t}\right) - \theta = p_t - p_{t-1}.$$

The new NAIRU would be less than $\bar{U}$ because it takes a lower value of U_t $(U*)$ to make the middle of 7c equal to zero. Specifically:

(16) $$U* = \frac{h}{h + \theta} \bar{U} < \bar{U}.$$

Intuitively, the increased downward pressure on w_t due to the TIP incentive effect will now counter the upward pressure from this lower U_t, causing w_t to equal, rather than to exceed, w_{t-1} in 7c at this U_t.

Given the monetarist assumption concerning nominal income and the wage-price system adjusted for TIP, it can be shown that a specific rate of monetary growth would continue to cause the system to converge to the same long-run, equilibrium inflation rate.[14] TIP would not permanently reduce the inflation rate, but rather would permanently reduce the NAIRU.

A numerical example of TIP's impact is provided in table 2. There, without TIP, the system would remain in its initial equilibrium indefinitely, in the absence of shocks, with s kept at 7 percent. Now suppose that a penalty TIP were introduced, and that m and n_t were set so that w_i would be 2 percentage points less than it would otherwise have been for the average firm. Suppose that the h parameter were 0.04. Then from 16 the new NAIRU under TIP would be 4 percent.

One approach to disinflation would be initially to set s_t each year so that U_t remained at 6 percent. Then each year w_t and p_t would decline 2

14. Ibid.

Table 2. A Disinflation Path under TIP[a]

Percent

Year	U_t	w_t	p_t	s_t	n_t	t_i
0	6.0	8.0	6.0	7.0	...	48
1	5.6	6.3	4.3	5.7	6.3	48
2	5.2	4.9	2.9	4.3	4.9	48
3	4.8	3.9	1.9	3.3	3.9	48
4	4.6	3.1	1.1	2.3	3.1	48
5	4.4	2.6	0.6	1.8	2.6	48
6	4.2	2.3	0.3	1.5	2.3	48
7	4.1	2.1	0.1	1.2	2.1	48
8	4.1	2.0	0.0	1.0	2.0	48
9	4.0	2.0	0.0	1.1	2.0	48
10	4.0	2.0	0.0	1.0	2.0	48

Source: Derived from the model presented in Laurence S. Seidman, "The Tax-Based Incomes Policy and the Monetary View of Inflation: A Reconciliation" (University of Pennsylvania, Department of Economics, November 1977; processed).

a. The variables are defined as follows: U_t = unemployment rate, w_t = rate of change in wages, p_t = rate of change in prices, s_t = rate of growth of the money supply, n_t = target rate of increase in wages with TIP, and t_i = the tax rate of a firm with TIP. Initially, s_0 = 7 percent, $U_0 = \bar{U}$ = 6 percent, and q_0 (the growth rate of real output) = 3 percent. It is assumed throughout that a, the trend growth rate of productivity, and v, the trend growth rate of the velocity of money, each are equal to 2 percent; and the trend growth rate of the labor force is equal to 1 percent.

percentage points and the interim target n_t would be adjusted downward by 2 points. At the end of three years, the permanent targets, w at 2 percent and p at 0 percent, would be achieved. Then s_t should be temporarily increased to reduce U_t to 4 percent. When U_t equals 4 percent, s_t would be set at 1 percent indefinitely, thereby maintaining this equilibrium in the absence of shocks.

This approach, however, makes no progress in reducing U_t until the permanent inflation target is achieved. Furthermore, it requires a rapid expansion at the end of the third year. An alternative disinflation path, shown in table 2, is likely to be regarded as preferable. In each period, n_t is adjusted downward so that, without TIP, $w_t{}^*$ would exceed n_t by 2 percentage points, but with TIP, w_t would approximate n_t. In the final equilibrium, n is permanently set at 2 percent, and w_t permanently remains at 2 percent. In the absence of TIP, when U_t equals 4 percent, $w_t{}^*$ would exceed w_{t-1} by 2 points; TIP just offsets that upward pressure on wage inflation, thereby keeping w_t equal to w_{t-1} (2 percent).

This simple illustration shows how a penalty TIP and monetary policy should ideally be coordinated to reduce gradually both inflation and unemployment rates. However, most of the key magnitudes required to obtain the desired values for m, n_t, and s_t are not known, and at best can only be imperfectly estimated. Thus, in practice, the path to equilibrium cannot be fine-tuned as in table 2. Moreover, other "shocks" will temporarily move the system away from its desired values, and countercyclical monetary and fiscal policies will be necessary to return the system to its targets. Nevertheless, if TIP becomes a permanent feature of the system, it should eventually be possible to achieve an average combination of inflation and unemployment that is lower than what could have been achieved without TIP.[15]

An Employee TIP

An employee TIP could be introduced either in place of an employer TIP or as a complement to it. Elsewhere I have analyzed the employee TIP.[16] In this section, the main issues will be treated.

An employee TIP is subject to the same penalty-reward permutations given earlier for an employer TIP. For example, employees at firm i could be given a tax cut if the average wage increase at i were below a threshold, a tax increase if the average wage increase were above a target, or both if the target equaled the threshold.

The reward or penalty for each employee at firm i must depend on the *average* wage increase at i, not on the individual employee's own wage increase, because the purpose of the incentive is to discourage increases in the entire wage structure of the firm, not to discourage promotion and upgrading of individual employees.

One method of implementing an employee TIP is to use the withholding system at each firm. For example, if the wage increase at firm i warranted a tax cut, the actual income tax withholding rate could be cut; but employees could be credited on their W-2 forms as if the withholding rate had not been cut. Under this method, the employee TIP would be fully administered by the employer and would place no additional compliance burden on individual employees. At the same time, employees could be made aware of the employee TIP tax credit or surcharge on each paycheck and on the W-2 form, so that the TIP might influence the bargaining posture of employees.

15. Robert S. Chirinko and Laurence S. Seidman, "The Tax-Based Incomes Policy and Optimal Control," discussion paper 390 (University of Pennsylvania, Department of Economics, February 1977; processed).
16. Seidman, "Payroll Tax-Credit."

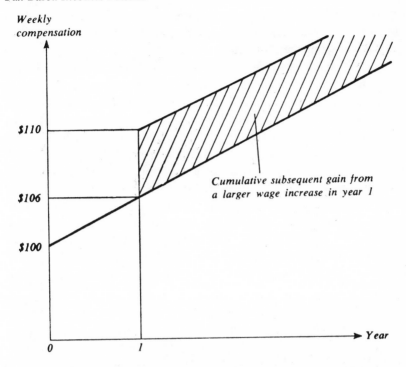

If the penalty completely eliminated the gain from exceeding the target or if the reward completely compensated employees for the shortfall below the threshold, the employee TIP would surely reduce w_i. Such an extreme penalty or reward would have harmful consequences, however. A future projection must be made to estimate whether the gain has been completely eliminated or the shortfall fully compensated. For example, suppose in year 0 the average employee at firm i received $100 a week, and the interim TIP target was 6 percent, or $106 for i. Under the penalty TIP, suppose 100 percent of the excess above $106 was taxed away in year 1. The average employee may still be better off in future years, the larger the wage increase in year 1. One possible projection is shown in the diagram. If the average employee made this particular projection, then to eliminate the gain, the year 1 tax would have to exceed 100 percent, so that the loss in year 1 balanced the gain in future years.

The tax penalty required to eliminate the gain, however, will vary among individual employees because the gain depends on how long the employee will work for firm i. For example, an employee who plans to work at i for only one year (year 1) would have his gain completely eliminated with a 100 percent tax. Thus, a tax penalty that exactly eliminates the gain for the average employee would more than eliminate it for some, and less than eliminate it for others.

A penalty or reward sufficiently large to eliminate exactly the gain for an employee with average expected tenure would produce serious equity and efficiency problems. How would a firm seek to expand its labor force in response to a rise in product demand? For example, suppose that for each $1 above $106, employees were taxed $2; and for each $1 below $106, they were rewarded $2. If $110 were granted, the tax penalty would be $8; thus, in year 1, the average employee would receive only $102; this loss in year 1 might be just balanced by the expected gain in future years from beginning year 2 at $110. Similarly, if $102 were granted, the tax reward would be $8, so in year 1, the average employee would receive $110; this gain in year 1 might be just balanced by the expected future loss from beginning year 2 at $102. Thus, the average employee looking ahead might be indifferent to the size of the wage increase in year 1.

Current and new employees who joined in year 1, however, would prefer lower wages if their expected tenure were less than average; and conversely, higher wages if their expected tenure were greater than average. Because some employees would be adversely affected by higher wages, while others would be adversely affected by lower wages, inefficient turnover would be encouraged. Whether the firm raises or lowers its rate of wage increase, it will cause employees who are so affected to consider seeking employment elsewhere. Moreover, potential new employees who might join in year 2 would be more attracted in year 2, the greater the w_i in year 1, because they would not bear the year 1 tax penalty. Without an employee TIP, an employer knows that the larger the wage increase he grants, the more attractive his firm is to all current and potential employees. Under an employee TIP that eliminated the gain to the average employee, this would not be the case.

Because of these equity and efficiency consequences, a permanent employee TIP should not completely eliminate the gain from exceeding the target or completely compensate for the shortfall below the threshold. An increase in wages must still benefit all employees to some degree. This means, however, that it is no longer clear that an employee TIP will provide a strong incentive.

The collective bargaining model can be used to analyze the impact of an employee TIP under which an increase in wages still provides some positive gain to employees. Earlier, four factors that influence the position of the union push curve were listed. Two additional factors must now be added. The height of the union push curve at a given wage increase will be higher: (5) the greater the increment in real (inflation-adjusted) after-tax income that results from a given increase in wages, and (6) the smaller the gain (from the past year to the current year) in real after-tax income from that wage increase.

Factor 5 is the substitution, or incentive effect, which motivates the employee TIP proposal. As in the case of an employer TIP, the same incentive effect can be achieved by a penalty or a reward employee TIP. Because an employee TIP, whether penalty or reward, reduces the after-tax gain from a given increase in wages, this substitution effect should shift down the union push curve in the first diagram in this paper.

Factor 6 is the income effect. To analyze its impact, consider an employee penalty TIP with an interim target of 6 percent, and suppose that without TIP, wage increases were 8 percent at the average firm (with p at 6 percent for the whole economy). First consider the optimistic view that employees believe that, in response to TIP, the rate of price inflation will be reduced by the full 2 percentage points sought by the program. Then a partial TIP penalty (less than 100 percent) would lead employees to expect a higher real after-tax income for an 8 percent raise with TIP than without it. The expected slowing of inflation under TIP would add 2 percentage points to their real income, outweighing the reduction of real income from the partial TIP penalty. Thus, the income effect would reinforce the substitution effect, helping to shift down the union push curve at 8 percent.

Now consider the pessimistic view that employees do not believe TIP will lower inflation below 6 percent. Then, because of the penalty, a wage increase of 8 percent will be expected to yield a smaller gain in real after-tax income with a penalty TIP than without it. In this case, the income effect would work against the substitution effect. While the substitution effect may still dominate, the result is no longer unambiguous.

An employee TIP must operate through a penalty, with an employee tax rate in which $t_i(w_i^*)$ is greater than b if the average tax rate on employees is to remain unaltered (assuming that TIP succeeds in reducing wage inflation). If the government could afford to reduce the average tax rate on employees, an employee reward TIP might be implemented.

Consider an employee reward TIP with t_i given by equation 2, g equal to 8 percent, and the same b and m as the penalty TIP. Then even under the pessimistic view, such a program should unambiguously reduce wage inflation. The substitution effect is the same as for a penalty TIP, and any income effect associated with a reward will reinforce the substitution effect. Even if employees believe that p will remain 6 percent, the gain from an 8 percent wage increase (which incurs neither a penalty nor a reward) will be unaltered; with no income effect, the substitution effect should reduce wage increases.

It seems doubtful that an employee TIP could be a reliable substitute for an employer penalty TIP. As explained earlier, an employee TIP must not eliminate the gain to employees of increasing wages, and hence it is not clear how strong an incentive it would provide. Under an employer penalty TIP, the firm must reduce w_i below $w_i{}^*$ to avoid a net profit squeeze. Management is obliged to respond to an employer penalty TIP because the consequences of not doing so are severe. Under an employee TIP, employees will merely gain less from an increment of wages, and may not be very responsive to the TIP incentive effect.

Nevertheless, an employee TIP should be a useful complement to an employer penalty TIP. In the discussion of income distribution, it will be suggested that if the decline in price inflation does not match the decline in wage inflation (contrary to theory and econometric evidence), employees might be compensated for their wage restraint. Such compensation could be naturally integrated with an employee TIP if it were in effect. Under the employee TIP, the tax cut or surcharge for employees of each firm would already be computed. Compensation could be implemented by raising the tax cut for employees and reducing the surcharge on them at each firm, perhaps by adjusting the income tax withholding rate, as suggested earlier. An employee TIP would therefore facilitate the implementation of compensatory tax rebates to protect labor under TIP.

The Welfare Economics of TIP

Two aspects of the welfare economics of TIP are considered: its impact on allocative efficiency and on income distribution. Both have important implications for the design of tax-based incomes policies.

ALLOCATIVE EFFICIENCY

As has been argued above, the institutional features and ethical norms of modern labor markets and the income-maintenance programs of the welfare state have had the socially undesirable effect of raising the NAIRU above the social optimum; but these deviations from a classical, atomistic labor market have also had socially desirable consequences. Imagine an unorganized labor market in which workers compete individually with one another for jobs in intense, atomistic rivalry. Unconstrained by ethical norms, employers encourage this competition among individual workers and do not hesitate to replace an employed worker with an unemployed rival who will accept a lower wage. Moreover, there are no income-maintenance programs. The consequence of prolonged unemployment is catastrophic.

In such an economy, the NAIRU would be significantly lower than that of the current economy. Each worker would weigh the wage offered against the value of leisure or job search, and offer to work as long as the former exceeded the latter. The equilibrium unemployment rate, or NAIRU, would be optimal with respect to allocative efficiency (the trade-off of work versus leisure-search).

Many economists, including me, believe that the development of trade unions, ethical constraints on employers, and income-maintenance programs on the whole have significantly advanced social welfare, even though they impair allocative efficiency and convey a distorted signal of the work versus leisure-search preference of individual workers. From this perspective, the appropriate response is to investigate whether or not policy can be designed to reduce the NAIRU while preserving the positive contributions of existing institutions.

From a microeconomic perspective, the problem is that the average individual firm grants a larger wage increase, at any given unemployment rate, than is optimal. The standard microeconomic approach to this externality would be to charge each firm for raising the NAIRU through its "excessive" wage increase. A TIP would attempt to do this. It would add one new incentive, but would not eliminate the market forces that continue to shape relative wage and price patterns and help guide resources efficiently.

An example will illustrate TIP's impact on relative wage and price patterns. Suppose that firm A had a labor shortage because demand for its product was increasing, while firm B (equal in size to firm A) had a labor surplus because demand for its product was declining. Without TIP, at the excessive NAIRU suppose A granted a 10 percent wage increase, and B, 6 percent, so that the average was 8 percent. If TIP were introduced with an interim target of 6 percent, A might grant 7 percent, and B, 5 percent, so that the average would be reduced to 6 percent. Ultimately, when the permanent inflation and unemployment targets are achieved, A might grant 3 percent, and B, 1 percent, so that the average would be 2 percent. Because TIP would not influence labor shortage and surplus and would leave each firm free to make its own decisions, basic relative wage and price patterns should still emerge.

The objective of preserving the allocative function of relative wage changes does, however, tend to limit the size of the TIP multiplier m and hence the extent to which the NAIRU can be lowered. There is a social cost to a high m. Raising m not only reduces the average wage increase, but also reduces the variance around it, thereby impeding the allocative function of relative wage changes.

Consider three alternative tax schedules for an employer penalty-reward TIP (with a target of 2 percent) and for the NAIRU that each would hypothetically achieve:

Schedule	t_i (percent)	NAIRU (percent)
1	$48 + 0(w_i - 2)$	6
2	$48 + 5(w_i - 2)$	4
3	$48 + 10(w_i - 2)$	3

If the unemployment rate were at the NAIRU, an illustrative dispersion of w_i between the firms might be:

Schedule	Firm A, shortage (percent)	Firm B, surplus (percent)
1	4	0
2	3	1
3	2½	1½

Under schedule 1, in effect without TIP, the firm's tax rate is uniformly 48 percent. Under schedule 2, however, the firm's tax rate would rise to 58 percent if it gave a wage increase of 4 percent, and would fall to 38 percent if it gave 0 percent. As a result, the optimum wage increase for firm A should be less than 4 percent, say, 3 percent; the wage increase for firm B should be greater than 0 percent, say, 1 percent. Under schedule 3, the firm's tax rate would be higher than under schedule 2 at each w_i above 2 percent, and lower at each w_i below 2 percent; and the dispersion of wage increases between A and B would be even more compressed.

In the extreme case, if m is large, no firm can afford to give more than 2 percent; and employees would not tolerate less than 2 percent because the reduced corporate income tax under a penalty TIP would give management a large increase in net profit. This case is virtually equivalent to uniform wage control at 2 percent. A key advantage of TIP over wage controls is that the market forces that shape relative wage patterns would continue to operate automatically, provided that m is not too large. But a large m overwhelms these forces and approaches uniform wage control. Thus, there is a trade-off.

The cost of a large m lies in slowing the speed with which the equilibrium pattern of relative wage levels required for efficient allocation is attained. The more compressed the distribution of wage changes, the longer it takes to reach the desired pattern of wage levels. Similarly, TIP should somewhat slow the speed of adjustment of the relative size of two firms, like A and B in the example above, by reducing the retained earnings with which A may finance its expansion. Thus, more time will be required for the desired ratio of capital stocks to be attained for the two firms. It should be emphasized, however, that once the new relative wage is achieved, the tax rates will again be equalized. The cost of a larger m is therefore the reduced speed of adjustment, not a permanent misallocation of resources.

The case for TIP rests on the plausible assumption that neither an m of zero (in effect, no TIP), nor a large m (in effect, uniform wage control) is socially optimal; but rather, some intermediate m will best promote social welfare, optimally balancing the gains of a lower NAIRU against the loss from slower responses to market forces.

Concern for allocative efficiency has a number of important implications for the design of TIP. First, TIP should be fully continuous, rather than discontinuous. Under a fully continuous TIP, any increment of wages would raise the tax rate, and any decrement would reduce it. In contrast, under the completely discontinuous, all-or-none TIP, unless the firm can go all the way to the target, there is no incentive to go part way. Moreover, once the target is reached, there is no incentive to go further. It is likely that only firms close to the target will slow wage increases under such a TIP, and thus the incentive will be less effective on the average and will cause a greater distortion of relative wages. By similar reasoning, a partly continuous TIP is less desirable than a fully continuous one.

Second, allocative efficiency would be affected by the coverage of TIP. If the pattern of relative wages and prices were allocatively efficient without TIP, then to minimize the distortion of this pattern, TIP should exert comparable downward pressure on all wage increases. This would argue for broad coverage. However, if the pattern of wages were regarded as distorted without TIP, excluding from TIP small firms with low wages might improve allocative efficiency, as well as holding down administrative cost and improving equity.

Allocative efficiency would call for inclusion of large firms in the public and nonprofit sectors as well as in the private profit sector. The feasibility of such inclusion should therefore be carefully investigated. For example, federal general revenue sharing to state and local governmental units might be varied inversely with the size of the wage increase.

Third, the method of measuring the wage increase may affect allocative efficiency. Perhaps the most straightforward method of computing the average wage level at any firm would be to divide total compensation by total man-hours. As Wallich and Weintraub recognized in their original article, this method would enable a firm to reduce its average wage (and hence reduce its TIP penalty) by shifting its labor skill mix from high-wage to low-wage workers. However, the incentive may not be strong. The firm must weigh a one-time tax gain (in the year of the shift) against a permanent distortion in its labor skill mix. If the firm maintained the new skill mix in subsequent years, it would receive no further TIP benefit. If it shifted back to the original skill mix, it would incur a TIP loss, subsequently offsetting its initial TIP gain.

Furthermore, some shift in the composition of labor demand toward low-skilled workers may be socially desirable. An argument can be made that the wages of these workers relative to those who are highly skilled are too high for allocative efficiency because concern for equity tends to narrow the wage differential.[17] The result is an excess supply of low-skilled workers at the same time as there is a shortage of high-skilled workers. Employment programs for low-skilled persons try to induce employers to shift their skill mix. From this perspective, it is possible that the in-

17. J. R. Hicks, "Economic Foundation of Wage Policy," *Economic Journal,* vol. 65 (September 1955), pp. 389–404.

centive to shift the mix of workers under TIP could improve, rather than harm, allocative efficiency.[18]

If further analysis indicates that excessive shifting is likely, one method to contain it would be to use a weighted wage index such as that suggested by Wallich and Weintraub.[19] Recently, Weintraub has suggested an alternative approach of corrected-average-product.[20] As this example illustrates, implications of the method of measuring the wage increase for allocative efficiency require further investigation.

Another aspect of allocative efficiency that warrants study is the issue of whether TIP will induce the substitution of labor for capital, and of debt for equity, because the tax penalty is levied on the accounting profit of the firm, which includes returns to equity capital. Only if a firm expects to grant above-average wage increases would it have an incentive to reduce its equity capital. Under a penalty-reward TIP, a firm that expects to grant below-average wage increases would have an incentive to increase its equity capital. If a firm chose its capital-labor and debt-equity ratios based on long-run considerations, it may be unaffected if it assumes that a penalty-reward TIP will not affect its average tax rate over the planning period. In contrast, a penalty-only TIP would be expected to raise the average tax rate (assuming the base rate remains constant) and would therefore presumably reduce equity capital. It appears likely, therefore, that a penalty-reward TIP would be less harmful to allocative efficiency in this respect than a penalty-only TIP. Concern for allocative efficiency therefore calls for both penalty and reward.

In general, analysis should attempt to go beyond the detection of a possible distortion from TIP to an estimate of its magnitude. Is the distortion of a penalty-reward TIP likely to be large relative to the benefits of such a policy? This assessment should be an important task for future research.

INCOME DISTRIBUTION

Because TIP provides an incentive to reduce wage increases, it is sometimes suggested that it will shift the distribution of income from labor to capital. As long as TIP does not alter the growth rate of the markup of

18. Laurence S. Seidman, *The Design of Federal Employment Programs* (Lexington, 1975), pp. 77–146.

19. Wallich and Weintraub, "Tax-Based Incomes Policy."

20. Weintraub, *Capitalism's Inflation and Unemployment Crisis*, p. 128.

price over standard unit labor cost (k), however, the decline in wage inflation caused by TIP will be matched (perhaps after a short lag) by an equal decline in price inflation. There is no obvious reason why TIP should alter k, though this warrants careful study.

On the other hand, TIP would not "freeze" the distribution of income shares. As noted earlier, if k were nonzero, the distribution of income would change gradually over time. For example, suppose that the degree of competition in the economy increases over time, so that k is slightly negative. The share of labor income in national income will then have an upward secular trend. If TIP does not affect this negative value of k, it would not alter the secular trend in labor's share.

Even though there is no obvious reason why TIP should reduce labor's share of income, wage earners and their union representatives may remain concerned that the reduction in price inflation will not match the reduction in wage inflation. Although a tax incentive for price restraint is administratively infeasible, two methods of protecting labor appear feasible and deserve careful consideration. They are set forth in the concluding section below.

Conclusions and Recommendations

This paper presents an analysis of alternative tax-based incomes policies. To summarize, a TIP is a tax penalty, a reward, or a combination of both that provides an incentive to the employer or employees at each firm to reduce the firm's own wage increase. The microeconomic impact of TIP is analyzed in a value-maximization model and in a collective bargaining model. A macromodel consistent with the micromodel is then used to analyze the impact on the macroeconomy.

A central conclusion is that a permanent TIP should permanently reduce the NAIRU of the economy. Rather than considering TIP as a policy that seeks to reduce the inflation rate permanently, even in the presence of excessive monetary growth, TIP should be viewed as a policy that attempts to reduce permanently the unemployment rate at which the inflation rate will remain constant. The proper average growth rate of the money supply would be required, over the longer run, to achieve an average inflation rate near zero.[21] Thus, TIP is fully compatible with a flexible

21. It might well be desirable to vary the money supply growth rate around its average for countercyclical purposes.

monetary view of inflation. At the same time, the wage view of inflation, which holds that prices closely follow unit labor costs, is a key element of the macromodel.

The case has been made that the current NAIRU is above the social optimum and is economically inefficient. The institutional features and ethical norms of modern labor markets and the income-maintenance programs of the welfare state have raised the NAIRU so that, when the unemployment rate is at the NAIRU, the value of leisure or job search to the marginal unemployed worker is significantly less than the value of his marginal product. Thus, policy should attempt to reduce the NAIRU while preserving the benefits of modern labor markets and the welfare state.

A distinctive feature of TIP is that it attempts to reduce the NAIRU by a method that seeks to maintain the influence of market forces on relative wages and prices, thereby minimizing the reduction in allocative efficiency and preserving decentralized wage and price decisionmaking. It therefore appears likely that the benefit of reducing the NAIRU by this method will exceed the cost in allocative efficiency.

A major objective of this paper is to compare alternative TIPs and to provide guidance for design. An important implication of the micro-analysis is that a continuous, penalty-reward employer TIP, implemented through the income tax of the firm, appears most likely to succeed. In particular, the penalty is essential to assure a high probability of effectiveness. A reward-only employer TIP is likely to be weaker and less reliable. An employee TIP is not likely to be an effective substitute for an employer TIP. An employee TIP, however, implemented through the withholding system at each firm, should reinforce the impact of an employer TIP and therefore be a useful complement to it. Allocative efficiency is impaired least if both employer and employee TIPs are fully continuous, so that any reduction in the wage increase reduces the penalty or increases the reward.

The following design for TIP is consistent with the conclusions of the analysis. It combines elements from the Wallich-Weintraub employer TIP and the Okun employer-employee incentive package. Currently the U.S. average annual wage increase is 8 percent; the average trend growth rate in labor productivity is 2 percent; and the basic inflation rate is 6 percent. Suppose that TIP set as its interim targets a wage inflation rate of 6 percent and a price inflation rate of 4 percent. Then the TIP might consist of the following two incentives. The first is an employer incentive, in which a firm that granted a wage increase in excess of 6 percent would receive a surcharge on its income tax for that year in proportion to the size of the excess. If it granted less than 6 percent, it would receive a proportionate tax cut; if it granted 6 percent, its tax rate would remain at the base (currently 48 percent for many corporations). The second is an employee incentive. Employees at a firm that granted an average wage increase in excess of 6 percent would receive a tax increase for that year in proportion to the size of the excess. If the firm granted less than 6 percent, the employees would receive a proportionate tax cut; if it granted 6 percent, their tax rate would remain at the base. The penalty or reward would depend only on the *average* wage increase at the firm so that individual promotions would not be discouraged.

The employee incentive could be implemented through the income tax withholding system, and the reward or penalty would be reflected in the actual withholding rate and in take-home pay, as described above.

Concern for both allocative efficiency and equity implies that coverage should be as broad as administrative and compliance costs permit. Small firms, however, should have the option of inclusion in both, or exclusion from both. If feasible, the equivalent of TIP should be applied to the nonprofit sector and to state and local governments (for example, by varying general revenue sharing inversely with the size of the wage increase).

For both incentives, the tax surcharge for exceeding 6 percent must be significant but not prohibitive, so that when market forces warrant a relative wage increase, the firm will still find it worthwhile to exceed 6 percent, though by less than it would have without TIP. For example, two firms that might have granted 10 percent and 6 percent, respectively, without TIP might grant 7 percent and 5 percent with it.

Because TIP is an unprecedented incentive, there is no reliable method for initially estimating the size of the penalty or reward required to achieve the interim target of 6 percent. Two kinds of information, however, should be useful in choosing the initial size of the employer TIP. First, data on the distribution of wage increases across firms should be examined. For example, given the current mean of 8 percent, what percentage lies between 6 percent and 10 percent, or 4 percent and 12 percent? Does the dispersion vary with the size of firms? Second, data on the distribution of profit rates across firms and fluctuations in profit rates for individual firms over time should be examined. Once again, do the dispersion and fluctuation vary with the size of firms? Together, these two kinds of data should help suggest the size of the penalty that would cause a significant, but bearable, temporary decline in the after-tax profit rate for firms that choose to be in the upper end of the distribution of wage increases. Once the initial sizes for both the employer and the employee TIP have been determined and put into effect and the actual response of firms observed, the sizes could be adjusted appropriately.

If these incentives, together with proper monetary and fiscal policies, succeed in reducing wage inflation to 6 percent and price inflation to 4 percent, the dividing line between the penalty and reward should be gradually reduced (over several years) to 2 percent, the average growth rate of labor productivity. As disinflation steadily occurs, the unemployment rate can gradually be brought down to the new lower NAIRU. With a permanent TIP exerting permanent downward pressure on wage increases, it should be possible to keep wage inflation steady at close to 2 percent and price inflation near 0 percent if the unemployment rate is kept equal to the new NAIRU. Experience with TIP will tell whether a NAIRU of perhaps 4 percent could be achieved with a TIP penalty that is sufficiently moderate to allow relative wages and prices to respond to market forces and guide resources efficiently.

To maintain the new NAIRU and price stability, the growth rate of the money supply prescribed by monetarists would then be essential, on average. Periodic disturbances will continue to move the economy away from its targets, and countercyclical policy will be necessary to counter these disturbances. Nevertheless, a permanent TIP should reduce the frequency and degree of stagflation in the economy.

Finally, TIP should have no significant impact on the secular trend in the distribution of income between labor and capital. Although TIP is applied only to wage increases, price inflation should decline as much as wage inflation. This conclusion does not depend on an assumption of perfect competition, but only on the assumption that TIP will not alter the degree of competition, or market power, in the economy.

Nevertheless, there are at least two methods of guaranteeing protection for labor under TIP that appear feasible and deserve serious consideration. Under "real wage insurance," suggested by Arthur Okun, if the wage target is met but the price target is not, a compensatory tax rebate can be provided to wage and salary workers.[22] My suggestion would be to link the tax rebate to an employee TIP, so that the tax cut is greatest for employees who exercise greatest restraint. A key aspect of the proposal is that the contingent compensatory tax cut must be authorized in advance, when TIP itself is enacted, so that protection is guaranteed. In addition, the rebate could be paid if wage inflation declined more than price inflation, even if the wage target were not met.

Under the second proposal, suggested by Lawrence Klein and Vijaya Duggal, if the wage target were met but the ratio of after-tax profits to labor income rose above some threshold for the entire corporate sector (or economy), the base corporate tax rate would be raised equally for all firms to keep the ratio for the corporate sector below the threshold for that year.[23] The threshold should reflect both the secular trend and the cyclical behavior of the ratio. Once again, a key aspect is that the corporate tax rate adjustment should be enacted in advance, so that protection is guaranteed.

Other feasible methods may be developed to assure that the distribution of after-tax income does not shift unfairly because of TIP. A tax-based incomes policy, together with such complementary policies, promises significant benefits for labor, business, and the public, and therefore deserves serious consideration.

APPENDIX

The Myopic Profit-Maximization Model
and the Value-Maximization Model

THIS APPENDIX presents the mathematics of the myopic profit-maximization model and the value-maximization model, which are described verbally in the text. In both, the firm is assumed to be a monopsonistic competitor in its labor market, facing an upward-sloping labor supply

22. See Arthur Okun, "Incomes Inflation and the Policy Alternatives," in "The Economists' Conference on Inflation: Report," vol. 1 (1974; processed), pp. 365–75.

23. Lawrence R. Klein and Vijaya Duggal, "Guidelines in Economic Stabilization: A New Consideration," *Wharton Quarterly*, vol. 6 (Summer 1971), pp. 20–24.

curve, and a monopolistic competitor in its product market, facing a downward-sloping product demand curve. It is assumed that current gross (before-tax) profit is a function of w, the percentage wage increase (given the wage of the previous period, the choice of the wage of the current period can be described as the choice of the percentage wage increase of the current period); and that the function has the following properties:

(A-1) $$\pi^G = \pi^G(w, \delta),$$

where δ is a product demand parameter. Terms that are not defined in this appendix are defined in the text.

(A-2) $$\frac{\partial \pi^G}{\partial w}(w', \delta) = 0,$$

(A-3) $$\frac{\partial^2 \pi^G}{\partial w^2} < 0.$$

From A-2 and A-3, w' is the wage increase that maximizes gross profit, as shown in the diagram.

The myopic profit-maximization model is as follows.

Without TIP, management chooses the w that maximizes current net (after-tax) profit according to the following:

(A-4) $$\pi^N(w) = (1 - b)\pi^G(w),$$

(A-5) $$\frac{\partial \pi^N}{\partial w} = (1 - b)\frac{\partial \pi^G}{\partial w} = 0.$$

A-5 follows from A-4 because without TIP, the tax rate b does not depend on w. Management will therefore choose the w' that satisfies A-2, as shown in the diagram.

If a continuous employer TIP were introduced, the tax rate t would be:

(A-6) $$t(w) = B + mw.$$

A-5 is therefore modified as follows:

(A-5a) $$\frac{\partial \pi^N}{\partial w} = (1 - t)\frac{\partial \pi^G}{\partial w} - \pi^G \cdot m = 0.$$

The difference between A-5a and A-5 is the change in $\partial \pi^N / \partial w$ due to TIP, and is called the TIP incentive effect:

(A-7) $$\left(\frac{\partial \pi^N}{\partial w}\right)_{TIP} - \left(\frac{\partial \pi^N}{\partial w}\right)_{No\ TIP} = (b - t)\frac{\partial \pi^G}{\partial w} - \pi^G \cdot m.$$

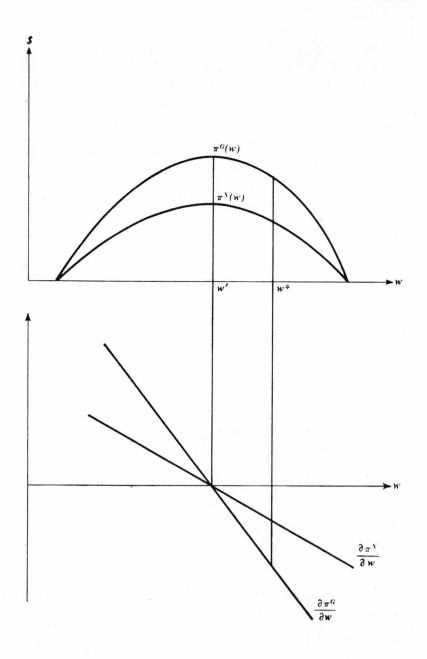

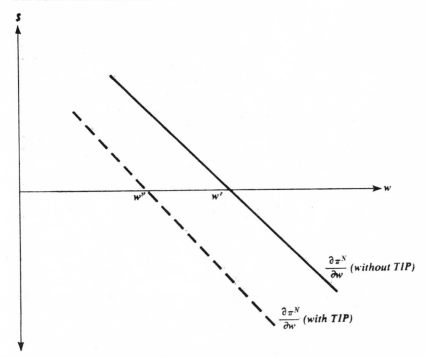

At w' the optimum without TIP, using A-2, A-5a becomes:

(A-8) $$\left(\frac{\partial \pi^N}{\partial w}(w')\right)_{TIP} = -\pi^G(w') \cdot m < 0, \qquad \pi^G(w') > 0.$$

The value of $\partial \pi^N / \partial w$ at w' measures the incentive provided by TIP—penalty or reward—to reduce w below w'. It depends on m—the TIP marginal tax penalty—and on $\pi^G(w')$; but not on $\pi^N(w')$. Because $\partial \pi^N / \partial w$ is negative at w', management chooses $w'' < w'$ to satisfy A-5a, as shown in the diagram presented above. But it also chooses a smaller volume of employment because it always optimizes at wage-employment combinations on its (positively sloped) labor supply curve.

The value-maximization model is as follows:

(A-9) $$V = V(\pi^N, I),$$

where

   V = the value of the firm (present value of current and future net profit), or the value of the income stream of management

   I = investment in personnel policy.

(A-10) $I = I(w)$, $dI/dw > 0$.

It should be noted that because I is defined as a function solely of w, it is independent of π^N.

The value function is assumed to have these properties:

(A-11) $$\frac{\partial V}{\partial \pi^N} > 0, \qquad \frac{\partial V}{\partial I} > 0,$$

(A-12) $$\frac{\partial V/\partial \pi^N}{\partial V/\partial I} \equiv \frac{dI}{d\pi^N}\bigg|_{V=constant} \equiv MRS > 0.$$

The *MRS* between personnel investment and current net profit is therefore positive as defined here (the negative of the slope of the iso-value curve).

(A-13) $$\frac{\partial MRS}{\partial \pi^N} < 0.$$

A-13 is the income, or profit squeeze, effect. When π^N declines, the impact of a specific decrement in I on V can be offset with a smaller increment in π^N. For A-13 to hold, the elasticity of the numerator of A-12 with respect to π^N must be less (more negative) than the elasticity of the denominator. This is shown as follows. Substituting A-12 into A-13 using the quotient rule yields:

(A-14) $$\frac{\partial V}{\partial I} \frac{\partial(\partial V/\partial \pi^N)}{\partial \pi^N} - \frac{\partial V}{\partial \pi^N} \frac{\partial V/\partial I}{\partial \pi^N} < 0.$$

Dividing by $(\partial V/\partial I) \cdot (\partial V/\partial \pi^N)$ and multiplying by π^N yields:

(A-15) $E_{\pi N} < E_I$,

where

    $E_{\pi N}$ = the elasticity of the numerator of A-12 with respect to net profit
    E_I = the elasticity of the denominator of A-12 with respect to net profit.

(A-16) $$E_{\pi N} \equiv \frac{\partial(\partial V/\partial \pi^N)}{\partial \pi^N} \cdot \frac{\pi^N}{\partial V/\partial \pi^N},$$

(A-17) $$E_I \equiv \frac{\partial(\partial V/\partial I)}{\partial \pi^N} \cdot \frac{\pi^N}{\partial V/\partial I}.$$

The more negative is $\partial(\partial V/\partial \pi^N)/\partial \pi^N$ in A-16, the more likely it is that A-15 and therefore A-13 will hold. For example, if $\partial(\partial V/\partial I)/\partial \pi^N$ in A-17 were zero, establishing that $\partial(\partial V/\partial \pi^N)/\partial \pi^N$ was negative would be sufficient to establish A-15 and therefore A-13. The discussion in the text concerning the cost of capital when V is the value of the firm and the signals of managerial competence when V is the value of management's own income stream provides rationales for why $\partial(\partial V/\partial \pi^N)/\partial \pi^N$ should be significantly negative, thereby increasing the probability that A-13 holds.

Management chooses w^* such that:

(A-18)
$$\frac{\partial V}{\partial w} = \frac{\partial V}{\partial \pi^N} \frac{\partial \pi^N}{\partial w} + \frac{\partial V}{\partial I} \frac{dI}{dw} = 0.$$

Dividing through by $\partial V/\partial I$ yields:

(A-19)
$$MRS \cdot \frac{\partial \pi^N}{\partial w} + \frac{dI}{dw} = 0.$$

Thus, at the optimal w^*, because both the MRS and dI/dw are positive, $\partial \pi^N/\partial w$ must be negative (not zero, as it is in the myopic model), as shown in the first diagram in this appendix. It is important to note that management does not choose w^* instead of a smaller wage increase because it seeks to attract a larger volume of employment and produce more output; it chooses w^* to invest in personnel policy. Thus, the firm will choose a wage-employment combination above (to the left of) its labor supply curve. A reduction in w below w^*, therefore, need not reduce employment.

Consider a particular $\pi^G(w,\delta)$ function such that when δ decreases, $\partial \pi^G/\partial w$ and $\partial \pi^N/\partial w$ are unaltered at each w. At the lower δ in A-19, $\partial \pi^N/\partial w$ and dI/dw are unaltered at w^*, but MRS is greater because $\pi^N(w^*)$ is less (from A-13). Because the left side of A-19 is now negative at w^*, $\partial V/\partial w$ at w^* is negative in A-18. It would therefore be optimal for management to reduce w below w^* in response to the decrease in δ. This contrasts with the myopic model, in which such a decrease in δ would not alter the optimal w (it would remain w' according to A-2).

The impact of TIP on A-19 is as follows. Under a penalty TIP, $t(w^*)$ is greater than b; because $\pi^G(w^*)$ is assumed to be unaltered, $\pi^N(w^*)$ declines. From A-13, the MRS term in A-19 increases. Because $\partial \pi^N/\partial w$ is negative at w^*, this increase in the MRS tends to make the left side of

A-19 negative, and thus $\partial V / \partial w$ negative at w^*. In contrast, under a reward TIP, $t(w^*)$ is less than or equal to b, so that the *MRS* stays constant or decreases, instead of increasing. The impact of a penalty TIP, in contrast to a reward TIP, on the *MRS* term is the profit-squeeze, or income effect. It is because a penalty TIP should raise the *MRS*, while a reward TIP should not, that it is probable that a penalty TIP will make $\partial V / \partial w$ more negative at w^*, and therefore provide a stronger incentive to reduce w below w^*.

Both a penalty and a reward TIP affect $\partial \pi^N / \partial w$ at w*, according to A-7. For a penalty TIP and a reward TIP with the same m, the second term in A-7 is identical at w^* and tends to reduce $\partial \pi^N / \partial w$ (making it more negative, thereby raising its absolute value). For a penalty TIP, b is less than $t(w^*)$, and because $\partial \pi^G / \partial w$ is negative, the first term is positive, partly offsetting the second term. For a reward TIP, the first term is either zero or negative, reinforcing the second term. Thus, the TIP incentive effect is actually somewhat greater for a reward TIP than it is for a penalty TIP at w^* because of the first term in A-7. Intuitively, the lower tax rate at w^* under a reward TIP causes the increment in π^N to be greater for a given decrement in w.

The intuition behind the value-maximization model, however, is that the differential impact on the *MRS* due to the profit-squeeze, or income effect, outweighs the differential substitution effect. If so, a penalty TIP would provide a stronger incentive at w^* to reduce w, as shown in the diagram below. Moreover, because the firm was operating above its labor supply curve prior to TIP, the lower w does not require a reduction in employment.

Under a penalty TIP, management chooses w^{**} less than w^* to satisfy A-19. It will now be shown that the TIP multiplier m can be set such that w^{**} will equal the TIP target n so that in A-20, $t(w^{**})$ equals b:

$$(A\text{-}20) \qquad t(w) = b + m(w - n), \qquad n < w^*.$$

If m can be so set, then a penalty TIP would reduce w below w^* without causing an actual increase in the tax rate, or an actual net profit squeeze at w^{**}.

If w equal to n is to be the new optimum, w^{**}, it must satisfy A-19 under TIP. Without TIP, at w equal to n the left side of A-19 would have been positive, since it was optimal to raise w to w^*. At w equal to n, TIP would not affect two of the three components of A-19, *MRS* and

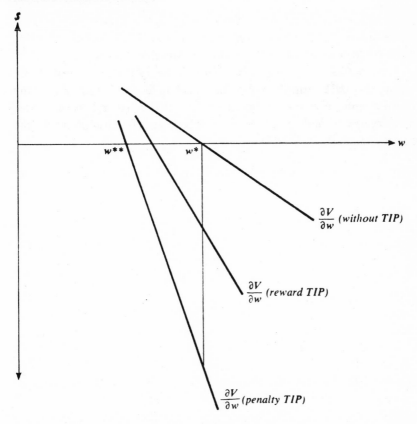

dI/dw. $MRS(n)$ is unaffected by TIP, regardless of the value of m because $t(n)$ equals b for all m, so that $\pi^N(n)$ is independent of m. The only component of A-19 that varies with m is $\partial\pi^N/\partial w$, according to the expression for $\partial\pi^N/\partial w$ given in A-5a. At w equal to n, $\partial(\partial\pi^N/\partial w)/\partial m$ equals $-\pi^G(n)$, so that $\partial\pi^N/\partial w$ varies linearly with m; any negative value of $\partial\pi^N/\partial w$ can be attained by raising m sufficiently.

The m required to make w equals n the new optimum under a penalty TIP is obtained as follows. First, solve A-19 for the required value of $\partial\pi^N/\partial w$ at w equals n, given $MRS(n)$ and dI/dw at n, which are both independent of m. Then the required value of m can be obtained by setting the expression for $\partial\pi^N/\partial w$ in A-5a equal to the required value of $\partial\pi^N/\partial w$, and solving for m, given t equal to b, $\partial\pi^G/\partial w$ at n, and $\pi^G(n)$.

The new optimum, w^{**} equal to n, is sustained solely by the TIP incentive effect—the change in $\partial\pi^N/\partial w$ at n—because a penalty TIP would not alter $MRS(n)$ or dI/dw at n. Thus, if m is set so that A-19 is satisfied at w equal to n, although a net profit squeeze would be threatened at w^*, none would occur at the w^{**} equal to n that results.

This contrasts with an increase in the ordinary income tax rate b. By raising the MRS term in A-19, this would reduce w below w^*. At the new optimum, however, the tax rate would still be higher, because b does not vary with w, and an actual net profit squeeze is required to sustain the new optimum.

Comments and Discussion

Robert J. Gordon: Laurence Seidman has presented a comprehensive and provocative analysis that attempts to persuade the reader that adoption of an employer TIP will reduce the natural (equilibrium) unemployment rate and, aided by an accommodative monetary deceleration, will slow inflation to a rate of less than 1.0 percent in a relatively short time. Along the way, Seidman argues that an employer TIP is to be preferred to an employee TIP. Although he claims that a penalty-based employer scheme is a more potent tool for wage deceleration than a reward-based plan, he nevertheless endorses a continuous flat-rate, tax-reward schedule applying both above and below the short-term wage guideline. Seidman's cursory review of allocative and distribution effects reveals no drawbacks sufficiently important to weaken his support of an employer TIP.

Several issues raised in the paper apply not only to TIP, but equally to any supply shift—whether a positive shift caused by a crop failure, a payroll-tax increase that raises the price at which firms are willing to supply a given output, a negative shift caused by bumper crops, or a successful TIP that reduces that price. First, for a given growth rate of nominal income, a supply shift changes the division of that spending between growth in real output and price increases. Bumper crops or a successful TIP would make possible, for any given growth rate of nominal income, a simultaneous reduction in the rate of inflation and increase in growth of real output. This, in turn, would allow the Federal Reserve to decelerate the rate of monetary growth without causing a recession or higher unemployment. In general, any government-induced price-reducing supply shift—whether in the form of price controls, TIP, or a reduction in payroll or excise taxes—creates an environment in which monetary deceleration is encouraged and, therefore, the administration and Congress indirectly "gain control" over monetary policy.

The principal sources of inertia in the U.S. inflation process, which make inflation so difficult to decelerate and cause monetary tightness to be translated into higher unemployment rather than a slowdown in inflation, are the institutions of three-year overlapping wage contracts in the unionized part of the economy and pattern-setting and emulation in much of the remainder of the economy. Before reading Seidman's paper, I found it difficult to understand the workings of an employer TIP that imposes a tax increase on firms, including those that are locked into existing wage contracts and those that have committed themselves to a given increase in wages over the following year. I doubted that such a program could reduce the inflation rate except by creating a crisis of business confidence and by increasing the amount of slack in the economy. Unfortunately there is nothing in Seidman's paper to allay my suspicion that the short-run impact of an employer TIP may be perverse.

While Seidman includes a collective-bargaining model, his primary analytical focus is on nonunion wage determination where the firm sets its own wage increase unilaterally to maximize its own net profit or utility. This is an important shortcoming of the paper. More convincing is the analytical framework in Rees' paper at this conference, which views the rate of wage change as the outcome of a clash between the differing interests of firms and workers, with a reconciliation brought about in many cases by strikes or by the threat of strikes. Seidman's myopic profit-maximizing model, in which TIP tilts the net profit schedule, presents a one-sided wage decision, not a two-sided wage bargain. Many firms cannot limit the wage increase to that which maximizes net profit because they face the threat of strikes as workers try to maximize their own utility. As Rees points out, TIP may increase the likelihood of strikes as employer pressure for small wage increases stands against the desires of workers, who have no such tax incentive to settle for less.

Seidman's second, value-maximizing model makes the size of wage increases depend on the size of employer net profits. Thus, the empirical tests of the effect of net profits on wage behavior in U.S. time series data form an important part of Seidman's case for an employer TIP. If Seidman is right, the squeeze on net profits caused by higher corporate taxes levied on firms through an employer TIP will lead to lower wage settlements as workers react to the profit squeeze. If Seidman is wrong, and net profits have no such effect on wage behavior, an equally plausible sce-

Table 1. Coefficients on Detrended Net Profits in Alternative Wage Equations

	Dependent variable[a]	
Sample description	Average hourly earnings (1)	Compensation per man-hour (2)
Period 1955:2–1975:2		
1. Seidman specification	0.0103 (2.29)	0.0177 (2.06)
2. Lagged wage replaced with lagged price	0.0011 (0.22)	0.0094 (1.13)
Period 1954:1–1976:4		
3. Seidman specification	0.0029 (0.75)	0.0067 (0.92)
4. Lagged wage replaced with lagged price	−0.0067 (−1.65)	0.0026 (0.39)
5. Social security tax, personal income tax, minimum wage, and control dummy variables added to 3, using lagged wage	−0.0073 (−1.33)	0.0007 (0.07)
6. Same as 5, using lagged price	−0.0152 (−2.68)	−0.0061 (−0.60)

Sources: Bureau of Labor Statistics and author's estimates.

a. Sum of coefficients on detrended ratio of net profits to corporate product. Numbers in parentheses are t statistics. The dependent variable is in the form of a one-quarter rate of change.

nario is that firms will attempt to shift forward the burden of the higher corporate taxes in the form of price increases.

For the purposes of discussion, I have prepared table 1, which presents the coefficient on net profits (measured as the detrended ratio of corporate profits after tax to gross corporate product) in a number of different wage equations. Column 1 presents results for equations in which the quarterly change in the average hourly earnings index of the Bureau of Labor Statistics is the dependent variable, and column 2 presents results in which the dependent variable is the quarterly change in compensation per man-hour.

Only in the first line, for both wage variables in columns 1 and 2, is the coefficient on net profits significantly positive. In all other variants of the wage equations the coefficient on net profits is either insignificant or significantly negative. In line 2, Seidman's sample period is retained, but his lagged wage-change variable is replaced by lagged price changes. In line

3, the sample period is extended slightly; in line 4, the lagged wage is again replaced by the lagged price. In lines 5 and 6 additional independent variables are included that have proved to be important in my recent research on wage behavior, including changes in the effective social security tax rate, the effective personal income tax rate, the effective minimum wage, and dummy variables for the period of price and wage controls in the early 1970s.

Thus, Seidman's empirical conclusion that a net profit squeeze contributes to a wage deceleration does not appear to be robust. On the other hand, in experiments that add a corporate tax variable to a price equation, there is no conclusive evidence supporting forward shifting of the corporate tax. Although my empirical results do not suggest that an employer TIP will have any beneficial income effect to reinforce its substitution effect, there is no strong case to be made that it will have an adverse income effect.

While I am skeptical that an employer TIP will have a beneficial impact, I am more sympathetic to the idea of an employee TIP. As Seidman points out, an employee penalty creates conflicting income and substitution effects, with the possibility that the loss of income caused by a tax penalty may lead to higher rather than lower wage demands. But this cannot be an argument for favoring an employer TIP because the same possibility of an adverse income effect exists for an employer tempted to shift forward the tax penalty to recoup lost net profits. Instead, the major weakness of the employee TIP is the problem raised earlier of inertia due to multiyear wage contracts and pattern setting. Equity problems arise when TIP penalties are levied on unions that are locked into pre-negotiated contracts that call for wage increases at rates higher than the TIP guideline.

Because Seidman ignores the inertia phenomenon, his numerical simulations of the effect of TIP are overly optimistic. Policymakers following Seidman would be likely to set the TIP no-penalty guideline too low initially, ignoring the large number of workers who would receive wage increases exceeding the guideline and who would thus pay a penalty (directly in an employee TIP or indirectly in the case of an employer TIP). If policymakers are surprised by TIP's lack of effectiveness, they will be equally stunned by a substantial increase of tax revenue that will have a deflationary effect on the economy. Thus, far from achieving a simultaneous reduction in inflation and unemployment as assumed by

Seidman, TIP could actually have the opposite effect and increase unemployment.

Finally, Seidman is entirely too sanguine about the lack of impact of a wage-only TIP on the income distribution, due to the alleged lock-step correlation between prices and wages. My past work has indicated that price change responds to wage change with a substantial lag. The short-run impact of a wage deceleration would be to limit labor's share of the income distribution. The wage deceleration of the early 1960s in response to slack labor markets, together with wage guidelines, helps to explain why the share of profits in the gross national product was so high in 1964 and 1965. And the British experience with voluntary incomes policy in the past few years has indicated that prices follow wages with a lag sufficiently long to cause a squeeze on labor's share that lasts for a year or more. Because labor unions are familiar with this historical experience, they are likely to fight hard against the adoption of a TIP scheme that applies only to wages.

Arthur M. Okun: Laurence Seidman provides much microeconomic and macroeconomic insight into the way alternative TIP plans could work. I agree with most of his analysis, but I have some important reservations and so I would like to summarize his argument, indicating where I see things differently.

As a point of departure, Seidman considers a representative nonunion firm facing a standard maximization problem with respect to its labor market. Operating in a search labor market, it faces a positively sloped supply curve of labor and has some wage discretion. When a penalty TIP —an extra tax on the wage increase—is imposed, the firm finds it optimal to settle for a smaller wage increment. But in those circumstances, a penalty TIP simply moves the firm to the left on the supply curve of labor facing it. The firm, as a result, opts for a lower level of employment as well as a lower wage rate. Also implied are a lower level of output and a forward shifting of the TIP penalty into product prices. In that world, TIP is not distinctly disinflationary; it is contractionary.

To justify an employer TIP, Seidman must leave that world and include "employee satisfaction" as a consideration in the firm's value maximization, which adjusts the short-term measured profit of the firm by adding the present value of its incremental personnel investment. The point is that, even though the firm obtains enough workers when it holds down its wage, it may sacrifice valuable morale, which may mean lower current productivity or higher future quit rates. Any firm for which personnel investment is important will operate off its labor supply curve in a weak labor market. And therefore when it is induced by a penalty TIP to hold down wages, it does not cut employment. Moreover, so long as the firm can expand output by hiring one more available applicant at the same wage, the last unit of output that was a zero-profit unit before TIP incurs no extra tax and remains a zero-profit unit after the introduction of TIP. And hence there is no reason to expect a forward shifting of the TIP penalty; lower wage hikes mean lower price hikes. Hence, the employer TIP is distinctly disinflationary and not contractionary in that world.

I fully share Seidman's view that the value-maximization model is the right model for the world we live in. Unlike the myopic model, it explains why firms allow quit rates to fall in a slack labor market without slowing or cutting wages, and why firms raise their wages even when applicants are abundant at the existing wage. Indeed, any time a nonunion firm raises its wage when it has layoffs or a no-help-wanted sign, it must be deliberately operating inside (to the left of) its short-run labor supply curve. Clearly, most firms during a slump consciously "over-pay" labor relative to the wage required merely to evoke the number of workers they want.

Seidman stresses another and quite separate implication of the model, namely, the role of high profits in stimulating wage increases. He invokes a diminishing marginal rate of substitution between currently measured profits and present value of incremental personnel investment. His intuition on that score seems plausible to me: capital markets cannot fully appraise the value of the personnel investment; and when current profits are very low, the value of long-run investments in personnel or anything else becomes questionable. That implies that the higher the level of current profits, the more the firm should focus on its long-run investment in personnel, and hence the higher the wage it should be willing to pay, other things being equal.

Seidman stresses this point as one rationale for preferring a penalty TIP to a reward TIP on wages. But actually it is an argument for a higher tax rate on corporate income. That higher rate comes back to haunt Seidman when he conjectures quite plausibly that some firms may do their pricing on the basis of after-tax returns and, in that case, would pass through the TIP surcharge into higher prices. Of course, a penalty TIP need not entail a higher average corporate tax rate: one could estimate the likely TIP revenues, lower the basic corporate rate, and thus keep total expected revenues constant. In that case, the favorable "income effect" on wages is lost, but the danger of forward shifting of the corporate tax is avoided. Because of his strong emphasis on the income effect, Seidman would not make that trade. As a matter of judgment, it looks like a good trade to me.

While the TIP surcharge will not enter into the marginal cost of output for any firm with excess job applicants, it does have a flaw previously noted by Richard Slitor. It imposes different marginal incentive effects on firms with a high ratio of profits to wages as compared to firms with a low ratio, reflecting either differences in labor intensity or profitability of their capital. As Slitor suggests, *that* defect can be avoided by depriving firms of full deductibility of their payrolls as expenses if they exceed the hurdle wage increase in a penalty TIP. But Slitor's alternative places the entire penalty into the marginal cost of output, and that would be an even more serious defect in my judgment. Ideally, any deductibility penalty should be based on the employment of *last year* so that increased employment would not enlarge the penalty. But that clearly creates greater administrative complexity.

When Seidman develops the macroeconomics of the TIP system, he describes briefly the way TIP could be used to disinflate an economy that had reached its nonaccelerating-inflation rate of unemployment (NAIRU) with a high inflation rate. The TIP and the adjustments of monetary growth can lower the inflation rate without incurring the enormous output losses that Perry underlines in his paper. Seidman stresses in greater detail that TIP can lower the NAIRU, backing his claim with an ingenious juggling act of adjusting the TIP penalty and monetary growth to neutralize the first-round effect of each successive movement into territory that would otherwise accelerate the inflation rate.

Of the two predicted consequences of TIP, disinflating at a given NAIRU and lowering NAIRU, I feel more enthusiastic about the former. The interest in TIP and other cures for stagflation that created this conference was triggered by the stubbornness of the inflation rate at high unemployment rates. The second part of the story—lowering NAIRU through TIP—works in any plausible model of the NAIRU type. Seidman has convinced me that he is right in principle. But any substantial shift might require a very costly reward or a penalty so high that it would be nearly prohibitive, like controls. The nonlinearity of the short-term Phillips curve points to this danger. Furthermore, the markup of prices over wages may become significantly wider at high utilization rates; then, the TIP incentive must be strong enough to push down (and keep holding down) real wages to lower the NAIRU. The emphasis on disinflation points to TIP as a transitional remedy, while the emphasis on lowering NAIRU frames it as permanent. Operationally, however, I submit that this is a red herring. Any advocate of TIP should ask the Congress to recognize TIP as experimental and to legislate it for a trial period of a few years.

Let me conclude with a few comments on reward and penalty variants of TIP. For policy purposes, one should simply forget the logical possibility that Seidman records of giving rewards to employers for especially small wage increases and imposing penalties on workers based on the average wage increase paid by their firms. Such proposals would fail any reasonable test of equity in the political process. Henry Wallich has articulately defended the evenhandedness of his proposal by emphasizing that the penalty is on the *employer,* even though the tax is on excessive wage increases. Penalizing workers or rewarding firms on wages would remove any semblance of evenhandedness. Wage penalties must be imposed on firms, and wage rewards must be given (and made universally available) to workers.

Seidman loads the dice against the reward approach in a number of ways. The most obvious example of that is his use of the assumption that any worker accepting a wage-restraint reward would expect an equivalently lower (before-tax) wage level for the remainder of his career with a firm. I find that entire analysis totally unpersuasive. It claims that workers will shift to jobs that offer lower current take-home pay on the conviction that the before-tax level of wages is the best predictor of future after-tax wages. Workers must be more sensible than that! Furthermore, Seidman ignores two advantages of rewards—that they cannot raise marginal costs and that they avoid the forward shifting and labor-intensity problem. Finally, he does not take seriously the evidence of a lag from wages to prices stressed by Robert Gordon, which implies that during its first year a penalty-TIP would redistribute income from wages to profits. A reward-TIP would compensate for that on an after-tax basis.

Laurence Seidman: Gordon's profit variable gives mixed results in alternative wage equations, in contrast to the highly significant performance of my profit variable in table 1. His profit variable does obtain a t statistic just above two in a wage equation with the same right-hand variables that I used ("Seidman specification"), though his t value is less than mine (just above four). The performance of Gordon's profit variable generally deteriorates as he varies the specification of the wage equation.

Part of the contrast may result from the fact that Gordon and I test different profit variables. If this is correct, then it becomes important to assess the theoretical plausibility of each profit variable.

My variable is the ratio of the after-tax profit rate on equity in manufacturing to its trend value. It focuses on the detrended level of after-tax profit relative to stockholders' equity. The choice of this profit variable rests on the hypothesis that it is the rate of return on equity (relative to the rate regarded as "normal") that is important to a board of directors and stockholders, and therefore to management. The profit rate on equity is a widely quoted measure of the performance both of a firm and of its management. In a collective bargaining context, the union may also focus on it as the best indicator of the firm's "ability to pay."

Gordon's variable is the detrended ratio of the share of after-tax profits in value added for the entire corporate sector. The numerator is the rate of after-tax profits to gross product originating (value added). It is not clear to me why a board of directors or stockholders, and therefore management, should be concerned about the ratio of after-tax profits to value added, rather than to equity. Even unions may be more interested in rates of return on equity.

In sum, a fair test of the role of profits in wage determination requires a theoretically plausible profit variable and the specification of the wage equation. Gordon's mixed results underline the need for further research. They do not, however, change my current view that the profit rate on equity relative to trend appears to influence wage inflation; or my conclusion that econometric evidence appears to provide some support for the belief that an employer penalty TIP is likely to provide a stronger and more reliable incentive than an employer reward-only TIP.

General Discussion

Several discussants were concerned about the allocative consequences of the TIP plan. Martin Baily mentioned distortions that could be introduced by uniform across-the-board guidelines. Recognizing the administrative problems, he nonetheless saw the need for flexible rules and special exceptions that would take account of differing supply and demand conditions among industries. Bruce MacLaury suggested that some variation across firms might be permitted by gearing the penalty on excessive wage increases to a firm's historical performance on wages over several years rather than to a uniform percentage guideline on wage increases.

Frederic Mishkin suggested that Seidman's scheme might punish rapidly expanding firms unduly, because he thought they would be likely to have above-average rates of wage increase. James Tobin said that firms would still be free to grow rapidly and to pay higher relative wages under a TIP plan; if they chose to do so, they would simply have to pay higher taxes for a limited period during which they raised their relative wage. Edmund Phelps was concerned that, if the penalty was only a one-time tax on a permanent move to a higher wage level, as Tobin implied, the TIP penalty might not be an effective incentive to hold wages down. George von Furstenberg saw other implications of the one-time character of the penalty. For example, it treated rapidly growing firms least unfavorably if they raised their relative wage most when they were small and thus still had small profits subject to the penalty tax rate.

Michael Wachter stressed the importance of the internal labor market that firms use for promotions and upgrading; he thought that any TIP plan might distort the workings of that market and thus cause a serious inefficiency. Thomas Juster was concerned that, under TIP, unmeasured fringe benefits—including loafing on the job—would become more attractive. Sidney Weintraub was not persuaded that some of these predicted changes would occur to any significant degree, or that all of them would necessarily be distortions if they did occur. In any case, he emphasized, it was worthwhile accepting some microeconomic allocative inefficiency to correct the massive allocative inefficiency of unemployed resources.

Robert Hall contended that Seidman's externality argument assumed that the social cost of inflation was huge. That was a fundamental issue that was not clearly demonstrated by theory or empirical evidence. James Duesenberry countered that, although the costs of inflation may not be clear, it was clear that the costs of attempting to reduce inflation through restraint of aggregate demand were extremely large.

Duesenberry suggested that, to be effective, a TIP plan had to supplement a basic consensus in which the majority of citizens committed themselves to reduce inflation through a cooperative effort. Under those circumstances, which are required for any incomes policy, a penalty TIP would help by punishing the minority of holdouts and by coordinating the actions of those in the consensus. Michael Wachter commented that a minority of holdouts might undermine the effectiveness of any plan. He expected many holdouts, especially among people who felt that their incomes had lagged behind and that they therefore deserved an opportunity to catch up.

In line with Duesenberry's view of a penalty TIP as a "convincer," Arnold Packer suggested more generally that the line between persuasion, on the one hand, and TIP, on the other, was not so sharp as Seidman implied. People in social situations generally respond to persuasion and unenforced rules. The effectiveness of rewards and penalties under TIP would depend on whether or not people accept the reasonableness of the system and expect others to do so, too.

Another portion of the discussion examined the short-run and long-run potentialities of tax-based incomes policy. Was it to be viewed mainly as a device to effect a transition to a lower inflation rate or as one to lower the nonaccelerating-inflation rate of unemployment (NAIRU) permanently? Wachter was unpersuaded by Seidman's argument that the NAIRU would be actually reduced. He did not see how TIP would reduce the size of the pool of unemployed required to keep labor markets in balance. Wachter thought such a shift had to involve some change in relative wage patterns (including the relative return from wages and transfer payments) or some improvement in the efficiency of labor markets. Basically, the issue required a general equilibrium analysis, which Seidman had not provided. Similarly, Benjamin Friedman questioned how TIP could have a beneficial transitional effect without lowering the natural rate of unemployment. In response, Arthur Okun pointed to the explicit assumption in Seidman's model that the ratio of prices to standard unit labor costs was not raised by high utilization rates. That assumption could be crucial to the possibility of lowering NAIRU significantly with a penalty of reasonable size. But it was not crucial to the transitional benefits.

Franco Modigliani felt strongly that any TIP should be terminated as soon as the inflation rate wound down, even if the program in fact was capable of lowering the natural rate of unemployment. He feared that a permanent TIP would have serious distorting effects. On the other hand, Phelps argued that, since the natural rate of unemployment was not necessarily socially optimal, a permanent tax to lower it might well be justified on efficiency grounds. Seidman urged Modigliani to weigh the permanent gains from a lower natural unemployment rate against any permanent distortionary costs. Weintraub commented that both the analysis in Seidman's paper and the discussion of it by the participants leaned heavily on the natural-rate view—an equilibrium concept that Weintraub felt had little relevance.

Albert Rees agreed and extended Gordon's reservation about the modeling of TIP in the context of a nonunion employer maximizing an objective function. Collective bargaining would be the dominant mode of wage determination for the class of firms that would be covered by a penalty TIP plan. Rees felt that the original Wallich-Weintraub paper, although less elegant than Seidman's, had presented a preferable model that allowed them to come to grips with wage determination among large firms and unions. Weintraub expressed another reservation about the single-firm microeconomic analysis; he thought that the general increase in the money wage should be viewed as determined by the whole system rather than by the functions of a single representative firm.

Particular issues about the design of a TIP plan evoked some comments. Martin Feldstein supported the view that, because TIP was experimental, it should be regarded as temporary; hence he preferred penalties to rewards because it was much less difficult politically to terminate a penalty. John Shoven felt that the corporate tax rate was a poor instrument for a penalty TIP designed to moderate wage increases because ratios of total wages to profits differ so widely among firms. The punishments for large wage increases would depend on those ratios and would not correspond to the seriousness of the violation.

George von Furstenberg noted the possibility of a perverse effect on prices from a penalty TIP on wages. For a monopolistic firm engaged in short-run profit maximization and facing an upward-sloping labor supply schedule, the marginal profit would fall to zero at a lower output level.

Under these conditions, the TIP penalty would curtail the supply of output and thus actually raise prices. He noted that Okun had made a similar point in his comments, and that Seidman had conceded it in the paper. Unlike them, however, he was not ready to dismiss that model as irrelevant.

Some participants probed the distributional impact of Seidman's TIP plan. Weintraub doubted that any shift to profits would be quantitatively significant, even in the initial year of the program. A small shift might be acceptable, particularly if the program included some type of excess profits tax. Seidman elaborated on his specific proposals for insuring fairness to workers. Duesenberry suggested that a penalty TIP might be made more equitable and more acceptable to workers by simultaneously enacting a cut in income or payroll taxes that directly benefited wage and salary earners.

LARRY L. DILDINE
Department of the Treasury

EMIL M. SUNLEY
Department of the Treasury

Administrative Problems of Tax-Based Incomes Policies

ALTHOUGH 1977 was a good year economically, unemployment and inflation are still serious problems. Over the last few months the outlook for inflation has worsened. Many believe that traditional monetary and fiscal policies will not be sufficient to do the job, as George Perry makes clear in his paper in this volume. And as Laurence Seidman suggests, novel tax incentives or disincentives are being advocated to provide a carrot or a stick to hold down wage and price increases. These tax-based incomes policies (TIPs) would permit a more aggressive use of monetary and fiscal policies without having to rely on direct controls to moderate wages and prices.

While there has been some public discussion of the merits of various tax-based schemes such as those put forth by Arthur Okun or by Henry Wallich and Sidney Weintraub, little attention has been paid to the details of implementing them.[1] This paper focuses on the administrative problems of TIP. A workable scheme must permit the Internal Revenue

1. Two exceptions are unpublished papers by Gerard M. Brannon, "Technical Issues in an Incomes Policy with Penalties" (U.S. Department of the Treasury, Office of Tax Analysis, July 13, 1971; processed); and Richard E. Slitor, "Tax-Based Incomes Policy: Technical and Administrative Aspects," a report prepared for the Board of Governors of the Federal Reserve System (March 20, 1978; processed). In addition, experience with excess profits taxes and with wage and price controls sheds some light on the administrative problems of TIP. See, for example, U.S. Department of the Treasury, Office of Economic Stabilization, *Historical Working Papers on the Economic Stabilization Program, August 15, 1971 to April 30, 1974* (Government Printing Office, 1974).

Service and businesses to determine the amount of tax benefit or penalty a firm should receive. As one might expect, solutions to the administrative problems involve choices and trade-offs.

Preliminary Observations

The administration of TIP will depend crucially on five initial design decisions. First, the scheme may impose tax penalties on firms that grant excessive wage or price increases or tax reductions for firms or workers that restrain price or wage increases.[2] If the stick approach were taken— that is, if penalties were imposed—unincorporated businesses and small firms, which often employ only rudimentary accounting, could be excluded from the program. These exclusions could greatly reduce administrative problems without having a serious impact on the effectiveness of the program. If, however, Okun's carrot approach were adopted, which offers tax reductions, there would be considerable pressure to allow all business taxpayers and their employees and even nonprofit organizations and their employees to participate and thus potentially qualify for the rewards for good behavior. Thus, although a policy of targeted tax reductions may be politically more feasible, administrative considerations strongly argue for the stick approach. If the latter approach were taken, TIP could be limited to firms like those in Tier I of the Phase II wage controls, November 1971–January 1973. If large firms set wage patterns, then inducing these firms to moderate their wage and price behavior would win the battle.

The stick approach would presumably impose penalties on *firms* that increase wages above some threshold level. The carrot approach, however, would probably provide tax reductions for *workers* if wages have not exceeded the threshold. Providing tax reductions for workers raises a number of vexing administrative problems. Firms would have to inform workers somewhere on the W-2 withholding form that they qualify for the tax break. If an audit of workers indicated that they did not qualify for the tax break, the Internal Revenue Service would have to collect from the firm, leaving the tax breaks for the workers intact. The alternative, to have the Internal Revenue Service collect from every worker directly, would be administratively infeasible.

2. No one has suggested applying a stick approach to *workers,* and such a scheme is not discussed here.

Carrying this theme a step farther, Okun has suggested that firms or workers be invited to "take the pledge" to restrain wages and prices at the beginning of the tax year so that the rewards could immediately appear in withholding or estimated tax payments.[3] Perhaps some additional incentives would be offered to those who signed up in advance. Such prospective changes in estimated payments to account for accruals of tax incentives is customary practice. When the rate of the investment tax credit is increased, for example, estimated payments are adjusted accordingly. However, in the case of TIP, the uncertainty is greater. If the failure rate for TIP based on the carrot approach were fairly high, there would be potential collection problems due to underwithholding. For this reason, prospective rewards allowed to individual workers may need to be repaid by their employers. This solution is practical, but it seems to suggest that employees are responsible for successful wage restraint, while companies are to blame for any failure. Whether or not TIP is designed to affect advance payment of tax, we conclude that a stick approach that imposes penalties on firms is preferable on administrative grounds to a carrot approach offering tax breaks for workers.

The second initial decision with important administrative implications is whether the rewards and penalties apply over the full range of possible wage and price changes, such as that proposed by Laurence Seidman, or whether they depend on the firm remaining above or below a threshold or "hurdle." Under a continuous program, higher prices and wages reduce the rewards or increase the penalties according to a specific formula. As Seidman points out in his paper, a continuous program ensures that all covered firms are given an incentive to moderate wage or price increases at the margin. This incentive increases the efficiency of the program, but also requires that the exact increase in wages or prices is known for every firm.

The hurdle approach has rewards and penalties that depend simply on whether a firm's wage increases are below, say, 5 percent a year. This type of approach would present fewer administrative problems than the continuous one for either the carrot or the stick proposals. For many firms, it would be clear that wage increases were within some narrow range, say, between 4.0 and 4.5 percent. These firms would qualify for the reward or avoid the penalty, and the size would not depend on whether

3. Arthur M. Okun, "The Great Stagflation Swamp," *Challenge,* vol. 20 (November/December 1977), p. 13.

the firm increased wages by 4.0 instead of 4.4 percent, but rather on whether the increase was less than 5 percent. An advantage of this hurdle approach is that Internal Revenue Service enforcement could be restricted to firms that are near the hurdle. On the other hand, the approach can only succeed if firms cannot arbitrarily adjust their accounts so that an actual 5.9 percent wage increase is measured as a 4.9 percent increase. Under the alternative continuous approach, this kind of adjustment is less of a concern because it either reduces the penalties or increases the rewards; it is not an "all-or-nothing" proposition. On balance, we judge that the hurdle approach raises less difficult administrative problems than the continuous approach.

A third initial design decision is whether the program is a temporary or a permanent one. If a tax penalty were imposed for only one year, it might have arbitrary effects among firms, depending on when they customarily raise wages and prices. For example, a firm operating on a calendar year may increase wages in a base year by 9 percent on September 1, before TIP is announced. Even if the firm did not increase wages the following year, it could not pass a hurdle of less than 6 percent if the wage increase were measured by the change in the total annual wage bill. Under the hurdle approach, this type of intrayear timing problem would persist for a permanent policy because there would be an incentive to bunch wage and price increases. The intrayear problem would tend to wash out if the program were continuous and in effect for a number of years. For a temporary policy of any type, complicated intrayear adjustments annualizing wage and price increases occurring during the year may be needed to reduce the arbitrariness of the program. Special rules or exceptions may be needed for multiyear contracts that provide future wage or price increases.

Firms and workers participating in a temporary program may agree to compensatory wage increases or bonuses to be paid after TIP expires. This may be particularly true of small firms. The best way to avoid this problem is to indicate initially that a temporary program might well be extended if it were successful in moderating inflation.

The fourth initial decision is whether the basic accounting unit for wage and price increases should be the plant, the corporate entity, or the conglomerate. In the case of a TIP that applies only to wages, the basic accounting unit could also be the bargaining unit or class of workers.

Many tax and financial accounting systems may not easily permit a division of the wage bill among plants of one firm. Data, however, are available on the wage bills of particular corporate entities within a corporate group. For these entities, data may also be available by bargaining units or classes of workers.

Disaggregation by employee groups within a corporation may be desirable if wage restraint is to be regarded as a "pact," or social contract, among employers, employee bargaining units, and the government. This type of disaggregation was followed in the Phase II wage controls of 1971–72. In that program, the designated "appropriate employee unit" was the bargaining unit; in the case of nonunion employees, it was a recognized class of employees. Reports and notifications were required to be sent to the Pay Board and were signed by the employer and a union representative. Because of this classification of accounting units (employee units), one group of employees that has greater demands or a stronger market position would not penalize a separate union or class of workers. However, such a classification would be administratively more complex than a policy that consolidated accounts to the level of the taxpaying unit. In nonunion situations, the designation of the employee units would also be subject to manipulation if left to the business firm, or would complicate administration if prescribed by regulations.

In the case of price increases, no compelling reason appears to exist for disaggregation of employers below the group of related corporations that file a consolidated income tax return.[4] Any disaggregation below the level of the consolidated group would require policing of transfer prices between related entities. This is an administrative quagmire to be avoided.

It is assumed in what follows that the basic accounting unit is a group of related corporations that file a consolidated return and that the time period is the accounting period of the group. These rules for the accounting unit are by far the simplest to administer as part of the existing tax system. Corporations may use a calendar year or a fiscal year.

If the basic accounting unit is the consolidated group, it must be recognized that the corporate tax return of the current year may include plants or corporate entities that were included on another corporate tax return in the previous year. And plants or corporate entities included in the previ-

---

4. The privilege of filing a consolidated return is extended to an affiliated group of corporations, generally corporations in which at least 80 percent of each class of stock of each corporation is owned by one or more of the other corporations included. If a corporation is eligible, it is generally advantageous for it to file a consolidated return.

ous year may no longer be part of the consolidated group. Furthermore, it is possible to sell a plant but not the corporate shell and vice versa. New firms, mergers, and other reorganizations raise special problems that are discussed at the end of this paper. Here, in passing, it should be said that the hurdle approach provides an incentive for corporate mergers between firms a little above and a lot below the hurdle.[5]

The fifth initial design decision is to specify the nature of the TIP penalty or reward. Most TIP proposals have been cast in terms of changes in the rate of the income tax. Thus, the Okun proposal suggests that a percentage of the income tax be rebated for firms and employees of firms that pass the hurdle, while Wallich and Weintraub suggest a surtax on income for firms that fail the hurdle.[6] Seidman, in his paper in this volume, suggests a variable system with rebates for firms that do better than a specified standard and a surtax for those that do worse.

An economic case may be made for tying a wage restraint to the federal payroll taxes. A payroll tax variant of TIP would then be directly related to a measure of labor cost rather than to capital income. As a consequence, many firms would not have a zero or negative tax base, and there would be no potential dilution of TIP incentives by income tax credits.[7]

In 1973, 56 percent of corporate taxpayers paid no federal income tax. A TIP that alters the income tax rate for the current tax year would have no consequence for such firms. If businesses are subject to TIP, regardless of the amount of income tax currently paid, some approach other than altering the income tax rate should be proposed.

An alternative TIP based on the penalty approach was recommended

5. There are similar incentives already in the Internal Revenue Code. For example, a firm subject to the minimum tax on preference income may want to merge with a firm paying a large amount of standard income tax, and a firm with unused investment tax credits may want to merge with a firm that has sufficient income tax liability to use the credits.

6. "The Great Stagflation Swamp," p. 13; Henry C. Wallich and Sidney Weintraub, "A Tax-Based Incomes Policy," *Journal of Economic Issues,* vol. 5 (June 1971), p. 2.

7. If the TIP penalty were defined as an income surtax (or if the reward were a rate reduction) the availability for some firms of excess tax credits would partly offset the immediate effects of the penalty (or reward). This possibility could be precluded by treating the penalty as a separate tax (or the reward as a tax refund) that would not affect the credit limitations. Presumably the penalty or reward would be based on income taxes after the foreign tax credit but before other credits.

by Franco Modigliani. He would disallow deductions for wages to the extent that the firm's wage increase exceeded a prescribed rate. This approach would affect deficit firms by reducing the amount of net carryover of operating loss, thus producing either a smaller immediate refund of taxes from previous years or higher tax payments in subsequent profit years. However, this method would require an exact determination of the rate of wage increase for all firms that exceed the hurdle rate. It would thus be much more costly to audit than would proposals for "all-or-nothing" penalties or rewards.

The most easily administered type of TIP incentive that would also apply to deficit companies is a credit or surcharge applied to one of the payroll tax bases. These incentives could be defined as additional income tax liabilities or credits so that they would not affect trust funds.

TIP could apply to wages or prices only or to both. The next two sections discuss the administrative problems of determining the extent of wage and price increases. In each case, there are problems of defining the base and measuring the increase beyond that base. The administrative problems are considerable, particularly in the case of prices, unless simplified procedures are adopted. These procedures would be somewhat arbitrary and could distort business decisions such as the choice between debt and equity or between wages and fringe benefits.

Measurement of Wage Increases

In aggregate terms, wage inflation may be said to occur when there is an increase in the average unit labor cost. The amount of wage increase that can be granted without increasing unit labor cost will vary among firms, depending on the rate of growth in labor productivity. In an economy of stable prices, labor compensation would rise roughly according to the average productivity increase; prices would fall in industries in which productivity gains were high, and vice versa. Hence, a policy to control price inflation might operate by attempting over time to limit the rate of wage increase for every firm to the average increase in productivity throughout the economy. It is certainly simpler to administer an incomes policy based on measurement of wage increases than one that hinges on measuring changes in unit labor costs for every firm, especially if there were no parallel price-restraint program that required the calculation of output-quantity weights.

In the remainder of the paper it is assumed that the wage-restraint program would be based on a measure of increases in hourly compensation. An average level of productivity increase would be allowed by setting the threshold wage increase above the target rate of price inflation.

A comprehensive measure of pay increases would include all elements of labor compensation that could be reasonably valued in dollars. That is, the numerator of the hourly wage rate would be the sum of money wages and salaries, including overtime; accruals of pension rights; profit sharing and other incentive awards; contributions to annuities and group insurance; commissions and bonuses; and any other valuable compensation. The denominator would be the annual total man-hours worked. Such a detailed definition of wages is desirable unless there is some reason to promote the substitution of nonwage benefits for money wages. The Phase II wage controls specifically exempted a number of components of total labor costs, for example. Among these were productivity incentive programs, longevity and automatic progression increases, employer contributions to social insurance, increases due to promotions, increases that resulted in an hourly wage level less than $1.90 (subsequently raised to $2.75), and increases in certain qualified benefit plans. All these exempted items are elements in labor cost and are substitutable, to some degree, for more direct compensation. If the main concern of the program is for cost-push inflation, these "loopholes" in the measurement of compensation are to be avoided. Exceptions for deferred compensation may be reasonable if the purpose is primarily to restrain current purchasing power, but in that case, more traditional fiscal policy would be needed.

All the practical problems of measuring nonwage compensation are encountered in defining and administering the income tax. For employees, the incentives to seek substitution of certain tax exempt or unreported nonwage benefits already exist. The strength of these incentives is proportional to employees' marginal tax rates. For employees in high tax brackets, the extra inducement of TIP may often be small. For corporations, there is a strong incentive to avoid understatement of deductible labor costs because these directly reduce corporate tax liability. In the case of pension plans, the understatement of current cost would give no direct tax advantage to employees, but would result in additional corporate taxes. However, most types of current nonwage compensation such as health insurance and fringe benefits are fully deductible for the corporation as costs of doing business, but are not included as income to employees. Unless these benefits are considered compensation, expanding fringe benefits will help the firm to qualify under TIP without incurring additional income tax liability. Under a policy based on the hurdle approach, the payoff at the margin for reducing measured increases in compensation may be large indeed. For some versions of TIP, if the wage hurdle is set at 6 percent, any device that allowed a firm to reduce the measured increase from 6.1 percent would result in a tax rate reduction on the entire income of the firm. Because of this "notch," firms that are near the margin of the target wage increase would have a strong inducement to underreport increases in compensation, even if the average rate of the TIP penalties or rewards were small. It may even be worthwhile to invite the extra current corporate tax liability associated with understatement of pension costs. A similar potential notch problem exists on the price side of TIP.

PENSIONS

For most firms, the largest nonwage element in labor compensation is pensions. In the national income accounts this element of compensation is measured by employer and employee contributions to the pension plan in the case of funded plans, and by actual benefits paid in the case of nonqualified or unfunded plans. However, neither current benefits paid nor current contributions is a good proxy for the year-to-year increase in the expected present value of future retirement benefits—that is, the increase in the actuarial value, which is in principle the correct measure of the current labor costs attributable to pensions.

Most pension plans are qualified plans, and the companies must currently fund future benefits. The tax law requires that firms meet certain minimum funding requirements. For firms that do not liberalize pension plans during the current year, contributions plus the earnings on pension trust funds would be a reasonable approximation for the year-to-year increase in the present value of expected future benefits. However, when pension plans are liberalized, companies are not required to fund past service benefits that accrued in the current year. Instead, companies may generally amortize these past service benefits over a period of thirty years.

Thus, using current contributions as a proxy for accrued benefits understates the increase in compensation whenever a pension plan is liberalized. This will encourage substitution of pension liberalizations for regular increases in wages or current compensation. If TIP were expected to be temporary, workers could receive an increase in future pension benefits when the program was in effect; after TIP expired, ordinary wage increases could again be provided.

Firms may view pension contributions of the current year as the only present labor cost associated with a pension plan that must be passed through in higher prices. The increase in unfunded liabilities or the earnings on previous contributions would not be viewed as a current cost, and consequently would not exert pressure on prices. If this is correct, pension contributions for qualified plans might be considered as the pension element of compensation. Firms above the minimum funding rate, however, should not be permitted to reduce their funding rates.[8] Alternatively, when qualified pension plans are liberalized, the required periodic actuarial report may provide a basis for estimating increased actuarial value. This method would require regulations to prescribe the choice of a discount rate and to specify a method for determining expected future retirements and the likelihood that the pension will vest.

A wage definition that overlooks accruals of future benefits and takes into account only benefits paid will understate current labor costs. Yet for unfunded retirement plans, benefits currently paid would have to suffice because it is probably the only information available.

OTHER NONWAGE BENEFITS

Stock options present a problem similar to pensions. Ideally, options would be valued at the time of grant. The right to purchase shares of stock at an established price at any time over, say, five years is clearly worth something at the time this right is created. For tax purposes, stock options granted after May 1976 are generally taxed when the option is exercised. The amount of income recognized is the difference between the value of stock at the time the option is exercised and the option price. Corporations

8. Current law provides a minimum funding rule and a maximum tax deduction for a qualified plan. If contributions were considered as the only pension element of compensation, firms above the minimum funding requirement would have an incentive to reduce the level of current funding.

are permitted an ordinary deduction for this difference. These tax rules are justified mainly on grounds of expediency, although it is generally recognized that the taxation of compensation is deferred until the option is exercised. Under TIP, tax rules would probably determine when compensation could be recognized. Corporations thus would have an incentive to grant stock options instead of cash wage increases.

Other nonwage benefits should be included in the wage definition of compensation, according to the current outlays of the firm. These benefits would include contributions to group insurance policies, profit-sharing plans, and paid vacations. In the case of paid vacations, the treatment of vacation pay that is earned but unused in a current year may be an issue. For plans that allow accumulation of annual leave and terminal payments on separation, vacation pay may be counted as it accrues, not as it is used. For contingent plans, adjustment to accruals should be allowed for experience. These rules are in line with tax accounting rules.

A more difficult problem is presented by employee benefit plans that are wholly unfunded, such as medical reimbursement plans. The amount of benefits paid by small firms, which is the only market measure of their value, may vary significantly from year to year because of a random variation in claims, rather than because of changes in coverage. Proper inclusion of these plans in the measure of compensation would require an estimate of the annual market premium for a comparable policy, but this is impractical.

A number of time-honored devices exist for increasing labor compensation without incurring additional tax consequences. Work rules may be liberalized; fringe benefits, such as company cafeterias, improved; and perquisites extended. Such changes would bedevil any wage restraint program. If they are not considered as compensation, TIP would add to the pressure to substitute on-the-job conveniences and company-paid luxuries for money wages. The administrative problems associated with fringe benefits are less severe under TIP than under the income tax because the former would not require that the value of the benefits be allocated to particular employees.

General rules for the evaluation of these benefits are relatively easy to formulate, but they are difficult to administer in detail. Consider such items as expense accounts, low-rate loans, use of company automobiles, discount goods and services, and the like. These privileges should be included in the wage measure to the extent that they are not directly related to job performance. They should be valued at the market price or at the difference between the discount price and the market price.[9]

Irregular compensation such as commissions, piecework wages, and bonuses should be included in total compensation as if they were regular wages. Measuring these kinds of compensation and also the salaries of professional and management personnel presents the problem of defining the denominator of the hourly wage fraction rather than the numerator. In the case of salaried employees, the simplest device is to specify a fixed number of hours per week, possibly 40, to be ascribed to each "full-time equivalent" employee. The same kind of rule may be applied to employees paid on a commission or a piecework basis unless explicit records of hours worked are kept.

ADJUSTMENTS AND EXCEPTIONS

Another set of wage measurement issues involves the extent to which gross increases in hourly compensation should be adjusted for such considerations as year-to-year variations in the amount of overtime, changes in the skill mix, changes in the average length of service, explicit escalator provisions, and incentive awards.

Equity might suggest that a firm with more overtime than the average in the current year should not be penalized under TIP. This would require that an adjustment for overtime be made both in the base period and in the current year. Many firms, however, would not have records to support the amount of overtime pay in the base period. We would recommend that no adjustment be made for overtime.

TIP would provide an incentive for firms to contract out for high-wage labor services. Suppose, for example, that a small construction firm, consisting of five laborers and two engineers, wishes to hire an additional engineer. Under a strict hourly wage hurdle with no adjustment for classes of workers, hiring the engineer outright could cause the firm to incur the TIP penalty or forgo the reward. Hiring the additional engineer as a

9. The Securities and Exchange Commission requires that listed corporations disclose the total remuneration of certain executives. Some of the flavor of the administrative difficulties and range of issues involved in defining the value of fringe benefits in a wage measure can be gained by perusing the interpretive responses of the SEC to questions about its disclosure rules. See *Federal Register,* vol. 43 (February 13, 1978), pp. 6061–62.

consultant would allow the firm to qualify unless there were regulations to count consultants as employees. Ordinarily it would be impossible to make adjustments for service contracts because such contracts typically do not specify hours worked.

In dealing with adjustments for changes in the skill mix, the recent wage controls interpreted the meaning of the term "wage increase" rather narrowly to mean increases in the regular compensation for the same level of job held by employees with the same length of service and quality of performance. A similar meaning is implied by Wallich and Weintraub, who suggest that a "fairly water-tight specification of a wage increase" would be given by the weighted average of hourly wages and related payments in each job classification and grade.[10]

However, the specification of such an index adds significantly more to the compliance and administrative burden than a simple average hourly wage measure and relies heavily on the job classification system of business organizations. If the coverage of TIP is to be nearly universal, most small firms would need to develop a classification system and all firms would be tempted to alter their classification in order to achieve the specified standard. Under such a system, for instance, "paper" promotions from editorial assistant to junior editor may be used to provide wage increases without penalty or to earn the rewards.

For example, suppose that the prescribed method is to calculate the weighted average of percentage increases in hourly compensation among all classes of workers, where the number of workers in the base period is the weight for each class. Unless classes are defined very narrowly or in a strict hierarchy according to the level of compensation, it is always possible to "promote" an individual while leaving his relative pay unchanged, and thereby to lower the average wage in each class. This simple kind of manipulation could be used to offset a portion of aggregate average wage increases.

To the extent that employee incentive awards, increases for length of service, and promotions are intended to reflect increased productivity, these changes in compensation already are allowed for in setting the wage-increase hurdle. Actual shifts in the mix of employment toward classes that receive higher pay will be penalized if TIP is based only on the change in aggregate hourly compensation. Also, firms in a cyclical downturn may

10. "A Tax-Based Incomes Policy," p. 14.

be arbitrarily penalized if layoffs affect primarily employees with fewer skills who receive less pay.

A final issue in the definition of a wage index is whether exception should be allowed for employees earning low wages. At the beginning of the Phase II wage controls, for example, any increase in wages up to the statutory minimum wage was exempt from wage controls. Apparently the presumption there was that the social policy of raising or maintaining income shares for the workers earning the lowest wages overshadowed the importance of wage control. Certainly if the wage increase were mandated by an increase in the minimum wage, it would be difficult to argue that the affected employers, or employees, should bear the penalties or be denied the rewards of TIP as a consequence. Nonetheless, any such exceptions will complicate administration and compliance.

AN OUTLINE FOR REPORTING WAGES

A useful way to summarize and further focus the discussion of wage measurement is to describe a possible reporting form or a tax return schedule for TIP. The reporting forms used during the Phase II wage controls are a useful example in this regard. In broad outline, these forms required the employer, or the employer and the bargaining unit jointly, to establish a base-period level of wages, including certain benefits; to calculate the amount of explicit wage increases, including the secondary effect of these increases on benefits; and to estimate the value of certain benefit increases. The total of these increases was then calculated as a percentage of the wage base. The emphasis in the Phase II reporting was on adjustments during the period. There was no requirement to calculate total wages—projected or actual—over the reporting period.

Some of the difficulties of using the Phase II experience as a model for TIP can be appreciated by reading the instructions to the wage control forms. For example, to estimate the value of benefits and of benefit increases the instructions advise "if exact expenditures are not available, report your best estimate, and indicate by entering 'EST.' " This level of precision is not appropriate as the basis for a tax or a tax credit.

The simplest, most readily administered wage reporting form would be one that required the reporting of total wages and nonwage benefits for the current period and for a base period, with each divided by total hours worked in the respective period. TIP rewards or penalties would then be based on the ratio of the compensation per hour for the current period to that for the base period. In broad outline, the reporting form would include:

	Base	*Cur-rent*
1. Total cash compensation paid (including but not limited to wages, salaries, bonuses, commissions, tips, vacation pay, sick pay, overtime pay, incentive awards, and allowances in excess of work-related expenses).	____	____
2. Contributions to premiums for life, health, accident, disability, or other private insurance (for unfunded plans, the cost of benefits paid would be reported).	____	____
3. Contributions to saving and thrift plans.	____	____
4. Other valuable compensation (including but not limited to the amount of employee discounts, goods and services provided by the employer for personal use, stock options, and the subsidy element of low-interest loans).	____	____
5. Total compensation (the sum of items 1 through 4).	____	____
6. Total hours worked (all hours worked by full-time and part-time employees, including salaried, commissioned, and piece-rate workers; excludes vacation and other leave).	____	____
7. Compensation per hour (item 5 divided by item 6).	____	____
8. Average percentage change in compensation per hour (the current-period figure for item 7 divided by the base-period figure for item 7 minus 1.0).	X	____

The worst injustices resulting from shifts in the employment mix could be accommodated without adding greatly to administrative burden if this type of calculation were made separately for certain broad and recognizable classes, and then averaged, using full-time equivalent employment in the base period as weights. Classes might be limited, for example, to hourly employees, salaried and commissioned employees, and corporate officers or partners.

Measurement of Price Increases

Extending TIP to prices increases the administrative problems several-fold. In the case of wages, a basic unit of labor, or man-hour, can be adequately defined. Total compensation, however defined, can then be divided by total man-hours to obtain compensation per man-hour.

In the case of product prices, there is no such basic unit. Thus, it is not possible to divide total sales revenue by total units of output to obtain price per unit of output. Instead, a price index must be created for each covered firm. This is not a simple task when some companies such as Dow Chemical produce over 100,000 separate products.

What makes matters even more difficult is that a firm may have raised its price only because it was passing through an increase in the cost of purchased materials. Consider the following data for a firm that produces only one product and uses only one purchased input:

	1977			1978		
Transaction	*Quantity*	*Price*	*Quantity* × *price*	*Quantity*	*Price*	*Quantity* × *price*
Sales of output	10	10	100	12	15	180
Materials purchased	20	2	40	24	4	96

Between 1977 and 1978 this firm increased the price of its output by 50 percent, but the price of its purchased materials doubled. Does this firm qualify for a tax reward or should it be subject to a tax penalty?

The firm knows that its 1978 sales totaled $180, of which $60 was due to increases in the price of the product. The firm also knows that its 1978 cost of purchased materials was $96, of which $48 was due to the doubling of the cost. Thus, the value-added price increase was $12 ($60 less $48) or $1 per unit of output. If the price of the product in 1978 had been $14, there would have been no value-added price increase. The $4 increase in the price of the product would have just passed through the $2 increase in the cost of the purchased material.

VALUE-ADDED PRICE INDEX

To determine whether there has been a value-added price increase, the firm must know the previous year's prices of purchased materials and output. The price of a product of the previous year is likely to be a weighted average of the prices at which the product was sold during the previous year, and special rules may be required for temporary special allowances offered during the base period. The firm would then measure the total value added using prices of the previous year and compare that with the total value added using the prices of the current year. In short, the firm would construct a value-added price index using quantity weights of the current year for both outputs and purchased materials. Constructing such an index would raise all the traditional problems involved in preparing a price index.[11]

The first problem in developing a value-added price index is to define a product or an input by statute or regulation. For example, how many kinds of automobiles does General Motors sell in one year or how many kinds of steel does Bethlehem Steel produce? In the case of a stationery store, are felt-tipped pens different from ball-point pens? Separate products or inputs would have to be defined with sufficient clarity that the firm and the Internal Revenue Service could easily compute the value-added price index.

New products or newly purchased inputs would have no price for the base period, and special rules would be required to establish one. (A similar problem exists with respect to certain products, such as special equipment that was last produced two or three years previously.) These products could be assigned a price for the base period equal to cost plus the net operating profit the firm received on the most nearly similar product it sold during the base period. If the firm had no similar products in the base period, the price could be set by the amount charged by other firms for similar products in the base period. If no similar products existed in the base period, the price could be determined by the firm's customary pricing practices during the base period.

These suggestions for handling new products parallel the recent price control rules.[12] Yet they raise as many questions as they answer. What is a "similar" product? How is "net operating profit" measured for a particular product? What are "customary pricing practices"? Presumably the

11. Using the quantity weights of the current year understates the true price increase, but we assume that this bias does not discriminate against particular firms and industries. We do not intend to debate here the relative merits of the Paasche, Laspeyres, or other indexes.

12. See *Historical Working Papers on the Economic Stabilization Program*, pt. 1, p. 257.

answers to these questions would come from either the statute or the regulations promulgated by the Department of the Treasury.

One possibility for handling new products would be to omit new products and new purchased inputs from the calculation of the value-added price index. This would still leave the problem of determining what is a "new" product or a "new" input, and there would be considerable pressure to alter products or inputs to make them "new."

Closely related to the problem of new products is the problem of quality changes. An automobile manufactured in the current year is different from that of the previous year. Some adjustment would have to be made for product improvement such as disc brakes, safety equipment, and more durable bumpers. Some of these improvements might be allowed by using the price of each item when it was first introduced as optional equipment. The cost of producing these items, however, might be reduced when they became standard equipment. And consumers might value them at less than the optional price. Again, the statute or the regulations would have to provide specific guidelines for quality improvements that both businesses and the Internal Revenue Service could follow easily.

An additional problem with constructing an index is that the base period may not be a typical year. Companies whose base prices or wages are abnormally low would seek an exception or special relief. For example, the major firms in the steel industry raised prices before the freeze of August 15, 1971. These firms thus had a high base price. The smaller firms in the steel industry did not raise prices. These firms as a result were doubly penalized because they purchased raw steel from the major firms and sold finished products in the same market. Although it may be desirable to provide no special relief and to rely on competitive pressures to constrain the prices of the major firms, the political pressure for special rules is probably irresistible.

One possibility for constructing a value-added price index would be to double-invoice all sales and purchases. Firms would then know the prices of sales to customers and of purchased materials for the current year and the previous year. An index could be computed as follows:

$$\frac{\Sigma P_1 Q_1 - \Sigma p_1 q_1}{\Sigma P_0 Q_1 - \Sigma p_0 q_1},$$

where P and Q are prices and quantities of final sales, and p and q are prices and quantities of purchased materials. The problem with this approach is that materials purchased in the current year may only have increased inventories, or sales made this year may have been from inventories. Complicated inventory rules would thus be needed to determine the value added associated with final sales for the current year and the previous year.

COST PASS-THROUGH

Allowing a pass-through of cost increases is a simple concept, but it raises a number of issues, in particular the problem of which costs should be included.

In general, firms should be permitted to pass through the costs of inputs if the firm is a price taker. However, if the firm has some control over the price of the input, pass-through should not be permitted. This suggests that increased labor costs, for example, would not be included.

Costs that have a continuing benefit for the firm present a difficult problem. For example, a firm might increase the costs of advertising or of research and development, and if such costs were allowed to be fully passed through as a cost increase in the current period, the firm could raise prices by more than would otherwise be warranted. One solution to this problem would be to exclude such discretionary costs from both the current period and the base period. Phase II generally did not permit pass-through of research and development costs or marketing costs above the level of the previous period.

Another problem of cost pass-through involves the treatment of interest, rent, and capital recovery. If interest were treated like the cost of purchased materials and allowed to be passed through, firms would have an incentive to increase the amount of debt financing to reduce their value added. If interest were not treated like the cost of purchased materials, firms that must refinance at higher interest rates would not be able to raise their prices without being subject to tax penalties (or loss of tax benefits). Under Phase II, pass-through was permitted for interest on short-term debt but not on long-term debt, which is a closer substitute for equity. This, however, introduced a discrimination between short-term and long-term debt.

Rent, especially on long-term leases, causes problems similar to those of interest—that is, the choice between ownership and leasing is similar to the choice between equity and debt. If rent increases were allowed to be passed through, firms would have an incentive to rent rather than to own. If rent increases were not passed through, firms that are required to renew leases might be penalized.

Capital recovery permitted for tax purposes is not likely to reflect the decrease in the value of the plant and equipment during the year. It may be too generous for some firms and not generous enough for others. Even for a particular firm, it may be too generous at times and not sufficiently generous at other times.

Although there are several ways to handle interest, rent, and capital recovery, it would probably be acceptable to permit a full pass-through of these items. The justification of this position is that firms generally are price takers with respect to these items. Full pass-through does not involve serious administrative problems.

In the long run, firms must set prices to earn a rate of return, recover their capital costs, cover operating costs, and pay income taxes. This suggests that firms should be permitted a cost pass-through for federal, state, and local taxes based on income. However, in the short run, firms may have a large increase in profits and income taxes due to a large increase in productivity. An income tax pass-through would provide these firms with more room for price increases. On balance, we conclude that income tax increases should not be passed through unless there are rate increases.

Mandated cost increases such as those necessary for occupational safety or pollution control should be passed through. The problem is to identify these costs separately. For example, part of the plant manager's time may be devoted to occupational safety. Should part of his salary increase be allowed to be passed through in higher prices? Presumably mandatory cost increases should be passed through only if they are identifiable. Thus, the cost of hiring additional safety inspectors could be passed through, but no allocation would be made of the plant manager's salary.

LESSONS FROM RECENT PRICE CONTROL EXPERIENCE

The problems of measuring average price increases arose during Phase II and later phases of the economic stabilization program. How the administrative problems were handled may suggest how the price side of Okun's proposal could be implemented.

During Phase II of price controls the concept of term-limit pricing was developed to permit Tier I firms some flexibility in pricing, provided they committed themselves in advance to a relatively low average price increase, usually over the following year. This greatly eased the Price Commission's administrative burdens of controlling price ceilings for individual products. Under a term-limit pricing agreement, a firm could raise prices on some products based on cost increases in other products.

Determining whether a firm fulfilled its commitment under a term-limit price agreement raised all the issues surrounding the construction of a value-added price index. For example, a firm would have had to maintain detailed price and quantity records to document its weighted-average price increase.

A firm that had entered into such a term-limit pricing agreement was required to make a quarterly report on form PC-1. However, this form, assuming it was correctly filled out, did not provide the information that would have permitted the Price Commission to determine whether the firm had actually fulfilled the agreement. For example, no data were requested on actual product mix. The official history of the economic stabilization program concludes: "The forms were not specific enough in their requests for information, so companies naturally provided the minimum detail possible . . . . Designed in a short time period and utilizing untested accounting techniques, the forms, while perhaps the best available under the circumstances, often gave the analyst inadequate tools with which to assess a company's situation."[13]

During Phase IV of the economic stabilization program the method for calculating the weighted-average price increase was provided in the regulations. The instructions for form CLC-22, the new reporting form, provided guidance on how to compute that increase. The basic rules are summarized as follows:

The parent and consolidated entities filed as a unit.

The basic accounting period was the quarter. The base period was the firm's last fiscal quarter ending before January 11, 1973.

The base price and current price had to be computed for each item. Firms, however, could employ sampling techniques and aggregate by-

13. *Historical Working Papers on the Economic Stabilization Program,* pt. 1, p. 595. For an evaluation of the term-limit pricing procedure and its administrative problems, see Fredric L. Laughlin, "An Evaluation of the Price Commission's Policy of Term Limit Pricing during Phase II of the Economic Stabilization Program" (Ph.D. dissertation, George Washington University, 1975). See also Robert F. Lanzillotti, Mary T. Hamilton, and R. Blaine Roberts, *Phase II in Review: The Price Commission Experience* (Brookings Institution, 1975), pp. 40–50.

products. (Product aggregation could lower the weighted-average price increase if the product mix shifted toward products with lower prices. For example, the average price of Dodges would decrease if compact sales became relatively more important.)

No cost pass-through was permitted.

When computing the base price, prices charged pursuant to temporary special deals or temporary special allowances could be excluded from the computation. (This was a potential source of much controversy, particularly in industries that always offered special deals.)

Firms were required to maintain documentation of the method used in computing the weighted-average price adjustment.

Unfortunately, the experience during the economic stabilization program gives little guidance on the administrative difficulties that might be encountered with TIP because little auditing of company reports was ever done. Firms were essentially on an honor system, and the Cost of Living Council generally accepted the reports as filed.

We conclude at this point that computing a value-added price index for each firm would involve considerable complexity. There is no easy way to define separate products or inputs or to handle new products, quality improvements, and the various issues surrounding cost pass-through. Sampling techniques could ease the administrative burdens for large businesses but would be beyond the capabilities of a small retail firm with many different products. If it is desirable to apply TIP to prices, consideration should be given to a scheme that does not involve the construction of an index.

PROFIT-MARGIN LIMITATION

During wage and price controls, a profit-margin limitation was employed as a supplemental device to allowable cost pass-through. It was assumed that a firm that had not increased its profit margin—the ratio of profits to sales—had not increased its prices excessively.

A profit-margin limitation would solve many of the problems of a value-added price index. No special rules would be required for new products or quality improvements. All costs could be passed through including increases in wages. Presumably the wage portion of TIP would provide a brake on excessive wage increases.

A profit-margin limitation would have some of the problems associated with cost pass-through. Firms would have an incentive to increase expenditures for advertising and for research and development to shrink profit margins. Unless the test were applied to *gross* profit margins—that is, profits before debt service—firms would have an incentive to substitute debt for equity financing. Base-year problems would also remain, although they would be mitigated because the base period could be an average of several previous years and not merely the preceding year. Special exceptions would have to be made for losses or extremely low profits in the base year. One possibility would be for the government to establish minimum profit margins for specific industries based on industry averages.

The major advantage of a profit-margin limitation is that the Internal Revenue Service could administer it more easily than it could a price limitation. Sales revenue and profits, either net or gross, are concepts with which the Internal Revenue Service has had long experience.

The major political drawback is that a profit-margin limitation would resemble price controls, although a test for gross profit margin might not. Like any excess profits test, a profit-margin limitation would be a penalty on efficiency. It would also penalize industries that are becoming more capital-intensive. A profit-margin test with little real bite, however, might be acceptable to business as part of a TIP that applied real restraint on wages. It is possible that a weak profit-margin limitation would not reduce the effectiveness of TIP. This assumes that if wages were successfully restrained, competitive pressures would restrain price increases.

Special Rules

Whether TIP applies to wages or prices, it may require a number of special rules relating to exports, coverage of particular industries, and corporate mergers and other reorganizations.

EXPORTS

The objective of TIP is to hold down *domestic* wages and prices, but not necessarily foreign wages paid by American companies or export prices. Thus, firms should probably be permitted or required to exclude exports in determining the value-added price increase or the gross profit margin. Because the value-added price index would depend on the quantity weights of the current year for purchased inputs and sales, the exclusion of exports from the calculation would not cause much additional complexity.

Calculating a profit margin on only domestic sales would, however, require an allocation of profits between export and domestic sales. One possibility might be to use special rules such as those for allocating taxable income between a domestic international sales corporation and its related suppliers. These rules are highly arbitrary and for the purposes of TIP probably are not much better than including all exports in the calculation of the overall gross profit margin. Another possibility would be to require only firms with exports of more than 10 or 20 percent of sales to determine the gross profit margin on domestic sales alone. Firms without significant exports would not be required to exclude them. Firms that were required to do this would have to allocate all costs between domestic and export sales. Special and probably somewhat arbitrary rules still would be required to allocate such costs as overhead, interest, and research and development expenses.

Because TIP is aimed at domestic wages and prices, foreign wages should be excluded, whether paid by a foreign branch or by a foreign subsidiary. However, wages paid to Americans working abroad who are subject to U.S. social security taxes could be included, although this may involve considerable complexity.

EXCEPTIONS

As indicated at the beginning of this paper, if TIP provided tax benefits, all business taxpayers and even nonprofit organizations would want to participate. If, however, tax penalties are to be provided, a number of exclusions that would greatly simplify the administrative complexities would be possible. An effective TIP could exclude new firms, unincorporated businesses, small corporations, and certain industries.

Determining prices and wages for the base period would be a considerable burden on new firms if they were included in TIP. New firms would have to assign base-period prices and wages on the basis of what other firms charged for similar products or paid for similar labor during the base period. If the firm began midway through the year, an intrayear adjustment might also be required.

Excluding small firms would greatly simplify the compliance and administrative problems of TIP. For example, applying the program only to firms with more than 100 employees would cover more than 60 percent of total employment, but would eliminate 99 percent of businesses from the record keeping, reporting, and auditing requirements. Given the high one-time costs of disseminating information about the TIP regulations and establishing accounting rules and procedures within firms, it would be especially undesirable for a temporary TIP to have comprehensive coverage. Moreover, if anything more than the most perfunctory auditing were to be contemplated for small firms, the necessary paperwork for those firms and for the Internal Revenue Service would make comprehensive coverage difficult. This kind of paperwork was encountered in administering Phase II controls, and it was eventually accommodated by the exemption of most firms having fewer than 60 employees.

Small firms are most likely to make use of the potential for contracting out for relatively high-cost labor. In addition, small corporations present significant opportunities to reduce salaries and increase corporate taxable income when the owners are also employees. This is particularly true when a small corporation is subject to only the 20 or 22 percent corporate tax rate.

Exemption for small firms and possibly certain industries is also recommended on economic grounds. The proportion of cases for which some special relief from the rules may be needed is probably much larger for small firms. These firms would be more likely to have variations in the skill mix, outlays for unfunded medical insurance, amount of overtime, and so on in the calculation of wage increases.

Exempting small firms would exclude most sectors of the economy in which wages and prices are the most market-sensitive. Even a rather low employment cutoff would exclude most enterprises in agriculture, retail trade, services, and real estate, where administered prices are the exception rather than the rule. However, an exclusion based on employment would also eliminate most private medical services and the construction industry, although large price increases often are associated with these two industries.

Including unincorporated businesses in TIP will require special rules to determine the appropriate amount of compensation. For example, the compensation paid by a law firm or medical partnership should include the income earned by the partners. Partnership income earned by a real estate syndicate, however, is more likely to be unearned income and thus should not be included in the amount of compensation paid by the partnership. The problem is that the income of a partnership or a proprietorship may include both labor and capital income. A reasonable way to separate the two would be to follow the general rules applicable to the 50 percent maximum tax on personal service income. If capital were not a material income-producing factor, all the income of the unincorporated business would be considered as earned income and thus as compensation paid by the business. If both labor and capital were material income-producing factors, not more than 30 percent of the income of the business would be considered as earned income.

Similar problems exist with including Subchapter S corporations, which are treated for tax purposes like partnerships. We conclude that unincorporated businesses and Subchapter S corporations should be excluded from a stick approach to TIP.

Mergers and other acquisitions raise special problems. Consider four possibilities. First, Bendix buys an Ann Arbor subsidiary from another auto supplier. Second, Bendix does not buy the subsidiary, but instead buys the Ann Arbor plant and equipment from the other auto supplier. In this case Bendix hires many of the workers who previously worked for the other auto supplier. Third, Bendix leases the Ann Arbor factory, including equipment, and retains the employees. Fourth, the other auto supplier closes down its old plant. Bendix then builds a new plant in Ann Arbor and hires many of the workers who had lost their jobs. Should the base period for the two auto supply companies be adjusted for the amount of compensation paid to employees in the old plant during the base year? Clearly no adjustment would be made when Bendix built a new plant because tracing the new workers to the old plant would generally be impossible. An adjustment should probably be made when Bendix acquires the subsidiary, buys the old plant, or leases the plant.

Rules for handling mergers and other acquisitions under TIP would have to be somewhat arbitrary. One possibility would be to follow the rules for the new-jobs credit. According to these rules, adjustments are required for acquisitions or dispositions of a major portion of a trade, business, or a separate unit of a trade or business. For purposes of these rules, certain leases are considered acquisitions or dispositions.[14] Making

14. As of this writing, final regulations on the new-jobs credit have been proposed but are not final. The examples used in the regulations indicate the problems of drawing reasonable lines. See *Federal Register*, vol. 42 (December 14, 1977), pp. 62932–34.

base price adjustments is clearly more difficult than making wage adjustments. Firms are likely to have information on compensation paid by a subsidiary. But reconstructing the base prices of a subsidiary would require policing of transfer prices between the subsidiary and other related entities.

Concluding Comments

We conclude that TIP would entail significant administrative problems for the Internal Revenue Service and compliance problems for businesses. These problems could be reduced to a manageable size if TIP were applied only to business taxpayers, if it were limited to wages, if the hurdle approach were adopted, and if it did not apply to small companies. The administrative and compliance problems, however, still would be significant.

There would be a strong incentive for firms near the hurdle to pass the test by substituting forms of compensation that are not included or are undervalued in the wage index. Experience with wage measurement problems of the income tax suggests that opportunities for substituting forms of compensation that understate the true increase in labor cost cannot be completely eliminated. Establishing the base-period wage level is another problem. Adjustments are required for firms that reorganize or add major new activities. Further adjustments may be demanded for year-to-year changes in the skill mix, overtime pay, or wage increases mandated by law or by previous contracts.

If a parallel program of price restraint were adopted, there would be strong administrative reasons for preferring a profit-margin limitation rather than an explicit price index.

The remaining administrative and compliance problems must be weighed against the expected gains from TIP in moderating wage and price increases. An evaluation of such a trade-off is beyond the scope of this paper.

Comments
and Discussion

Joseph A. Pechman: Dildine and Sunley make a serious attempt to lay out the administrative and compliance problems of tax-based incomes policies, which its proponents have so far virtually ignored. It would be impossible for me to comment on everything they cover. I limit myself to what I regard to be the five most important problems.

First, there is the issue of prices. The original Wallich-Weintraub proposal increased taxes on profits of firms with excessive wage increases; prices were not involved at all. However, Arthur Okun suggested that his carrot approach might be expanded to provide reductions of profits taxes for firms with price increases below the average. It is clear from the paper by Dildine and Sunley that any kind of tax penalty or subsidy that depends on a change in average prices of particular firms is simply impractical. All the problems of constructing price indexes would emerge, such as treatment of new products, quality change, and measurement of costs to be passed through, and there is no easy solution to most of them. It would be possible to substitute a limitation on gross profit margins for the penalty on price increases, but this approach has many of the earmarks of a tax on excess profits (penalty on efficiency and increased capital utilization, encouragement of advertising and other unnecessary expenses, and lack of representativeness of the base period), which is anathema for business and Congress alike. I conclude that tax penalties or subsidies based on price changes are unworkable. I leave it to Albert Rees to explain how labor would react to a TIP that applied only to wages and not to prices.

Second, there is the matter of the type of coverage a TIP would entail. The latest available data on the number of business firms in the United States are for the year 1975. About 13 million firms filed tax returns in that year, including 10.9 million sole proprietorships, 1.1 million partnerships, and 2.0 million corporations. And there were 0.5 million returns of nonprofit organizations and over 78,000 governmental units. Most of the business firms had no employees; many report no net income; and all but a relatively small number of large businesses do not keep detailed personnel records. Yet, if a tax penalty or tax subsidy is to be designed, the law must be explicit about how every one of these units is to be treated.

Dildine and Sunley state that a penalty would be easier to administer than a subsidy because it would be possible to limit the penalty to large firms; if there are "goodies" to be handed out, it would not be possible to limit eligibility to employees of such firms. But this does not imply that the problems of a penalty can be overlooked. As I shall indicate below, I am not persuaded that it is feasible to measure average wage changes for all economic units in a manner that would be appropriate for a tax-based wage penalty or subsidy.

If the carrot approach were adopted, I assume we would not ask the average farmer, or the average corner drugstore owner, or most self-employed professionals who have a few employees to report man-hours on a tax return. To avoid the administrative problems, the wage subsidy would probably be given to all employees in such establishments and to the owners also. This is not fatal for the wage subsidy plan on administrative grounds, but I wonder what effect the plan would have if a substantial fraction, if not a majority, of all workers received the subsidy whether or not they behaved.

A third issue is the economic unit. The unit for tax accounting purposes is a legal entity which, in our complex economy, often bears little relationship to the unit that enters into wage bargains with its employees. Large corporations generally file consolidated returns that include the operating results of many, but not necessarily all, of their subsidiaries. I assume that the wage behavior of foreign subsidiaries is of little relevance to wage behavior of their counterparts in the United States, so those foreign units would not be covered by the wage subsidy or penalty.

While the foreign subsidiary is the extreme case, there are numerous other instances of branches or subsidiaries located in the United States which, as far as wages are concerned, bear virtually no relationship to one another or to the parent firm. What about the oil firm that owns one of the largest retail and mail-order houses in the country? Or the textile firm that owns a Hollywood film manufacturer? Or the electronics manufacturer that owns a bread manufacturer? If the wage subsidies or penalties of one of these firms depended on the wage bargains of all the other firms included in the consolidated return, labor and management would have no way of making wage decisions in one place unless they knew what the decisions were to be elsewhere. Accordingly, the rules would have to be sufficiently flexible to permit the unit of calculation to be relevant to the wage-setting process. Under wage controls, the business firms themselves made this decision, and I assume the control agency could modify that decision if it were necessary. But for purposes of a wage subsidy or penalty, definite rules would have to be established, either in the legislation or in the regulations, so that labor and management would know exactly which wage bargains were included. If there are any usable guides on how these rules can be written, I am not aware of them.

Once such rules were prepared, it would be necessary to prescribe other rules to make interyear wage comparisons. Dildine and Sunley suggest the range of problems: new firms, mergers, spin-offs, sales of facilities, changes in product mix, and other developments that occur in a dynamic economy. This is what is referred to in the tax lingo as "the excess-profits tax problem": that is, the problem of estimating the tax base when it depends on events and conditions in two or more adjacent years. The decisions made for the excess profits tax in the United States have been the subject of extensive and time-consuming litigation every time the tax was used, and no one on the government or the business side was ever satisfied. I can imagine a set of arbitrary rules that a group of economists or tax administrators might agree to, but that does not mean that Congress would accept such rules. For example, it has been suggested that, for new firms, a base-year wage structure might be constructed from averages for other firms in the same industry. But the only data of this type that exist are those of the Bureau of Labor Statistics, and they could not possibly be applied to a particular firm. In the end, the legislation would be complex and, like the excess profits tax, would impose unforeseen costs on business that would lead to further legislation and litigation to moderate such costs.

The problem of timing a penalty or subsidy is a fourth issue of concern. From the standpoint of administration or compliance, it would be much easier to impose a penalty or provide a subsidy after the end of the accounting period. If the proposal is for a penalty based on profits, it should be possible to rely on the business firms to take the penalty into account in its wage decisions.

The opposite is true for a subsidy to workers accepting a wage increase below the guideline percentage. To appeal to workers to accept the constraint, the subsidy must be prospective and must be incorporated in the current tax withholding tables so that the workers will have immediate tangible evidence that their disposable income will not be impaired by the policy. (Of course, this would require two sets of withholding tables, but this is only a minor complication compared to the others.)

The basic problem is that labor and management would find it extremely difficult to incorporate a prospective subsidy in their wage bargaining. Unless the bargaining unit were coterminous with the unit for determining the subsidy, no worker or group of workers would know whether the deal they made would actually trigger the subsidy until negotiations are completed with the other bargaining units in the same firm. Management would be in the same situation: how can it be sure that the construction workers will accept a wage increase that, together with the agreement with coal miners, will trigger a subsidy to both groups?

Suppose also that the firm and its workers take a chance and accept wage bargains that result in a wage subsidy effective at the beginning of the firm's taxable year. Suppose that later there is a miscalculation: after the fact, the average wage increase for the firm actually exceeds the guideline. How could the excess wage subsidy be collected? The firm would have no way of collecting from workers who had left, and the workers who remained would be up in arms to find that income already spent was really not income at all. Or the firm might be made responsible, but this could lead to excessive hardship, if not bankruptcy. Alternatively, the government might require workers to make up the excess wage subsidy by reducing their refunds or by increasing their balances of tax due when they filed their returns. To accomplish this, firms would be required to inform their workers if there were excess subsidies in time for them to fill out their tax returns, a requirement that would be highly unrealistic because most large firms take many months to complete their final tax returns. The firm could make estimates, but if these were incorrect, the workers would be even more furious.

I conclude that a penalty on profits based on wage changes is feasible, but it would have to be retrospective. For prospective subsidies to workers, there are numerous pitfalls. Frankly I do not see how the solutions can satisfy labor or management.

A fifth issue is controls versus tax-based incomes policies. I believe it is not productive to argue whether or not TIPs are another form of controls. The questions are which approach is feasible and what are the costs relative to the alternatives?

It is true that a tax-based incomes policy can be disregarded by any firm and its workers. But the rules and regulations must be written to ensure that all economic units in the country understand them and make their decisions accordingly. Even if it is agreed that some of the rules must be arbitrary, I doubt that it would be possible to arrive at such arbitrary rules through the tax legislative process as we know it today.

Under controls, Congress avoids the hard decisions and lets the controlling agency make the arbitrary rules. One reason controls seem to be acceptable is that relatively few firms are ever involved in disputes, whereas a tax penalty or a subsidy would apply to all or a large number of firms, and the perceived hardships and disputes will be numerous. Both controls and tax-based incomes policies lead to capricious results, but I am at a loss to understand why the proponents of the latter believe that their approach would be more acceptable than the other to labor, management, the public, and Congress.

Richard E. Slitor: The sponsors and designers of this panel have singled out for attention one of the most critical problems of our time. In keeping with this objective, the paper by Larry Dildine and Emil Sunley does an efficient job of highlighting and assessing the administrative and compliance aspects of tax-based incomes policies.

My first reaction to their excellent paper was one of discomfiture over the deft way they handled a broader assignment—covering TIP applied both to wages and to prices—than the one that pushed me to write four times as many typescript pages (a paper prepared under other auspices). But this personal reaction was quickly balanced by gratification that their basic conclusion on the administrability and feasibility of TIP applied to wages seems to be not too far from mine.

TIP is designed to help create jobs without inflation. In more exact terms, TIP will aid in the substitution of employment and production growth for small increases in the wages of currently employed people and in the prices of an existing flow of production.

As most of us have come to realize, the Keynesian cornucopia of the early years was part illusion and part the creature of historic circumstance. The blind spots, the oversimplification, and to some degree the vulgarization that occurred are now being corrected. The process of making our macroeconomic models more realistic and reliable must go on.

But in terms of immediate policy, TIP must cope with a stubborn and resistant problem of spiraling costs and prices. To decelerate these spiraling forces effectively, TIP must be constructed carefully to be sturdy, workable, and reliable.

The Dildine and Sunley paper deals with five initial design decisions: the carrot versus the stick approach; the continuous range versus the hurdle format; the temporary versus the permanent TIP; the question of the basic accounting unit—the plant or establishment, the corporate entity or conglomerate, the wage bargaining unit, or other class or sector of employees; and the specification of the nature of the penalty or the reward.

Following the review of initial design issues, Dildine and Sunley devote the major portion of their paper to a helpful and illuminating review of problems and issues in the measurement of wages and wage increases and a counterpart discussion of the more prickly task of measuring increases in price or profit margins. Their canvass of definitional, identification, and quantification problems is impressive and constructive. There is considerable ground to be covered here and that task needs to be worked out carefully, but that does not lead to a conclusion that compliance and administration are overly burdensome.

Dildine and Sunley regard the treatment of pensions as the most difficult problem in the measurement of compensation per hour. This is partly because of the cited problems of actuarial valuation of liberalizing funded plans, which seem to go beyond current concepts of taxable wages or salaries. The employer's contribution would seem adequate to measure the compensation element under prevailing concepts. The difficulty is also attributed to the possibility of liberalizing unfunded pension arrangements when data on benefits currently paid are the only information the tax administrator may have available. It may be necessary to recognize benefits as paid after-the-fact, but gross infringement of guidelines by this approach could be singled out for special treatment—that is, actuarial valuation—if the legalities permit TIP penalization of unfunded promises of future payment. The pension area presents intellectual problems, but somehow I doubt that pension liberalizations, funded and qualified or unfunded and unqualified, would constitute a massive threat to the workability and economic effectiveness of a TIP applied to wages.

The overall conclusion reached by Dildine and Sunley is balanced and in line with their analysis. However, I feel that the flavor of their concluding comments, particularly with respect to TIP based on wages, is too negative in the light of the practical and technical difficulties they uncovered.

Basically, their rating of TIP from the practical and administrative standpoint is that these problems, while "significant," can be reduced to a manageable size if the scheme is (1) applied only to business taxpayers, (2) limited to wages, (3) implemented with the hurdle or threshold approach, and (4) not applied to small companies. I regard this evaluation as granting a thoroughly passing if not an honorable grade to the Wallich-Weintraub TIP proposal.

The adjective "significant" applied to TIP administrative problems gives pause. Where does it stand in the spectrum of ratings that administrative experts on taxation apply both to various new proposals, plans, and schemes and to existing or even longstanding tax provisions that elicit comment, favorable or otherwise, on their administrative cost and feasibility? What kind of semantic overtones does it carry?

Tax administrators have a fairly wide spectrum of ratings they attach to tax provisions and proposals. These ratings are as follows, on a scale of 1 to 7 in descending order of administrative difficulty: (1) "administrative nightmare," (2) terribly difficult, prohibitively costly, (3) difficult but not intractable, (4) difficult but manageable by capable and experienced personnel, (5) routine, (6) "piece of cake," and (7) almost self-operating: collection is "slick as a whistle."

It is neither frivolous nor cynical to express the conjecture that ratings of administrative difficulty change with the administrator's attitude—spontaneous or inculcated—toward the underlying policy. A policy proposal that is not "sound" or in keeping with the perceived role of tax administration will tend to be given a higher rating on the scale of administrative difficulty.

On the whole, the rating by Dildine and Sunley of "manageable" applied to TIP's administrative and compliance problems would seem to be rather favorable, subject to the listed structural specifications and interpreted in the light of the somewhat subjective adjective "significant."

One can understand their hesitation about a cost-benefit calculation. This would call for an evaluation not only of TIP's effectiveness but of its benefits in terms of stabilization, employment, and the general welfare of decelerating the wage-cost-price spiral. If TIP has even moderate effectiveness and benefits, the payoff would be enormous in relation to the administrative and compliance costs (a few million dollars) implied in the "manageable" rating assigned to the compensation TIP plan by Dildine and Sunley.

The real issue in a practical evaluation of TIP, particularly if it applies to wages, is not design problems or compliance and administrative difficulties. These can be managed at moderate and acceptable costs. The more difficult question is whether or not the public and sometimes intransigent economic interest groups are prepared to accept action that goes beyond anti-inflation rhetoric. I believe the prognosis will be favorable. The firm, insistent pressure of a genuine economic incentive will be more acceptable and effective and far less administratively complex than a system of rigid, hard-line regulations or controls to decelerate the inflationary spiral.

General Discussion

Donald Nichols observed that the authors had concluded it was administratively more feasible to operate a TIP based on average compensation per man-hour than on weighted wage measures with categories of employees. He asked the proponents of various TIP plans for their reactions to that conclusion of the paper.

In response, Arthur Okun said that he favored allowing firms to select the method they would use—whether it was aggregate compensation or particular classification—but would require them to specify the method in advance. Joseph Pechman objected that it was unrealistic to ask a firm to determine its wage structure so early. But Okun replied that firms need not have foreknowledge of the wage structure in order to choose their measurement basis. He went on to explain that, while he had previously emphasized advance pledges for firms, he felt they should be allowed to apply for TIP bonuses at the end of the period without a prior pledge, so long as they had already specified the method of computation. Sidney Weintraub said he would support any method of measurement provided that consistency could be assured over time and that his scheme would be applied on an ex post basis. He felt that distorted reporting could be identified by some arithmetic cross-checks, such as keeping an eye on the implied movement of average product per worker.

Franco Modigliani felt that Pechman had exaggerated several administrative difficulties, like the problem of choosing the reporting unit for tax purposes. Modigliani favored allowing the firms to choose the reporting unit and argued that there would be an incentive on the part of corporations to make these as large as possible to allow the maximum scope for maneuver. But Pechman reiterated that it would be difficult to decide who should be penalized if excess wages were actually paid. James Duesenberry suggested that some of the problems in a reward plan might be avoided if the reward came through a rebate after the end of the year rather than in lower taxes withheld during the year. Okun felt that both routes could be kept open by rewarding firms that qualified their workers in advance for the withholding benefits, thereby taking on some risks and administrative burdens.

Nichols noted that there had been little discussion about how the number of hours was to be measured and audited by the Internal Revenue Service. Emil Sunley replied that an arbitrary assumption of 2,000 hours per full-time employee might suffice. Nichols stated that using average hourly compensation would provide an incentive for hiring low-wage workers. Okun agreed but said that this did not bother him. He noted that the ceiling on the payroll tax base now gives firms a marginal incentive to prefer high-salaried workers.

Alan Greenspan said that although he appraised TIP plans to be unworkable overall, the particular problem of measuring wages and hours could be overcome. He expected this to generate a substantial amount of distortion in the reporting of wages to the Internal Revenue Service— perhaps a discrepancy of 1 to 2 percentage points below the figures of the Bureau of Labor Statistics. Others were even more skeptical. Arnold Packer remarked that even defining compensation might be a task comparable to defining income, and it would have to be undertaken in a short period of time. Robert Hall felt that the TIP plan was unworkable because the government could not possibly provide firms with suitable classification categories, and it would have to accept those devised by the firms themselves. The firms would then have an incentive to juggle with classification methods, whereas the Internal Revenue Service would have the insurmountable problem of ensuring the consistency of the categories over time. He compared this with the difficult problems encountered by the Internal Revenue Service in policing the classes of assets that firms use for depreciation purposes.

Pechman's prediction that a TIP plan would generate a large amount of litigation was endorsed by others. Daniel Mitchell noted that, unlike the controls of 1971–74 in which the Justice Department had been reluctant to go to court without being reasonably certain of success, alleged violators of a TIP plan would frequently appear in the tax courts. Sunley reminded the panel that the Internal Revenue Service only recently closed the last litigation involving the excess profits tax of the Korean War. But Lloyd Ulman pointed out that the threat of complex litigation might induce employers to try to avoid tangles with the government by complying clearly with the standards of a penalty TIP. George Perry commented that the incentives to cheat were different under TIPs with rewards and TIPs with penalties: under the penalty scheme, the firm benefited directly from deceiving the Internal Revenue Service; but under a reward TIP, a firm would be unlikely to risk punishment simply to make its employees better off. Modigliani agreed with Perry that a reward TIP had this advantage, but noted that it had the disadvantage that it could not be limited only to the largest firms. He added that some discussants were mistakenly assuming that firms would try to give workers as much as possible and then would hide the bonuses. In fact, a penalty TIP would assist them by giving them a rationale for resisting higher wage demands.

Other distortions that might be generated by TIP plans concerned some participants. William Poole suspected that, because firms would not be liable for a penalty TIP when they had no profits, firms with cyclical profitability patterns would try to time wage increases in trough periods. Mitchell observed that, in contrast to a controls program that could be introduced by administrative proclamation, the extensive period of debate required for the introduction of TIP by the Congress would provide an incentive for destabilizing large wage hikes to "beat the gun." Mitchell also noted that being involved with a temporary scheme within the Internal Revenue Service would not be an attractive assignment for any of its officials. Thus, like the temporary controls in the 1971–74 period,

TIP would be staffed with the less competent Internal Revenue Service administrators.

Sidney Weintraub said he had been encouraged by Richard Slitor's optimism on the feasibility of TIP. Some slippage and distortions were inevitable; but with experience the administration would improve, and the big prize—full employment—could become a reality. Ulman suggested that the assessments of various participants on the seriousness of the administrative difficulties mirrored their convictions on the importance of the anti-inflationary gains from TIP.

ROBERT W. CRANDALL
Brookings Institution

Federal Government Initiatives to Reduce the Price Level

THEORIES of the origins of inflation and the effects of price increases on a mixed market economy abound; as a result, there is no widespread consensus as to how to restrain inflation efficiently while maintaining high employment levels and a healthy rate of economic growth. There is little dispute, however, that the government's varied microeconomic policies have substantial price effects. At a time when inflation is a major concern and there is no accepted general policy for its containment, the federal government should explore ways to lower the price level through a variety of basically microeconomic policy decisions.

This paper focuses on options that are currently available to the federal government for lowering the price level. While these options are disparate and not easily synthesized into a simple framework, most have a similar theme: pursuing objectives through direct rather than indirect taxation, where "indirect taxation" includes government-mandated cost increases for producers of private goods and services. For a number of reasons, government programs are often financed through increases in producer costs rather than through direct payments from general government revenues. In some instances, such as when user taxes are levied, there is an equity or efficiency reason for doing so. In others, such as health and safety regulation, the reason is largely pragmatic: mandating cost increases for producers is simply the easiest (not the most efficient) means of achieving the desired objective. But in still other cases, such as agricultural policies or minimum wage legislation, programs are financed

Note: I wish to thank Jeffrey A. Goldstein for his research assistance.

165

through increases in the price level because direct payments to the targeted population might not pass the scrutiny of the electorate.

In this paper I do not analyze the efficiency gains that could be derived from various proposals. These gains are likely to be large and are often related to price-level effects, if only imprecisely. For instance, a less "inflationary" farm policy is also likely to increase allocative efficiency. The same is true for deregulation of the airline industry. In a few cases, such as the deregulation of natural gas, crude oil, and petroleum products, however, the efficient policy would lead to higher deregulated prices, and the inflationary cost of such a policy shift would then have to be weighed against its benefits. But these are the exceptions. Most of the initiatives discussed here can be embraced both by those interested in eliminating economic waste and by those concerned with containing the upward movement of the price level.

Calculating the Effects of Policy Initiatives on the Price Level

In addition to monetary and fiscal policies, the federal government has a major influence on the price level through the payroll taxation for old age and survivors, disability, and health insurance; indirect taxation, agricultural price supports; economic regulation of such industries as communications and transportation; social regulation of the environment, health, and safety; trade protection; minimum wage legislation; and subsidization of health insurance. In a single paper, it is impossible to estimate the full effects on the price level of all policies pursued in these areas. However, I present estimates for some elements of each and suggest alternative policies that might achieve the same goals at a lower social cost and with a smaller effect on the price level.

In the sections that follow I attempt to estimate the effects on the price level of various policies, using a consistent methodology. In each case, I calculate an initial (first-round) effect on the price of the affected good or service produced in the private sector. I then pass this price effect through to finished goods on a dollar-for-dollar basis and calculate its share of gross private domestic product. The relative importance of the price change is deduced from:

$$\left[\frac{\Delta p_i q_i^0}{VA_i}\right]\left[\frac{VA_i}{V_p}\right] = \frac{\Delta P_p}{P_p},$$

where p_i is the price of output in the ith sector; q_i^0 is the initial output of the ith sector; VA_i is valued added in the ith sector; V_p is the value of private domestic product; and P_p is the domestic private deflator. I essentially calculate a Laspeyres index of the effect of various microeconomic policies on the price level. In only a few cases are substitution or own-price effects computed.

I specifically avoid estimating any effects from these changes in the price level throughout the economy over time because there is no general consensus about the appropriate structure of wage-price equations in a macroeconomic model. It remains an open question whether prices affect wages through their influence on workers' expectations, through increases in the nominal marginal-value product of labor, or through escalator provisions.[1] In fact, whether such a feedback between prices and wages exists at all is a subject of debate.[2] In another paper in this volume George Perry provides new insight on this question, and concludes that there is some evidence of a price-wage effect in recent U.S. wage behavior. He argues for government cost-cutting measures as an important component of a comprehensive anti-inflation policy.

Social Security

The 1977 amendments to the Social Security Act were designed primarily to place the old age and survivors, disability, and health insurance (OASDHI) trust funds in a more solvent position. Except for health insurance, these funds were running large deficits in 1977. The deficits were projected to grow substantially in the next few years, in part because of the rapidly rising benefit levels and the increasing cost of disability benefits. To amend the act, the Congress could choose among raising the payroll tax rates, increasing the taxable wage base, or tapping general revenue for the trust funds. Moreover, if it chose to increase payroll taxes, it could increase employee contributions, employer contributions, or both. The Senate bill and the administration's proposal would have placed more of the burden on employers, but the final legislation more nearly paralleled

1. See Robert J. Gordon, "Inflation in Recession and Recovery," *Brookings Papers on Economic Activity, 1:1971*, pp. 105–58. (Hereafter *BPEA*.)
2. See Robert E. Hall, "The Process of Inflation in the Labor Market," *BPEA, 2:1974*, pp. 343–93.

Table 1. Effect of the Social Security Revisions of 1977 on the Tax Rate and on the Taxable Wage Base, 1978–81

Year	OASDHI[a] tax rate (percent)			Taxable wage base (dollars)			Total cost of revisions (billions of dollars)
	Old law	New law	Change	Old law	New law	Change	
1978	6.05	6.05	0	17,700	17,700	0	...
1979	6.05	6.13	0.08	18,900	22,900	4,000	6.4
1980	6.05	6.13	0.08	20,400	25,900	5,500	9.4
1981	6.30	6.65	0.35	21,900	29,700	7,800	18.4

Source: *Summary of the Conference Agreement on H.R. 9346: The Social Security Amendments of 1977* House Committee on Ways and Means, 95:1, WMCP: 95-61 (Government Printing Office, 1977).
a. Old age and survivors, disability, and health insurance.

the House version of the amendments, which required equal increases in employer and employee taxes.

It is reasonable to assume that employer contributions are reflected in product prices because they raise the total costs of compensating workers and thus unit labor costs. Employee taxes are simply a mildly regressive form of income taxation, which reduce employees' after-tax incomes.[3] Placing less emphasis on employer contributions and more on employee taxes or general revenue financing is therefore likely to have more beneficial effects on price levels in the short run if labor supply is price inelastic.

The final bill enacted by the Congress, which delayed the increases until 1979 and raised employee and employer taxes equally, is among the less inflationary choices it could have made from the major proposals before it. The changes in the tax rates and the new ceilings for the income base are shown in table 1. The total cost of these changes in terms of additional contributions to OASDHI is $6.4 billion in 1979, $9.4 billion in 1980, and $13.4 billion in 1981.

At present there is growing support for utilizing general revenue financing of the disability and health programs. In 1977, tax receipts for these two programs totaled $25.7 billion.[4] It has been argued that health insurance differs from old age and survivors insurance and disability insur-

3. However, Gordon, in "Inflation in Recession and Recovery," p. 121, finds that about one-seventh of employee direct taxes are shifted forward by workers.
4. *Background Materials for Hearings on Social Security,* Subcommittee on Social Security of the House Committee on Ways and Means, 95:1, WMCP: 95-40 (GPO, 1977), p. 3.

ance because it does not pay benefits in proportion to a worker's past contributions and because benefits are not based on this wage experience. Thus, severing health insurance funds from payroll-tax funding would not impair the structure of the old age retirement system in social security. However, general revenue financing of disability insurance would create problems of justifying current eligibility requirements and of distinguishing it from the supplemental security income program, which provides benefits to the elderly, blind, and disabled. If the disability and health insurance contributions from employees and employers were replaced by general revenue financing—as specified in H.R. 10754, which is now being debated—the employer contributions would decline by approximately $14.6 billion in fiscal year 1979.[5] This would place downward pressure on unit labor costs and therefore prices, approximately offsetting the forthcoming employer tax increases in the OASDHI for 1979–81.

Substitution of Direct for Indirect Taxes

There can be little doubt that indirect taxes, such as general sales taxes, manufacturers' excise taxes, customs duties, and sumptuary taxes add directly to the price of the market basket of goods purchased by consumers. Moreover, changes in these taxes should be reflected in prices rather quickly. Okun has suggested that the federal government substitute direct taxation for sales taxes in order to achieve a one-time reduction in the price level.[6] The potential effects on the price level of such a reduction are the most pronounced of any of the microeconomic proposals in this paper.

Most indirect taxes are levied at the state and local levels. In 1977, the federal government received only $17.4 billion in excise taxes and $5.3 billion in customs duties, a total of 6.1 percent of its tax receipts.[7]

At the state and local levels, sales taxes account for approximately 30 percent of all tax receipts, a total of $63.8 billion in 1977. Some of these are sumptuary taxes that would not easily be given up for direct

5. Congressional Budget Office, "Comparison of the Impacts of a Cut in the Hospital Insurance and Disability Insurance Payroll Taxes with Those of the Administration's 1978 Tax Cut Proposal" (CBO, February 24, 1978; processed).

6. Arthur M. Okun, "The Great Stagflation Swamp," *Challenge,* vol. 20 (November/December 1977), pp. 6–13.

7. This includes social security contributions.

federal transfers, but the general sales taxes might be a target. Obviously, any program to reimburse states for rescinding their sales taxes could place the federal government in the position of redistributing income across states. In 1976, Hawaii, for instance, collected sales taxes equal to 5.2 percent of its personal income while five states had no sales tax at all. Some minimum grant related to income could be paid to states without sales taxes. But in order to avoid major redistributions across states, the amount of sales tax for which federal grants were substituted would have to be limited.

For instance, if every state were to reduce its sales tax receipts by 1 percent of personal income originating in the state, with the revenue to be replaced by, say, half (0.5 percent) in state income tax and the remainder in federal revenues, there would be little if any redistribution across states. The federal tax system is mildly progressive in terms of personal income per capita.[8] The substitution of federal revenues for state sales taxes would most likely result in an increase in the progressivity of the general tax structure.

How much of state sales taxes could be bought back? In 1976, all state and local sales taxes, including sumptuary taxes, amounted to 4.1 percent of personal income, or 5.2 percent of personal consumption expenditure. General state sales taxes were approximately one-half of this total. The distribution of the ratios of these general sales tax receipts to personal income is shown in table 2. Most states cluster between 0.015 and 0.030. Therefore, a buyback of sales tax revenues up to 2 percent of personal income might be feasible without major redistributive effects. If the federal government offered 50 percent of each reduction up to 2 percent of personal income, the Treasury's bill would have been $12.4 billion in 1976.[9] The total reduction in sales tax available from such a buyback would be an estimated $27.4 billion in 1977 or 1.6 percent of gross

---

8. The personal income tax, which generates nearly one-half of federal government receipts, is related to personal income per capita as follows:

$$\frac{\text{personal income tax}}{\text{personal income}} = 0.0569 + 0.928 \times 10^{-5} \text{ per capita income,}$$

based on a 51-state cross-sectional regression using 1974 data. The elasticity of the tax rate with respect to personal income per capita is 0.46 at the point of means.

9. If the five states not utilizing a sales tax were given 1 percent of personal income as part of the program, the federal outlay would have risen by only $0.3 billion to $12.7 billion.

Table 2. Distribution of Ratios of State General Sales Tax Revenue to Personal Income of the State, 1976

Ratio of sales tax revenue[a] to personal income of the state	Number of states	Share of total U.S. personal income (percent)
0 (no sales tax)	5	2.32
0.01 to 0.015	4	6.45
0.015 to 0.02	13	41.57
0.02 to 0.03	20	43.57
0.03 to 0.04	4	1.90
0.04 to 0.05	4	3.74
0.05 and over	1	0.45

Sources: U.S. Bureau of the Census, *Quarterly Summary of State and Local Tax Revenue*, various issues, and *Survey of Current Business*, vol. 57 (August 1977).

a. General sales taxes and general gross receipts taxes. The latter are analogous to the former in their effects on the price level, but are levied on all business receipts rather than on retail sales.

domestic private product.[10] If the federal government were to rescind its excise taxes in favor of an income tax, it might gain another 1.0 percent reduction in the private domestic deflator. In total, the federal government could potentially reduce indirect taxation by $44.8 billion, based on 1977 revenues, yielding as much as a 2.7 percent reduction in the private domestic deflator.

Even if a substitution of direct for indirect taxes reduced the price level in the short run, problems in the long run could undermine this policy. In particular, a federal policy to buy back general sales taxes could be offset over time if the states selectively imposed indirect taxes—hotel occupancy taxes, licensing fees based on revenues, increases in sumptuary taxes, or specific excise taxes of other forms. Given the present apparent preference for indirect over direct taxes in many states, this difficulty cannot be ignored.

Agriculture

The past five years have provided some breathing space for the formulation of a rational policy for agriculture. After the Russian wheat purchases in 1972–73 and a subsequent reduction in world grain stocks,

10. Assuming that taxes on general sales and gross receipts increased at the same rate as personal consumption expenditures from 1976 to 1977. *Survey of Current Business*, vol. 58 (January 1978).

Table 3. Realized Net Farm Income of Farm Operators and Prices Received by Farmers, 1969–77

Income and index items	1969	1970	1971	1972	1973	1974	1975	1976	1977
Realized net farm income					Amount				
Billions of current dollars[a]									
Excluding government payments	10.88	10.89	10.49	14.35	27.67	27.27	20.10	21.26	18.70[c]
Including government payments	14.19	14.15	13.24	17.80	29.94	27.74	20.81	21.91	20.40
Billions of 1972 dollars[b]									
Excluding government payments	12.42	11.73	10.84	14.35	26.05	23.13	15.62	15.62	12.91[c]
Including government payments	16.19	15.25	13.68	17.80	28.19	23.53	16.18	16.10	14.08
Price index				Price received by farmers (1967 = 100)					
All farm products	107	110	113	125	179	192	185	186	183
All crops	97	100	108	114	175	224	201	197	193
Feed grains and hay	96	103	108	104	163	243	230	218	182
All livestock and products	117	118	118	136	183	165	172	177	175

Sources: U.S. Department of Agriculture, *Farm Income Statistics*, Statistical Bulletin 576 (July 1977), p. 30; USDA, *Agricultural Prices: Annual Survey 1976* (June 1977), p. 6; USDA, *Agricultural Outlook* (GPO, March 1978); and *Survey of Current Business*, various issues. Figures are rounded.

a. Excluding the net change in farm inventories.
b. Converted to 1972 dollars by using consumer price index, all items.
c. Author's estimate.

prices of wheat and feed grains rose sharply. In 1973, the average price received by farmers for crops climbed 53.5 percent; and in 1974 it rose another 28.0 percent (see table 3). Resources were then rushed back into agriculture after farm incomes rose to record levels in 1973. As a result, for a brief period the emphasis in farm policy proposals shifted somewhat from price supports to price stabilization.[11]

INCOME SUPPORTS: THE CHOICE BETWEEN
DIRECT PAYMENTS AND PRICE ENHANCEMENT

Unfortunately, the respite was brief. The old problems in farm policy returned in 1977–78 after farm income declined from its 1973–74 plateau. The emphasis turned once again to raising farm incomes through price supports and direct government payments. A combination of political and budgetary pressures again imparted an inflationary bias to agricultural policy. While some progress was made toward establishing a rational mechanism for managing a price-stabilizing reserve program, the income-support policies adopted in 1977–78 have been unnecessarily inflationary with an emphasis on redistributing income to large farmers, rather than on supporting the small, family-owned farm.

The 1977–78 Policy Setting. In 1977, because of mounting pressure from farmers whose real income from farming (excluding capital gains) had fallen to approximately one-half of its 1973 level, Congress faced a choice of raising farm income through direct government payments or through price supports. It chose a little of each, raising the target prices for wheat and corn to $2.90 and $2.00 a bushel, respectively, and raising the loan rate for corn to $2.00 while keeping the loan rate on wheat at $2.25 a bushel.[12] This reflected a decision to peg target prices on which government payments are calculated at or near the "cost of production," while keeping the loan rate for wheat (which effectively becomes a price-support floor) substantially below the level of estimated costs. When calculating the cost of production, however, Congress ac-

11. See, for example, *Government and the Nation's Resources,* Report of the National Commission on Supplies and Shortages (GPO, 1976), chap. 7.

12. The loan rate is the price at which the secretary of agriculture is authorized to make loans or purchases of the relevant crops. It therefore serves as a support price for commodity sales by all farmers. The target price is the price guaranteed to those farmers who participate in the program and is the basis for calculating direct government payments.

Table 4. Estimates of the Annual Costs to Consumers of 1977–78 Changes in
Agriculture Policy
Millions of 1977 dollars

Increase in price supports[a]		Set-asides[b]		March 1978 wheat, feed grain, and soybean initiatives[c]	Total
Feed grains	Milk	Feed grains	Wheat		
810	140	445	445	1,775	3,615

Sources: Milk, Council on Wage and Price Stability; March 1978 wheat, feed grain, and soybean initiatives, USDA; other figures are author's estimates.
a. Assumes that the price of feed grains rises by 15 cents per bushel of corn equivalent.
b. Based on a participation rate for feed grains of 25 percent and an elasticity of demand of −0.5; for wheat, these figures are 75 percent and −0.5, respectively.
c. Average of low and high yields.

cepted a methodology that included a return on the current value of land, which continued to rise despite declining farm income (see below). Thus, income supports were structured at least partially to ratify the inflationary expectations indicated in agricultural real estate markets.

The Food and Agriculture Act of 1977 created predictable problems for the administration. Feed grain stocks rose in response to the sharp increase in the loan rate while deficiency payments for wheat (the difference between the target price and the market price) placed considerable pressure on the Department of Agriculture budget. The administration's reaction was the use of acreage "set-asides."[13] In early 1978, set-asides were announced of 10 percent of feed grain acreage and 20 percent of wheat acreage. These added nearly $900 million to consumer costs in addition to the $800 million from the increased loan rate on feed grains created by the 1977 act (see table 4). In March 1978, the administration announced further output-limiting policies, including payments for diverting feed grain and cotton acreage and additional incentives to graze wheat rather than to harvest it. The effect of the March initiatives was to increase the cost of farm commodities by $1.78 billion annually. In addition, milk price supports were raised to add another $140 million to annual food costs.

Why have these various forms of price enhancement been chosen for supporting farm incomes and stabilizing prices? If the objectives of agri-

13. The term "set-asides" refers to the requirement that farmers retire a specified percentage of their acreage during the crop year in order to participate in price support and disaster programs.

cultural policy are price and income stability and the support of the small family farm, why not allocate government payments to the smaller, struggling farmer in periods of generally low farm income, while managing a commodity reserve program to stabilize prices? Part of the answer is, quite simply, that the apparent objective of current farm policy is to maintain the incomes of all farmers—particularly the large farm operators.

Agriculture is obviously not a sector dominated by small family farms. Since 1973, roughly the top 5 percent of farm operators have received between 55 and 60 percent of total cash receipts. These large farmers, with annual receipts of $100,000 or more, averaged $93,748 in net farm income in 1973, $9,406 in off-farm income, and $94,116 in capital gains (the accrued rise in value of farm real estate), or a total of $197,270 per operator (see table 5).

The decline in farm income from 1973 to 1976 (the most recent years for which detailed data are available) was most pronounced among large farmers. The farms with the largest sales in table 5 show the sharpest decline in total income, with or without capital gains. But despite this decline in fortune, farmers with annual receipts in excess of $40,000 a year continued to earn healthy returns on their investment. The return on equity shown in table 5 is not adjusted for the opportunity cost of the operator's labor, but even if, say, $15,000 a year were deducted from income for this purpose, the return would not fall below 16 percent for the two largest categories of farms. On the other hand, a similar allowance would reduce the return to a low level for smaller farmers. In short, the largest farmers continued to prosper in 1976 while returns on capital for the smaller farmers were much less satisfactory. But it was the decline in income for the large farmers that generated the impetus for the 1977–78 farm policy approved by Congress and the administration.

Alternative Mechanisms for Supporting Farmers' Incomes. In 1977, Congress could have chosen to increase farm incomes by relying on deficiency payments, price supports, or direct payments scaled in proportion to the perceived economic needs of different farm operators. Direct payments, however, whether in the form of deficiency payments or other mechanisms, are so visible that Congress feels it must impose ceilings on the level of payments per farm. In the 1977 act these ceilings vary from $40,000 to $52,250 a year, depending on the crop. Previous experience with large expenditures on direct payments to farmers demonstrates that large farmers have obtained a major share of the payments, but they have

Table 5. Distribution of Farm Operators' Cash Receipts, Income, and Equity, by Size of Farm, 1973 and 1976

Description	Farm sales (dollars)						
	100,000 and over	40,000–100,000	20,000–40,000	10,000–20,000	5,000–10,000	2,500–5,000	Less than 2,500
Distribution of cash receipts from farming (percent)[a]							
1973	56.3	20.6	11.2	5.8	3.0	1.5	1.6
1976	59.6	20.3	10.1	4.9	2.4	1.3	1.4
Distribution of net income (percent)[b]							
1973	43.2	22.5	14.1	7.6	4.3	2.5	5.8
1976	39.4	23.2	14.1	7.2	4.1	2.5	9.5
Total income per farm-operator family (dollars)[c]							
Excluding capital gains							
1973	103,154	28,445	17,147	12,324	10,771	9,918	13,399
1976	69,026	23,464	15,384	12,308	12,154	12,067	17,551
Percent change	−33.1	−17.5	−10.3	−0.1	+12.8	+21.7	+31.0
Including capital gains on farm real estate							
1973	197,270	63,162	37,562	26,793	21,618	18,551	19,186
1976	164,742	57,213	36,056	27,126	23,255	20,926	23,346
Percent change	−16.5	−9.4	−4.0	+1.2	+7.6	+12.8	+21.7
Farm operators' equity, 1976							
Value per farm (dollars)[d]	523,580	218,921	135,830	88,059	62,202	47,429	31,688
Return (percent)[e]	28.9	23.0	22.3	22.8	22.7	22.4	24.3

Sources: USDA, *Farm Income Statistics* (July 1977); USDA, *Balance Sheet of the Farming Sector, 1977*, Agriculture Information Bulletin 411 (USDA, October 1977).
a. Including other farm income and excluding capital gains.
b. Realized net farm income, excluding capital gains.
c. Total income, including nonmoney income from farm food and housing, income from government payments, and off-farm income.
d. Calculated using farm operators' 1975 share of total farm operators' and nonoperator landlords' equity, from unofficial U.S. Department of Agriculture estimates.
e. Realized net farm income plus capital gains as percentage of farm operators' equity.

Table 6. Returns per Farm from Alternative Hypothetical Policies for Distributing $4.4 Billion to Farmers, by Size of Farm
1976 dollars

	Alternative policies		
Farm sales	Pure price enhancement (A)	Target-price income supports with 1970 government payments distribution (B)	Income supports with equal payments distribution (C)
100,000 or more	16,842	8,567	1,577
40,000–100,000	2,896	3,716	1,577
20,000–40,000	1,382	2,346	1,577
10,000–20,000	711	1,585	1,577
5,000–10,000	353	918	1,577
2,500–5,000	182	553	1,577
Less than 2,500	57	217	1,577

Source: USDA, *Farm Income Statistics* (July 1977).

not enjoyed payments in proportion to their share of total receipts. In 1969–71, for example, the top 8 percent of farmers received approximately one-third of all direct payments from the government; their farms received more than 50 percent of all cash receipts from farming.

To compare the distributional effects of alternative mechanisms for supporting farmers' incomes, I assume that Senator Talmadge's objectives represent the 1978 consensus in the Congress.[14] His initial proposal would have increased domestic farm commodity marketings by an estimated $4.38 billion, compared to the prices that could have been expected without set-asides. This is enough to restore total real farm income to more than its relatively high 1972 rate. Policy A in table 6 assumes that a pure price-enhancing set-aside policy will raise farmers' incomes in proportion to their 1976 gross cash receipts. A second alternative is a policy that would distribute income support payments in the same relative proportions as those that occurred in 1970 when there were high price supports (policy B); a third is one that would distribute $4.38 billion equally across all farms (policy C). The results show that a price-enhancement strategy greatly benefits the farmers earning more than $40,000 at the expense of virtually all the others. The 1970 pattern of price-support payments would give farmers with sales in excess of $20,000 a year (1976 dollars) more than an equiproportional share of the $4.38 billion.

14. *Emergency Agricultural Act of 1978*, S. Rept. 95-699, 95:2 (GPO, 1978).

Thus, a direct payment scheme, using either income-support payments subject to a ceiling or an equal payment per farm, would benefit the small farmer considerably relative to a price-enhancement strategy. Moreover, the direct payments would not translate directly into price-level effects as would a commodity price-enhancing strategy. The combination of high loan rates and acreage set-asides is not only inflationary but is also designed to convey most of the benefits to large farmers who continue to enjoy large average returns on their investments.

Land Values and the Cost of Production. Given the tendency of Congress to use price enhancement as a means of redistributing income to farmers, it is unfortunate that it has now settled on a standard based on cost of production for setting target prices and, indirectly, loan rates. These estimates of the cost of production include a 3.5 percent return on the current value of land, which has risen sharply despite declining farm income.

Throughout the 1950s and 1960s, the value of cropland and dairyland climbed steadily. This increase followed a rise in net farm income with a short lag. In the 1970s, land values soared in response to higher farm prices and, therefore, higher farm incomes. However, when farm incomes began to decline in 1974, the price of land continued to rise. Predictions of 1972–76 land values were based on equations that estimated the effect of current and lagged net income on land values for 1955–71. The result was underestimation for 1974, 1975, and especially 1976 (table 7).[15] Actual land values in Iowa and Kansas approximately doubled between 1972 and 1976, while realized net income receded roughly to its real 1968–69 levels. Farmers were apparently expecting further income gains in the near future, perhaps from government initiatives.

PRICE STABILIZATION

While agriculture is a competitive sector of the economy, not necessarily subject to the downward price rigidity observed in many labor and product markets, there are major reasons why government policies are needed to stabilize food prices at some cost to economic efficiency. Food prices comprise a large share of the cost of living and may have major

15. Kansas, Iowa, and Wisconsin were chosen as typical wheat, corn, and dairy farming states, respectively.

Table 7. Actual and Predicted Values of Farm Land in Iowa, Kansas, and Wisconsin, 1972–76ᵃ

Indexes of average value per acre (1967 = 100)

Year	Iowa		Kansas		Wisconsin	
	Actualᵇ	Predicted	Actualᵇ	Predicted	Actualᵇ	Predicted
1972	122	118	118	130	148	138
1973	141	169	137	160	179	165
1974	189	168	178	159	214	167
1975	234	230	211	152	240	174
1976	294	126	235	125	271	159

Sources: USDA, *Farm Real Estate Market Developments*, CD-77 and CD-82 (July 1973 and July 1977); and USDA, *State Farm Income Statistics*, Supplement to Statistical Bulletin 576 (September 1977).
a. Land values regressed on current and two-period lagged net income, 1955–71.
b. March of each year.

effects on wage and price escalation in other industries.[16] In addition, government agricultural income support programs now contain features that may mean downward price inflexibility for farm commodities in future years. Sudden rises in agricultural prices are rather quickly translated into increased farm land values, which in turn increase the cost of production used to calculate support and target prices. Hence the inflationary cost of repeating the experience of 1972–73 would be enormous.

To argue that the government should stabilize farm prices does not mean that it can. It may be difficult to devise operational decision rules for government programs that are stabilizing in the presence of major exogenous shocks. Moreover, even if such policies were designed well, political forces may not allow them to operate to increase stability.[17]

On the other hand, there is a general consensus that private decisions do not always lead to the optimal level of agricultural stocks. There are two reasons for this: first, speculators will not hold stocks for the low probability of a large return because government policy will not permit them to realize market-clearing prices during periods of prospectively high returns and, second, private decisions fail to include the social cost

16. Food accounted for 23.7 percent of the consumer price index as of December 1976. Food accounts for 19.3 percent and 17.7 percent of the two new CPIs introduced in 1978.

17. During the 1970s, the volatility of the crude food and feedstuffs of the wholesale price index actually declined relative to other crude materials, despite the return to a less interventionist agriculture policy.

of inflation. As a result, it behooves government to subsidize or to accumulate stocks to augment those held by private investors and speculators.

The Food and Agriculture Act of 1977 recognizes this need by requiring the establishment of programs both to encourage producer storage for wheat and feed grains and to promote U.S. participation in international reserve programs. U.S. reserves are to be stimulated by government loans, payments for storage ($0.25 a bushel, as set by the Department of Agriculture), and penalties for sales from these reserves in advance of reaching prescribed "trigger points" when sales could begin. These points are defined in the act to be between 140 percent and 160 percent of the loan rate for wheat and at appropriate levels for feed grains. Wheat is to be accumulated in this planned reserve up to a total of 300 million to 700 million bushels. The purpose of these reserves is to "promote the orderly marketing of [the] commodities." Lacking, however, are instructions to insulate the management of this reserve from political forces.[18]

Although the reserve program may resemble the Houthakker program for entering future markets to stabilize agricultural prices, it is at present little more than a stockpile program.[19] Unanswered are questions concerning how the size of the stockpile should vary over time, when the secretary of agriculture should increase diversions through augmentation of storage payments, or when feed grains should be released from the reserve.[20] Congress could easily change the operation of the stockpile during a period of rising wheat prices by simply raising the (nonbinding) loan rate to within 40 percent of the market price. Finally, the pressure of political forces may lead to short-run decisions that are more destabilizing than the usual cycle of support payments, loan rates, and acreage set-asides.[21]

18. An example of these forces was an administration decision in March 1978 to forgive interest payments after one year for grain placed in government-subsidized reserves. This decision appears to have been based not on an assessment of the optimal reserve, but simply on the political necessities of the moment.

19. A description of the Houthakker program appears in Hendrik S. Houthakker, *Economic Policy for the Farm Sector* (American Enterprise Institute, 1967), chap. 7.

20. The secretary has considerable discretion in setting the level of payments to producers for storing the grain.

21. An example of such political pressure is found in the administration's new agricultural policy initiatives of March 29, 1978. While arguing that farmers' incomes rose 15 percent over the previous year and grain prices increased over 30 percent, the initiatives announced plans to increase reserves considerably through a reduction in interest charges.

SUMMARY

Declining real farm income has spawned a set of income support policies that are unduly inflationary because of the political necessity of directing the benefits toward large farmers. If the welfare of smaller farmers were the principal motivation behind 1977–78 policies, direct government payments could have been utilized effectively with much less effect on the price level. A new policy of building farm-commodity reserves indicates progress in the drive to stabilize farm prices, but even this policy is impaired by the short-term political necessity to maintain farm incomes.

Government Regulation

It is useful for the purposes of discussion to divide federal government regulation into at least two categories: economic and social. Economic regulation is the general rate-setting or price-setting form of regulation that has long been in existence. While the ostensible purpose of such regulation is generally to restrict monopolistic control over price, it often leads to implicit cartelization of the regulated firms and to prices (or rates) that are in excess of the cost of service. In energy markets, however, much of the current regulation represents an attempt to transfer economic rents from producers to consumers while acknowledging a loss in economic efficiency.

During the past decade, social regulation—largely environmental, health, and safety regulation—has grown so rapidly that it challenges and perhaps surpasses the economic forms of regulation in its impact on prices and economic efficiency. It is in this newer area that the greatest opportunities lie for changing the government's effect on the price level because Congress has generally chosen to have it implemented through the mandating of cost-increasing methods of control. This choice is a pragmatic one, but it is rarely coupled with a requirement that the regulation be efficient.

ECONOMIC REGULATION

Of the government-regulated transportation, communications, energy, banking, and securities industries, only the transportation industry offers important opportunities for reforms that would decrease the price level. Current energy regulation reflects an attempt to restrain the upward adjustment of energy prices in the short run, although there is some evidence that the regulation of gas pipelines raises prices.[22] Communications regulation is currently being reformed substantially through a variety of court tests and the inexorable progress of new technology.[23] The securities industry is already being persuaded by the Securities and Exchange Commission to increase competition, and the effect of banking regulatory reform cannot easily be measured in terms of the price level.

In the transportation sector, reform would mean deregulation of entry and fare setting. A step in this direction has been taken in the Kennedy-Cannon bill, which would provide greater fare flexibility and liberalize entry into the interstate airline industry. A similar approach is clearly possible for trucking, given the limited economies of scale in that industry. Finally, amending the current cabotage laws that restrict the coastal trade to vessels manned and built by U.S. labor would greatly reduce shipping costs in the coastal trade for the maritime industry. In each of these transportation sectors, the need for deregulation is evident. In the absence of regulation, competitive forces would operate satisfactorily in each, and there would be little reduction in service to small communities or small shippers. Only in the case of the maritime industries could national security be used as an argument for continuing to maintain rates above market levels, and even in this market there are other, less expensive means for promoting the nation's security.

The prospective net savings in fares from deregulating the airlines, trucking, and the coastal maritime trade appear in table 8. These estimates, based on existing studies, are at best approximate and do not include a measure of deadweight loss nor reflect the shifts among modes of transportation that would occur. Full deregulation—a political impossibility—would lower transportation costs by at least $5 billion and perhaps $10 billion a year.

22. Stephen G. Breyer and Paul W. MacAvoy, *Energy Regulation by the Federal Power Commission* (Brookings Institution, 1974).

23. By this I do not mean that rewriting the Communications Act of 1934 or a government victory in *United States* v. *American Telephone and Telegraph Company* will not change the pace of deconcentration, but only that competition is virtually inevitable in the telecommunications industry.

Table 8. **Potential Price Effects from Deregulating Transportation Industries, 1976**

Industry	Total revenue (billions of dollars)	Price impact from deregulation (percent)	Potential annual savings (billions of dollars)
Airline	16.8	−20 to −30[a]	3.4 to 5.0
Trucking	26.0[b]	−7 to −20[c]	1.8 to 5.2
Maritime[d]	n.a.	n.a.	0.10 to 0.15[e]

Sources: U.S. Civil Aeronautics Board, *Supplement to the Handbook of Airline Statistics, Covering 1975 and 1976* (GPO, 1977); and Interstate Commerce Commission, unpublished calculations. See also notes a, c, and e.

n.a. Not available.

a. Based on data in George W. Douglas and James C. Miller III, *Economic Regulation of Domestic Air Transport: Theory and Policy* (Brookings Institution, 1974), p. 90, and in Theodore E. Keeler, "Airline Regulation and Market Performance," *Bell Journal of Economics*, vol. 3 (Autumn 1972), pp. 399–424.

b. Motor carriers of property, classes 1, 2, 3.

c. Based on data in Thomas Gale Moore, *Freight Transportation Regulation: Surface Freight and the Interstate Commerce Commission* (American Enterprise Institute, 1972) and various studies cited therein.

d. Cabotage laws.

e. Gerald R. Jantscher, *Bread upon the Waters: Federal Aids to the Maritime Industries* (Brookings Institution, 1975), chap. 5.

SOCIAL REGULATION

The reform of social regulation may have important effects on the price level. While this type of regulation can and does bring substantial benefits to society, there is a need to provide the agencies responsible for its execution with an incentive to achieve these benefits at the lowest possible cost—an incentive that is currently lacking. A rather large number of regulatory authorities are entrusted with this newer type of regulation, including the Environmental Protection Agency, the Occupational Safety and Health Administration, the Food and Drug Administration, the Consumer Product Safety Commission, the Federal Aviation Administration, the National Highway Traffic Safety Administration, the Coast Guard, the Mining Enforcement and Safety Administration, the Department of the Interior, and the Forest Service of the Department of Agriculture.

Of all the agencies entrusted with social regulation listed above, the two having the greatest responsibilities across the breadth of the economy and the largest impact on business costs are the Occupational Safety and Health Administration and the Environmental Protection Agency. The prospective net social costs of their regulations is discussed below.

The Occupational Safety and Health Administration. There is no good source of the total prospective costs of OSHA's regulation. At best, the costs can be estimated for the regulations that have been promulgated since 1975 or those that have been proposed but not finally pro-

Table 9. Prospective Annual Cost of Major Regulations Proposed or Promulgated by the Occupational Health and Safety Administration, 1974–77

		Number of workers protected	Annual cost (1977 dollars)[a]	
Item regulated	Date proposed		Total (millions)	Per protected worker
Noise	October 24, 1974	206,700	1,985.3[b]	9,605[b]
Arsenic	January 21, 1975	7,400	125.3	16,932
Coke ovens	July 31, 1975	29,600	262.6	8,872
Sulfur dioxide	November 24, 1975	14,000	177.4	12,671
Lead	October 3, 1975	5,200	363.4	69,885
Deep-sea diving	June 15, 1976	1,500	23.0	15,333
Acrylonitrile	January 17, 1978	3,400	23.1	6,794
Benzene	May 27, 1977	191,000	503.6	2,637
All items	...	458,800	3,463.7	7,550
Addendum				
Cotton dust	December 20, 1976	314,000[c]	717.5	2,285[d]

Sources: Based on data in Occupational Safety and Health Administration, Dockets OSH-11A, OSH-37, H-017A, H-039, H-004, H-103, and H-052, respectively, for first six items and last item in the table; submission by the Council on Wage and Price Stability to OSHA, "Analysis of Proposed Benzene Standard," appendix, September 12, 1977, for benzene; unpublished data from the Council on Wage and Price Stability, for acrylonitrile.

a. Deflated using the implicit GNP deflator for producers' durable equipment from the quarter of proposal.

b. Assuming a 90/90 standard (scale of dBA noise level), where the first number indicates the noise level for the initiation of engineering and administrative controls and the second number, the noise level for the use of hearing protectors.

c. Total employment, not the protected population.

d. Minimum.

mulgated. Table 9 provides a summary of items affected by major regulations, with the estimated annual cost and the number of employees to be protected for each. Most data are drawn from the inflation and economic impact analyses performed for OSHA.

An important measure of the impact of OSHA is the cost per protected worker. In four of the eight cases in which this measure can be calculated, the cost of the agency's proposed regulations exceeds total average earnings per worker in manufacturing. The principal reason for this enormous cost is the reliance on engineering controls rather than on work practices and personal protective equipment. Clearly, such costly regulations— if promulgated—will drastically change the industries affected because many will find it unprofitable to continue operation without major reductions in output.

In 1977 dollars, the prospective costs of the nine major regulations listed are $4.2 billion a year—0.25 percent of the gross private product. Excluded are new regulations controlling toxic substances such as mandatory labeling, which could add several billion dollars a year, and the agency's general carcinogen policy now under development.

In a recent article, Edward Denison estimated that in 1975 the total annual cost of the OSHA's regulation of the nonmining, nonresidential workplace was $972 million, or 0.09 percent of the nonresidential net national product.[24] Thus, the prospective costs of regulations listed in table 9 are more than four times Denison's estimates for 1975. The impact of this type of regulation will undoubtedly grow in the next few years.

Environmental Regulation. To calculate the prospective cost of environmental regulation in the next few years, a slightly different approach is taken. The Environmental Protection Agency has recognized that its regulations governing air and water will have the greatest impact on six industries: electric power generation, petroleum refining, steel, paper, copper, and chemicals. As a result, the agency has funded analyses of the total cost of controls for each of these industries. Only the study on the chemicals industry is incomplete as of this writing.

It is estimated that the prospective cost of the first phase of environmental regulations, excluding new regulations promulgated in response to 1977 legislation, will be $7.83 billion a year in 1977 dollars (see table 10). If enforcement of these regulations were begun in a timely fashion, these costs, except for utilities, would have been incurred by 1977 and each year thereafter. By 1983 (1985 for utilities), these costs will rise to $13.81 billion a year, excluding new regulations under study currently at the Environmental Protection Agency.[25]

These estimates of environmental costs for five major industries, combined with earlier work on the industrial distribution of air control and water control (best-practicable-technology standard, or BPT) outlays, may be used to calculate a prospective total annual cost of air and water pollution controls in the near term (1977 standards) and in the mid-1980s. Assuming that the five industries contribute to total future costs in the same proportion as they do to current air and BPT water control costs, the prospective cost for air and water pollution control in the nonfarm business sector of the economy, excluding the cost of controlling

24. Edward F. Denison, "Effects of Selected Changes in the Institutional and Human Environment upon Output per Unit of Input," *Survey of Current Business,* vol. 58 (January 1978), pp. 21–44.

25. These include new standards for sulfur dioxide emissions from new sources, revision of ambient air quality standards, a new lead standard, revision of state implementation plans under the Clean Air Act, and new approaches to carcinogens.

Table 10. Prospective Annual Cost of Environmental Controls for Legislation in Effect in 1976, Five Major Industries and All Industries, 1977 and 1983[a]
Billions of 1977 dollars

Industry	1977	1983
Electric utility	4.28[b]	7.13[c]
Petroleum refining	1.79	2.96
Steel	0.90	2.36
Pulp and paper	0.69	1.07
Copper	0.17	0.29
Total	7.83	13.81
All industries	25.34	44.69

Sources: Estimated using U.S. Environmental Protection Agency, Office of Planning and Evaluation, "Economic and Financial Impacts of Federal Air and Water Pollution Controls of the Electric Utility Industry: Technical Report," EPA-230/3-76-013 (EPA, May 1976; processed); ibid., "Economic Impact of EPA's Regulations on the Petroleum Refining Industry," pt. 1, EPA-230/3/76-004 (EPA, April 1976; processed); Temple, Barker & Sloane, Inc., "Analysis of Economic Effects of Environmental Regulations on the Integrated Iron and Steel Industry," vol. 1, EPA-230/3-77-015 (EPA, July 1977; processed); Arthur D. Little, Inc., "Economic Impacts of Pulp and Paper Industry Compliance with Environmental Regulations," vol. 1 (ADL, nd; processed; available through National Technical Information Service); ADL, "Economic Impact of Environmental Regulations on the United States Copper Industry," submitted to EPA (ADL, January 1978; processed); all industries, estimated from L. P. Gianessi, H. M. Peskin, and E. Wolff, "The Distributional Effects of the Uniform Air Pollution Policy in the United States," discussion paper D-5 (Resources for the Future, March 1977; processed), table 1, and L. P. Gianessi and H. M. Peskin, "The Cost to Industries of Meeting the 1977 Provisions of the Water Pollution Control Amendments of 1972," Contract No. 68-01-2817 (National Bureau of Economic Research, January 1976; processed).

a. Assumes full enforcement of all control legislation in effect in 1976. Costs adjusted using implicit GNP deflator for producers' durable equipment.

b. 1980.

c. 1985.

nonbusiness automobiles, is $25.34 billion annually in the near term and $44.69 billion a year by the mid-1980s. This is decidedly higher than the latest forecast of the Council on Environmental Quality for private costs of water and stationary air-quality regulation in 1985. In 1977 dollars, the council's estimate is $24.4 billion in annual outlays in addition to those costs that would be borne without environmental regulation, and $34.9 billion for all costs, whether or not they are in response to regulation.[26]

The above cost estimates exclude mobile sources, although the costs of controlling these sources now exceed those of stationary ones. In addition, these estimates ignore the costs of public water treatment and solid waste management because these are largely funded from general revenues with little effect on the price level.

Denison's estimate of the incremental cost of pollution abatement to nonresidential business mandated by the Environmental Protection

26. *Environmental Quality—1977, The Eighth Annual Report of the Council on Environmental Quality* (December 1977).

Agency and state and local authorities is $9.55 billion for 1975, or approximately 0.7 percent of the net national product.[27] This is a remarkably small total, given the pervasiveness of environmental regulation and the above estimates. In part, its small size indicates that many enforcement deadlines for environmental standards had not yet been reached in 1975. As table 10 suggests, these outlays will rise substantially in the next few years.

In summary, the prospective costs of environmental, health, and safety regulation will undoubtedly be large by the middle of the next decade. In many cases, such as control of air emissions from stationary sources, the costs may be substantially less than the prospective benefits, but in others —such as control of mobile sources—the evidence is far less conclusive. Regardless of the merit of the strictness of environmental or social controls, the experience of OSHA and the Environmental Protection Agency in setting standards suggests that there may be considerable room for reducing the cost of achieving the desired benefit levels. A few examples of recent or pending decisions will serve to highlight the absence of cost-effectiveness in regulatory decisionmaking in various agencies.

Occupational Exposure to Coke-Oven Emissions. The standards promulgated by OSHA for coke-oven emissions are illustrative of the tendency for regulators to specify engineering standards (mandating the installation of given equipment) rather than performance standards (specifying the maximum allowed rate of exposure to the risk in question). In this case, OSHA opted for specific engineering controls instead of a combination of work practices and personal protective devices (respirators). The latter strategy would have been much less expensive but less easily enforced. Respirators are uncomfortable and are therefore likely to be ignored by many workers for substantial periods of time. As a result, OSHA requires them only when the engineering controls fail to achieve a desired maximum emissions level. If they were required for all workers, regardless of the effectiveness of the engineering controls, greater protection would be afforded the exposed population. On the other hand, if they were required as a substitute for the engineering controls, the annual cost of the standard would have been substantially less than $8,900 per protected worker.

Segregated Ballast. The Carter administration proposed in April 1977

27. This is an "incremental" cost over and above the expenditures firms would have undertaken in the absence of recent environmental legislation.

that all tankers serving the U.S. market should be required to segregate ballast from cargo. This regulation would apply to both existing and new ships. The cost of retrofitting ships and the effect of reducing capacity because of that retrofitting will be an estimated $360 million a year based on the administration's initial proposal. This cost would be incurred despite the availability of other less expensive techniques for controlling marine pollution.

National Forest Policy. The current timber policy of the Department of Agriculture has led to a substantial underutilization of the national forests. While the department is required by law to limit the number of trees that can be cut from these national forests to a level no greater than the long-run sustainable yield, temporary increases could be permitted in the cut of mature trees without any reduction in the long-run yield from younger, faster growing ones. However, environmental pressures have succeeded in preventing the Forest Service from increasing the cut in this manner. As a result, the supply of timber from national forests has not grown; it actually decreased by approximately 17 percent between 1970 and 1976.[28] It is difficult to estimate how much of an increase in the cut from national forests could be both economically feasible and consistent with the current timber policy requiring a nondeclining yield. Much of the underutilized timber is in wilderness areas that are expensive to exploit and valuable as environmental preserves. If the cut could be increased by at least 10 percent without violating the 1976 National Forest Management Act (and without exceeding the 1969 cut), the price of timber would decline by at least 3 percent, assuming a demand elasticity of -0.5, a 1.8 percent decline in private forest output, and a decrease in net imports of 0.4 percent. The impact would be to lower timber costs by approximately $300 million annually.

Passive Restraint Systems for Automobiles.[29] In 1977, the secretary of transportation announced a decision to require passive restraint systems for all front-seat positions on all new passenger cars, beginning with selected size classes in 1981. The decision, while not as costly as one that mandates air bags, will require at least passive safety belts at about $25 per car more than present belt systems. Alternatively, the Department of

28. These and the following estimates are drawn from the Council on Wage and Price Stability, *Lumber Prices and the Lumber Products Industry,* Interim Report (The Council, October 1977).

29. Air bags or passive safety belts.

Transportation has estimated the cost of air bags to be between $100 and $200 more than the present belt systems. The total cost of the standard, therefore, is between $250 million and $2 billion a year.[30] This standard was adopted despite evidence that safety belts were the most effective safety devices. If air bags diminish seat belt usage, the standard could increase highway fatalities.

"Rolled-in" Pricing of Natural Gas. The Federal Power Commission (now the Federal Energy Regulatory Commission) has issued initial rulings that imports of liquid natural gas may be rolled in with gas purchased domestically by pipelines so that the imported liquid natural gas does not reach final buyers at its true incremental acquisition price. The practical effect of this policy in a world in which domestic field prices are being regulated and customers are allocated the gas at less than market equilibrium prices is to transfer the rents from domestic owners of "old" natural gas to foreign producers or their agents. At present, it is difficult to place a cost on the policy of rolling in imported liquid natural gas at prices as high as $5.27 per thousand cubic feet because the full extent of importation has not yet been realized; approximately 5 percent of natural gas is now imported. The potential cost of this policy is equal to the difference between the full equilibrium market value of domestic gas and the regulated cost of this gas.[31] This difference is roughly $36 billion per year, or 2.2 percent of the gross private domestic product in 1977.[32]

Multiple-Point Source Regulation: Guidelines for Iron and Steel Effluents. In the absence of sophisticated monitoring techniques, the Environmental Protection Agency has promulgated regulations for both water and air emissions based on engineering performance standards for equipment at each "source" in an industrial complex. Because the goal of environmental controls is to reduce total emissions or discharges per unit of time, it would seem more efficient to specify emission levels (or pollution taxes) for entire industrial facilities and even to allow trading of rights between different companies in the same area.

30. This cost would not enter the consumer price index because the restraint systems are considered quality improvements by the Bureau of Labor Statistics. To the extent that air bags reduce the severity of accidents, they should reduce insurance rates as well.

31. The equilibrium market value of gas is assumed to be equal to $2.40 per thousand cubic feet.

32. Estimate based on data on prices and consumption in U.S. Department of Energy, *Monthly Energy Review,* various issues.

The effect of the Environmental Protection Agency's detailed approach to regulation may be illustrated by the guidelines for iron and steel effluents proposed in March 1976. A study by the Council on Wage and Price Stability found that the standards for removal of total suspended solids proposed for 1983 produced incremental costs for meeting the single standard that were nine times as high for some parts of a plant's operation as for other parts.[33] Clearly, a rational management, if allowed to minimize its costs in meeting an overall standard for an entire plant, would not allow the incremental costs to diverge so widely across various point sources. The same environmental cleanliness could thus be purchased at much lower costs if the Environmental Protection Agency would set standards for an entire plant as a unit.

Mandate for Best-Available-Control Technology in the Clean Air Act Amendments of 1977. In 1977, the Congress amended the Clean Air Act in several ways, one of which was to require the Environmental Protection Agency to mandate the "reasonably best available control technology" for emissions from all new stationary sources.[34] This requirement places the emphasis on the reduction in pollution, particularly sulfur, rather than on the *level* of sulfur emissions. Hence, it requires the Environmental Protection Agency to mandate the use of scrubbing (or another specific technology) in combination with virtually any type of coal. This means that a utility no longer will be given the choice between burning low-sulfur coal or scrubbing the stack gases from combustion of higher-sulfur coals. The goal of those proposing the amendment was to stimulate the demand for eastern and midwestern coal because previous standards for new sources (1.2 lbs of sulfur per million Btu) would lead to the importation of cheap, low-Btu, low-sulfur coal from western mining regions to north-central locations. The Environmental Protection Agency has not yet issued its standards for new sources to conform with this requirement, but it is likely to cost four to eight times as much per incremental ton of sulfur removed as the cost in the sulfuric acid or non-ferrous metals industries. The additional costs may therefore be between $1 billion and $2 billion annually.

33. See "Effluent Guidelines and Standards for Existing and New Sources in the Iron and Steel Manufacturing Point Source Category 40 C.F.R. 420," Comments of the Council on Wage and Price Stability before the Environmental Protection Agency (June 24, 1976; processed).
34. 91 Stat. 712.

IMPROVING REGULATION: A STRUCTURAL APPROACH

The preceding examples of regulation illustrate prospective policies with potentially important impacts on the price level. In many cases, they reflect political decisions of regulators who have little incentive to equate incremental social costs to prospective benefits. Allowing or disallowing a rate increase does not affect a regulator's budget. Similarly, the cost-effectiveness of social regulation is not systematically measured by the agencies promulgating the regulations, by the Office of Management and Budget, or by the Congress. As a result, administrators have little incentive to spend their agencies' scarce resources in the pursuit of economically efficient regulation. Invoking public health and safety is often sufficient to blunt the thrust of any critic who claims that the costs are too large for the benefits derived.

Faced with these obvious problems, the Ford and Carter administrations have attempted to require economic analysis from executive department regulatory agencies. President Ford launched the "inflation impact" program in November 1974. Under this program, each agency within the executive branch was required to prepare an economic assessment of the effects of major regulations—generally those with an aggregate impact of $100 million for one year or $150 million for two years. These analyses were intended to serve as a check on the efficiency of the regulations, but they did not achieve the planned result. Many agencies virtually ignored the program, while others perfunctorily had contractors perform the studies.[35] These analyses influenced agency decisionmaking in only a few cases. Moreover, they became the source of heated debate concerning the intent of the program. A congressional report suggested that cost-benefit estimates required in such analyses are counterproductive because they are likely to be biased and impossible to undertake with precision.[36]

35. For details of agency compliance, see the joint evaluation of the inflation impact program by the Council on Wage and Price Stability and the Office of Management and Budget, "An Evaluation of the Inflation Impact Statement Program," prepared for the Economic Policy Board (December 7, 1976; processed).

36. *Federal Regulation and Regulatory Reform,* Report by the Subcommittee on Oversight and Investigations of the House Committee on Interstate and Foreign Commerce, 94:2 (GPO, 1976).

In this climate of congressional hostility to the cost-benefit approach, regulators have not been pressing the frontiers of applied economic analysis. Nevertheless, the Carter administration has announced a policy of requiring economic impact analyses from each agency for major decisions. Less emphasis is placed on the benefit side of cost-benefit analysis, but the intent is similar to that of the inflation-impact program. Because administrators of the important agencies will continue to have little incentive to perform these analyses well, this policy is not likely to meet the goals set for it.

How could government regulation of health, safety, and environment be made more efficient and thus less "inflationary"? The only approach that will work must tie the economic efficiency of regulations to the agency's budget constraint. This could be done either by reversing the ownership of property rights in question or by developing a new "shadow" budget for each agency, by which it is limited to a specified amount of society's resources each year.

Reversing the Ownership of Property Rights. The suggestions that polluters should be compensated for reducing pollution or paid to increase worker or product safety are not new ones. Whether such mechanisms could work has been discussed at length by Coase and others.[37] As long as there are multiple sources of each externality in a given location, there could be a "market" with a regulatory agency as buyer—representing workers, residents, or consumers—and the producers of the externality as sellers. Presumably such a market would only require the buyer to calculate the clients' reservation price for the externality and to submit a bid for it at that price. If, however, there were few sellers of the externality in a location, the reversal of property rights might not work efficiently because of the possibility of monopolistic control.

Reversing property rights creates yet another problem. The supply of the offensive externality varies with the ownership of the property right. If the government owned the rights, for example, any new emitter of pollution would have to purchase those rights from it at a specified fee or under specified conditions or regulation. If the ownership resided with owners or lessees of land adjacent to the water or air in question, the supply of the undesired externality would become potentially unlimited.

37. R. H. Coase, "The Problem of Social Cost," *Journal of Law and Economics,* vol. 3 (October 1960), pp. 1–44.

Threats to pollute could be increased without limit in order to gain revenues from the public authority.

A solution to this problem is to pay the polluters for permanent reductions in their discharge rate and use this payment rate as the tax rate for new sources. The partial reversal of property rights would mean that large budget outlays would have to be made by the regulatory authorities to reduce these externalities. Increases in the price of pollution would mean that pollution from new sources would be less attractive, but only at a cost to the regulator. Moreover, the regulator would now search for the strategy with the lowest cost for reducing the externality to maximize his achievements for any given budget.

Use of Shadow Budgets. The most practical possibility for confronting regulators with the costs of their actions would be to construct a shadow budget to cover the resources that the agency requires private agents to consume in the pursuit of the regulatory goal. An agency such as the Office of Management and Budget would have to administer such a system, but Congress could specify the size of the budgets for each agency or even each program. Administrators would not be told how to value the benefits of the dangers they presumably would reduce. Instead, there would be a limitation on the cost that they could impose on firms in a given year; their function would then be to maximize the benefits of their regulations subject to that limitation. These cost limitations would be publicized each year in the budget message and would therefore be more visible to the public, which, in turn, would be less likely to assume that regulatory costs are minimal.

The administration of such a system would not be easy, for someone would have to arbitrate the differences in the estimates of costs. These estimates probably would be undertaken by a competent staff close to the administrator of each agency because his total accomplishments would be limited by the magnitude of the costs of each regulation. An inefficient choice of regulations in one area would reduce his ability to promulgate regulations in others. In addition, there would be much greater interest in equating the incremental costs of controlling the same externality from different sources. Because these costs are difficult to estimate ex ante, there should be provisions for carrying back and carrying forward cost limitations in each budget. Costs could be estimated ex post, and the difference between the estimates could be deducted from the budget of the current year in the case of cost overruns or added to the budget in the case of earlier overestimates of costs. A discount rate could even be applied to such carryovers.

FUTURE PROSPECTS

No proposal that fails to alter the incentives of regulators will cause the protectors of the environment, the guardians of carcinogens, or the preventers of highway deaths to take economics as seriously as they should. Present incentives, combined with imprecise statutory language about economic efficacy, cause administrators to be concerned with major, localized employment reductions (often through plant closings) rather than with other economic effects. A price mechanism or a budgetary process would change this system of incentives and have potentially salutary effects on the price level.

Foreign Trade Restrictions

A classic example of government support of prices to redistribute income can be found in trade policy. It allows the government to protect an industry and its employees without direct budget outlays. Protectionism is likely to be sought and granted during periods of economic recession or declining comparative advantage for individual industries. It is not surprising, therefore, that since 1975 there have been numerous new protectionist pleas from industries such as steel, textiles, footwear, electronics, copper, and zinc. Many of these pleas have led to successful rulings in cases presented before the International Trade Commission.

The costs and benefits of the major examples of trade relief granted by the commission or the administration from 1975 to 1977 are indicated in table 11. Each of these actions—tariffs, quotas, or minimum requirements for import prices—generates significant price effects. The estimate for steel may underestimate the total effects of trade protection, given the prospects of further voluntary reductions of exports to the United States. The price increase for sugar is the largest and thus affords the greatest amount of protection. The International Trade Commission's decisions for footwear and television sets have been replaced by "orderly marketing agreements," which may be less severe than the costs of the commission's original recommendations. The costs of these recommenda-

Table 11. The Effect of Recent Extensions of Trade Protection, 1975–77

			Annual total cost of protection			
			Millions of 1977 dollars		*1977 dollars*	
Commodity affected by extension	*Increase in jobs (number)*	*Increase in price (percent)*	*Cost to consumers*	*Deadweight loss*	*Consumer cost per job gained*	*Deadweight loss per job gained*
Sugar[a]	n.a.	28.6	660	56.6	n.a.	n.a.
Carbon steel[a]	20,000	3.0	1,254	105.5	62,700	5,275
Meat	n.a.	2–4	400–800	4.7–18.9	n.a.	n.a.
Initial ITC recommendations[b]						
Television sets	9,170	20.0	500	116.0	54,526	12,650
Footwear	21,000	20.0	1,200	75.0	57,143	3,571

Sources: Based on data in "Comments of the Council on Wage and Price Stability," submitted to the International Trade Commission, meat investigations TA-201-25 and 332-85 (CWPS-252, July 12, 1977); ibid., submitted to the ITC, television receivers investigation TA-201-19 (CWPS-227, January 18, 1977); and ibid., testimony before the ITC, docket TA-201-18 (importation of footwear) (CWPS-217, December 7, 1976).

n.a. Not available.

a. Author's estimates.

b. These recommendations were not implemented in full but were replaced by orderly marketing agreements, for which the cost estimates are not available. The costs of the initial recommendations by the International Trade Commission shown in the table are presumably upper limits of the ultimate costs of the agreements.

tions are included to demonstrate the degree of trade protection possible. The effect of the orderly marketing agreements cannot be estimated with data presently available. Excluded from the table are high tariff or non-tariff barriers from decisions reached in earlier years, such as those affecting textiles, because these have been fully accommodated by the market and are unlikely to be eased.

The cost of trade protection is generally large in relation to the increase in employment generated. In those cases for which data are available the average cost to consumers for each job protected is more than $50,000 a year. Deadweight losses are also large, ranging up to $12,650 per additional job per year.

If the intent of Congress is to protect inefficient U.S. industry, it is difficult to see how the above costs can be reduced materially. However, if protection is seen as a temporary political response to the employment difficulties created for a small number of workers, a less inflationary and less costly form of income support is available.

Temporary subsidies to labor could be made available in affected industries, although these subsidies should probably decline in time to insure that inefficient U.S. industry is not perpetuated unnecessarily. Moreover, the subsidies must not be in effect so long that they distort investment and production decisions. Lowering the cost of labor for an industry that is losing comparative advantage could lead to the creation of additional capacity and to the substitution of labor for capital. These effects would simply compound the difficulties of eventual adjustment to changes in comparative advantage.

Subsidies to labor could be targeted at those employees most likely to be laid off because of import competition, but such identification is undoubtedly difficult. Moreover, substitution would take place between subsidized and unsubsidized workers. As a result, a subsidy policy would probably have to be general to the industry. Assume that Congress decided that rehiring 20,000 steelworkers was desirable in 1977, and that a subsidy was offered to steel firms for all employees. Given approximately 360,000 hourly workers in the industry, an annual subsidy of more than $3,750 could be paid for every employee in the industry, and the total cost would be no higher than that of the import policy of the Trade Act of 1974. This would reduce the hourly cost of labor by approximately 14 percent, which should be sufficient to induce a 5.6 percent increase in employment. Moreover, the cost of steel would not be raised by this form of assistance.

Traditional trade assistance is designed to ease the transition of workers and firms to new lines of activity after import competition has affected them. Workers or employers are not provided benefits until excess capacity and unemployment becomes a reality. The Trade Act of 1974 liberalized the eligibility criteria for adjustment assistance and appeared to recommend that assistance rather than trade restrictions.[38]

Although trade adjustment assistance for employees can amount to as much as 70 percent of forgone wages, such assistance generally offsets only a small share of the capital losses suffered by a firm that has lost its market to imports. Both employers and employees will generally gain more from trade protection than from assistance. Thus, the assistance allowed under the 1974 Trade Act has not reduced protectionist pressures.

38. See Charles R. Frank, Jr., *Foreign Trade and Domestic Aid* (Brookings Institution, 1977), chaps. 4, 5.

The Minimum Wage

The minimum wage is an excellent example of the use of price-enhancing legislation to redistribute income in a manner that cannot be sustained politically through direct government payments. The beneficiaries of a legislated minimum wage are not principally the low-wage, low-income population, but a number of groups who compete in the labor market with these less fortunate workers.

At the beginning of the Carter administration, the AFL-CIO launched a major effort to increase the minimum wage from $2.30 an hour, which was established for 1976 as a result of the Fair Labor Standards Amendments of 1974. The minimum wage level, which had averaged 52 percent of straight-time (nonovertime) hourly earnings in manufacturing in the last half of the 1960s, had fallen to 44 percent of this benchmark by January 1977. There were proposals to increase it gradually by indexing it to the average manufacturing wage. Alternatively, one proposal given serious consideration (the Dent bill) would have raised the minimum wage to 60 percent of the manufacturing wage by January 1978.

The final legislation, the Fair Labor Standards Amendments of 1977, which became effective in November, raised the minimum to $2.65 an hour in January 1978, $2.90 in January 1979, $3.10 in January 1980, and $3.35 in January 1981. This replaced a Senate proposal to index the wage to 52 percent of the straight-time average hourly earnings of production workers in manufacturing in January 1979 and 53 percent in January 1980.[39] At the time of passage, these percentages were projected to yield minimum wages equal to those finally legislated. Thus, the final Senate and House agreement merely replaced the indexation approach with equivalent projected wages.[40]

None of the innovative suggestions designed to reduce the impact of the minimum wage on the employability ot low-income teen-agers was

39. *Fair Labor Standards Amendments of 1977,* S. Rept. 95-440, 95:1 (GPO, 1977).

40. There are a few other minor changes in the minimum wage. The tip credit is being reduced gradually from 50 percent to 40 percent. The exemption for small retail and service establishments is being gradually liberalized. The act also introduces a simplified form for certificating students.

adopted. The Senate report argues that there are no employment effects. Economic studies generally show just the opposite—that increases in the minimum wage result in unemployment for low-wage workers. Edward Gramlich shows that these effects may not be large and, with unemployment insurance, may not reduce the welfare of low-wage adult workers.[41] But minimum wages have a most undesirable effect on teen-agers, shifting employment from full-time to part-time work.

To estimate the price effects of the increased minimum wage, I employ Gramlich's result—that each 1 percent increase in the minimum wage increases average wages by 0.032 percent. The first-year increase to $2.65 an hour is a 15.2 percent rise, which should increase average wages in 1978 by 0.5 percent. This will produce an estimated increase in total private wages and salaries of approximately $3 billion.

If the purpose of enacting a minimum wage is to increase the income of low-wage workers, more efficient strategies could be found that would not adversely affect the price level or employment. A wage subsidy program, such as the one announced by the administration in its urban program, could be paid to those firms employing workers from certified low-income families. This would target the program at the desired population rather than raise the wage for teen-agers from high-income families who may be working in jobs near the minimum wage level. The only major drawback to such a program may be its tendency to induce employers to substitute eligible potential workers for existing workers, some of whom may only be marginally above the poverty level. But such a program financed from general revenues would have avoided increasing labor costs by $3 billion in 1978.

Other Policy Initiatives

The government could also undertake a number of other initiatives, a few of which are summarized in this section. Some proposals, such as hospital cost control, might have significant effects on the price level; others, such as pursuing a more aggressive antitrust policy, are likely to have less impact.

41. Edward M. Gramlich, "Impact of Minimum Wages on Other Wages, Employment, and Family Incomes," *BPEA, 2:1976,* pp. 409–51.

HOSPITAL COST CONTROL

Hospital cost containment, a regulatory policy designed to have salutary effects on the price level, was advocated by the Carter administration in 1977, but it has failed to win the support of the Congress. Because of the tax deductibility of health insurance, the lack of coinsurance and deductibility provisions in insurance payment policies, and the absence of market competition among hospitals, there is little market discipline in the provision of hospital services. Without any restraining forces, expenditures for hospital care have recently been rising at an annual rate of about 15 percent a year. A hospital cost-containment policy limiting the rate of growth in hospital revenues to the rate of increase in the gross national product deflator plus one-third the difference between the recent average annual rate of growth in hospital expenditures and the GNP deflator (approximately 3 percent) would have reduced the growth in hospital expenditures by 2.6 percent if it had begun in fiscal year 1978. Assuming that 80 percent of the reduction would be reflected as price changes, the net saving would be 2.1 percent of $72 billion, or $1.5 billion (in fiscal year 1978 dollars).

RESTRAINT IN FEDERAL PAY INCREASES

A large budget item for the federal government is its nondefense payroll—approximately $22.5 billion in 1977. These wages do not, however, enter directly into costs and prices; hence, reducing them or restraining the government's annual cost-of-living increases will not directly reduce the private deflator or the consumer price index. A reduction in the increase to be granted this year could, however, have some impact on wages in the private sector through its effect on wage demands and offers in skill markets in which government workers participate. (Moreover, any policy to limit these increases could provide a salutary example of broader wage-price policies.) The magnitude of this impact on wages in the private sector cannot be determined in a paper of this scope.

One suggestion offered to the President is that he reduce the annual increase by 0.5 to 1.0 percentage point from the target submitted to him based on "comparability" with the private sector. This reduction might be applauded, given recent evidence that federal workers are now paid

13 to 20 percent more than their counterparts in the private sector.[42] Based on the 1977 level of federal compensation of nondefense employees, the saving from such a cut would be in the range of $112 million to $225 million annually.

AGGRESSIVE ANTITRUST POLICY

A common view of inflation in the past few years has been that monetary and fiscal authorities are unwilling to hold nominal GNP to a steady growth rate in the face of sharp increases in oil, agricultural, or other commodity prices. Instead, they have been accommodating, allowing nominal GNP to rise as a result of these disruptive changes. Forcing other prices and wages downward through restrictive monetary and fiscal policies generates huge welfare losses in the form of unemployed resources, which occur because of the general inflexibility of these other wages and prices. The transitional costs of this unemployment are too much for a politically responsive administration to bear.

But if it is this inflexibility of wages and prices that so limits traditional policy tools, could some structural remedies be provided to increase price-wage flexibility? There are several reasons why the answer to such a question is decidedly negative.

First, the empirical evidence on the effects of concentration on price flexibility is at best mixed.[43] While there is some evidence that prices respond more slowly to changes in demand in moderately concentrated industries than in atomistic or highly concentrated industries, this pattern has not been consistent over successive business cycles.

Equally important is the sectoral structure of the U.S. economy. In 1976, more than one-fourth of all national income originated in government and regulated industries.[44] While some of these latter industries may

42. Sharon P. Smith, *Equal Pay in the Public Sector: Fact or Fantasy* (Princeton University, Industrial Relations Section, 1977), p. 132.

43. See Ralph E. Beals, "Concentrated Industries, Administered Prices and Inflation: A Survey of Recent Empirical Research" (Council on Wage and Price Stability, 1975; processed); and Phillip Cagan, "Changes in the Recession Behavior of Wholesale Prices in the 1920's and Post-World War II," *Explorations in Economic Research*, vol. 2 (Winter 1975), pp. 54–104.

44. Estimates of the sectoral structure are based on national income without capital consumption adjustment by industry. *Survey of Current Business*, vol. 57 (July 1977).

become more competitive over the next few years (stock brokerage and air transportation), there is little chance that much of this 26 percent will move to a nonregulated, competitive category with flexible wages and prices. Moreover, a good deal of mining and manufacturing—particularly the energy industries—may become less competitive as government regulation continues to supplant market forces.

Of the remaining 74 percent of national income, roughly 44 percent is currently derived from basically competitive sectors: wholesale and retail trade, most services, agriculture, and construction. There are concentrated industries within these categories, although competitive reform is unlikely to occur there.

Serious attempts to increase competition could possibly succeed in mining and manufacturing, which comprise only 27.5 percent of total national income. Manufacturing is already rather unconcentrated: only 1.8 percent of value added in manufacturing is found in industries in which the four-firm concentration ratio exceeds 67 percent. Another 18 percent derives from industries with concentration ratios between 50 and 66 percent. Antitrust policy aimed at less-concentrated industries would be exceedingly difficult to implement and might be counterproductive if the resulting firms were operating below their most efficient output level.

A Summary of Policy Proposals

As this paper has shown, a number of proposed policies could be launched as part of the effort to reduce the price level, while pursuing the search for the appropriate longer-run policy to control inflation. Given the heterogeneous nature of the proposals offered, it is difficult to summarize them neatly or concisely. Some cannot be quantified on the basis of present evidence and within the scope of this paper. Others could be modified in a number of ways to satisfy other policy goals and at the same time could have some beneficial effects on the price level. The effects of some prospective policies that can be quantified are tabulated in table 12.

Clearly, the largest potential effects—assuming the difference in incidence between direct and indirect taxation—are to be found in altering social security and sales taxation. The substitution of direct taxes for indirect state taxes could produce a 1.6 percent decline in the private

Table 12. Summary of Policy Proposals to Reduce the Price Level

	Potential reduction	
Proposal	Annual amount (billions of 1977 dollars)	In gross private domestic deflator (percent)
Social security		
Replace employer and employee payroll taxes with general revenue financing for disability and health insurance (fiscal 1979)	14.6	0.7ᵃ
Sales taxes		
Reduce state sales taxes up to 2 percentage points of personal income	27.4	1.6
Replace federal excise taxes with direct taxes	17.4	1.0
Agriculture		
Substitute deficiency payments for 1977–78 wheat, feed grain, soybean, milk initiatives	3.6	0.2
Substitute deficiency payments for set-aside proposals designed to raise farm income by $4.4 billionᵇ	4.4	0.3
Government regulation		
Pursue deregulation of airlines, trucking, and the coastal maritime trade	5.3 to 10.4	0.3 to 0.6
Impose a shadow budget on social regulatory agencies	Unmeasurable with present data	...
Increase federal timber cut	0.3	0.02
Require fully incremental costing of all imported liquid and synthetic natural gas	Unknown, but up to 36.0	Up to 2.2
Reassess best-available-control-technology amendment to Clean Air Act	1.0 to 2.0	0.06 to 0.12
Foreign trade		
Substitute direct subsidies for meat, steel, and sugar import restraints	2.3 to 2.7	0.1 to 0.2
Minimum wage		
Replace 1978 minimum-wage increase with employment incentives	3.1	0.2
Hospital cost control		
Impose limited cost controls (fiscal 1978)	1.5	0.09

Source: Compiled from information in the text.
a. Based on projection of fiscal 1979 gross domestic private product.
b. This is approximately the effect of some agricultural legislation being considered in the Congress as of this writing.

domestic deflator. General revenue financing of disability insurance and health insurance funding in social security could lead to another 0.7 percent decline in fiscal 1979.

The remaining policy initiatives are perhaps less important in terms of their prospective effects on the price level, but each one is to be strongly recommended on grounds of economic efficiency and internal consistency between stated policy goals and their attainment. For instance, changes in agricultural policy that would stress income supports instead of price supports could reduce the private deflator by a total of 0.2 percent (for the 1977–78 changes in agricultural policy), but such changes would also allow market forces to allocate agricultural resources far more efficiently. Avoiding the price increases in proposals now before the Congress would prevent another 0.3 percent rise in the deflator.

A reform of the basic constraints on regulatory agencies might have relatively minor effects on the price level (while increasing the benefits from reducing undesirable externalities), but it would improve the efficiency of regulators in mandating the flow of scarce resources for social purposes. Reform of transportation could lower the private domestic deflator by as much as 0.6 percent (without calculating any effect upon railroad rates), and it would clearly reduce economic waste in this vital sector of the economy.

Minor changes such as increasing the timber cut on federal lands or instructing the Federal Energy Regulatory Commission to pursue incremental pricing of synthetic natural gas or imported liquid natural gas would have relatively immediate effects upon the price level, but the latter policy could have much greater long-term benefits. Similarly, hospital cost control would not have a major impact on the price level, compared with other initiatives, but it would reduce the excessive flow of resources to a sector that is not governed by usual market forces.

A change from protectionism to adjustment assistance has been prescribed elsewhere. A reversal of the recent extensions of protection would have relatively small effects on the price level, but if older restraints (such as those applying to textiles and clothing) were replaced, the effect could be much greater. And the efficiency gains would be large if trade protection were removed in favor of easing the burden on displaced workers and capital.

Finally, the increases in the minimum wage legislated in 1977 could be repealed in favor of programs that more effectively and efficiently redistribute labor incomes. The effects on the price level of this change would be substantial as would the prospective effects on employment of teenagers.

None of these proposals solves the inflation problem, but a combination of a number of them might reduce the rate of increase in the price level for some time. They may be especially useful as part of a broader program aimed at wage-price moderation. Even if the effect of these initiatives on inflation proves to be minor or short-lived, most would have salutary effects on economic efficiency. The increase in gross national product should certainly be greater than the administrative and transitional costs required to put these reforms into effect.

Comments
and Discussion

Edward M. Gramlich: Robert Crandall has written a most useful species of what in government parlance might be called an options paper. He reviews a wide variety of actions the government could take to reduce price levels—many of these in fact reversing actions already taken to increase price levels—and provides the benefits and costs of these suggested actions and their effect on overall prices. In general, most of the actions appear to be attractive for their efficiency gains as well as for their inflation-reducing impact.

Because inflation is the subject of the conference, I begin by commenting on the relationship between one-shot reductions in the price level and inflation reductions. Assume the two-equation mainline model of backward-looking inflation (similar to the model in George Perry's paper and also used by Arthur Okun):

$$\frac{\Delta P}{P} = \frac{\Delta W}{W} - b$$

$$\frac{\Delta W}{W} = a_0 + a_1 \left(\frac{\Delta P}{P}\right)_{-1} + a_2 \left(\frac{\Delta W}{W}\right)_{-1},$$

where P refers to prices and W to wages. The parameter a_0 depends on unemployment, other proxies for demand, or both, and perhaps it also depends on whether a tax-based incomes policy exists. I assume that a_0 (and implicitly unemployment) is fixed because I am not considering demand: in particular, this implies that the one-shot increase in real money that follows any one-shot reduction in price levels is neutralized. The parameters a_1 and a_2 divide backward-looking inflation into price-wage and wage-wage components, and may either sum to one (if the model were accelerationist) or not. Most of the policies Crandall describes can be viewed as one-shot, nonmaintained increases in the shift parameter b.

It can be shown that if the model were accelerationist ($a_1 + a_2 = 1$), the permanent impact on the rate of inflation of a unit change in b would be a_1, the price-wage feedback component of the accelerationist model. If the model were not accelerationist ($a_1 + a_2 < 1$), there would be no permanent reduction in the rate of inflation, although for any path of real output, inflation will be slower for a number of periods, with the amount of slowdown declining in each period. If the model were forward looking, it is doubtful that there would be any price effect on wages. And there would be none if inertia were entirely a wage-wage process. Hence, it takes a rather particular view of inflation to translate one-shot price level reductions into significant permanent inflation reductions—it has to be accelerationist, backward looking, and primarily a price-wage type all at the same time. While many empirical models actually have this form, as Perry's paper indicated, that may be because with real world data it is difficult to draw a fine distinction between this form and others. But many people would question the applicability of this model of inflation in the case of one-shot, nonrecurring changes in price levels. If that is the case, the inflation-reducing potential of the measures Crandall discusses could be quite modest, although some of the measures may still be an important part of a whole package geared to alter near-term inflationary expectations in the United States in 1978.

My biggest surprise concerning the measures was the low potential given to antitrust policy. This results primarily from simple multiplication—only 27.5 percent of national income is generated in the relatively concentrated unregulated manufacturing and mining sectors, and less than 20 percent of that portion is concentrated. Moreover, after a possible one-shot reduction in price levels, all that could be expected from antitrust policy would be an increase in price flexibility, and this would be anti-inflationary on balance only when the unemployment rate averaged above the nonaccelerating rate of unemployment. Hence, apart from the subtleties that Crandall does not discuss—price leadership reactions and the fact that pass-through may not be dollar-for-dollar but may be disproportionately influenced by industries early in the production chain —there seems to be relatively little possibility of gain.

The most promising measure Crandall considers is the reduction of payroll tax rates by financing the disability and hospitalization portions of social security through general revenues. If done completely, this would reduce employer contributions by $14.6 billion in fiscal 1979 and, if shifted forward completely, it would lower price levels by as much as 0.7 percent. Whether the price reduction is this large or not, and the inflation reduction is permanent or temporary, such a measure clearly seems desirable on grounds of both economic efficiency and distributional equity.

The other potentially significant action, at least in dollar terms, is Okun's proposal for a general sales tax reduction. This one is not as appealing once Crandall holds it up to close inspection. There is not much scope for reducing federal excise taxes; the only important one remaining that is not justified by an obvious social externality is the telephone excise. There is no obvious reason why this should not be cut, but it will not amount to much in dollar terms. The bigger game is for state sales taxes: when, say, state sales taxes up to 2 percent of personal income are replaced with a combination of federal and state and local income taxes, price levels would be reduced as much as 1.6 percent or $27 billion in 1977. Crandall divides the replacement equally between the state and the federal income tax, but I believe the present state preference for sales taxes would be less strong than this implies, and the federal government should be able to accomplish its end with a grant of less than $13 billion. The calculation can be made even more attractive: because sales tax rates are rising over time, if a reduced rate had to be maintained, the effect on price levels would grow through time. But there is a fundamental and important problem with the measure that goes back to the difference between levels and rates of price changes: presumably to gain this revenue shift, the federal government would have to make continuing grant payments. Assuming only a modest permanent reduction in inflation rates from this policy, in 1982 the federal government would still be paying for a temporary reduction in the price level of 1978, while realizing little change in the 1982 inflation rate. The federal government could always stop payment, but then what is to prevent states from restoring their sales tax? Is the federal government, after stopping payments, going to sue states that got money back in 1978 but now in 1982 let sales tax rates rise again? If so, the government will have to write it into the law now, and then I think the odds that states will accept the grant and this future constraint on their fiscal policies are drastically reduced.

Finally, I would like to comment on the proposals Crandall considers for social and environmental regulation. I fully agree with him that there is a structural imbalance in the process for making these decisions: unlike most other programs where the cost is an observed budget cost and the antagonist is the Office of Management and Budget, social and environmental regulations impose unobserved social costs with no natural antagonists. Something should be done at least to factor these social costs into the decisionmaking process, but exactly *what* is unclear.

Crandall reviews two options, one of which I do not like and one I do. These options are reversing property rights, or making the government buy nonpollution from polluters, and providing regulators with a shadow budget. Crandall rejects the first as politically impossible. I would reject it as just plain wrong. To keep government costs down it is necessary to adopt an approach such as buying nonpollution only from current-day polluters; otherwise, anybody could say that they were intending to pollute and receive a payment for not doing so. Even this limited scheme has the disadvantage of rewarding those who behave in a socially undesirable manner. However, the second option—allowing an agency such as the Office of Management and Budget (OMB) to monitor social costs as well as budget costs—seems to me to be a great idea. A potential argument against it is that social costs are more difficult to estimate than budget costs; but it is not obvious that this is true or relevant. Costs of new programs (such as Medicaid and the C5A plane) are always difficult to estimate, and benefits cause even more problems. But if it is a budget expenditure, people tend to plunge ahead anyway, making decisions as well as they can. I see no underlying efficiency or equity differences between the average social expenditure program and the average social regulation program: in both cases, benefits are possibly important but often vague and unmeasurable, and costs can be stated in terms of resources given up —whether these resources are taxed away or are required to be spent on safety or antipollution. And in both cases, OMB might be the natural watchdog. Why not simply broaden the charter of OMB, have it ask all agencies for an estimate of the nonbudget costs of their regulatory actions, and then let the expanded budget process work as the regular process does now? This will not constrain new regulation programs any more than it now limits new budget programs. If the benefits of a regulation program are substantial and the costs minimal, the program ought to be successful. But the new procedure could alter a decision process that now ignores the social costs of regulation programs, national health insurance, and the like.

Robert E. Hall: Crandall's paper provides an opportunity to discuss the effectiveness of policies to reduce the consumer price index by shifting government finance from indirect to the direct taxation of income. The paper is written as if this were desirable on the grounds that it would give a temporary respite from inflation. I think that most participants at this meeting agree.

I find the argument for moving toward more taxation of income less convincing. It seems to me that the argument rests on an illusion created by the conventions of the CPI, which includes excise taxes and government-mandated high prices, but does not measure the adverse effect of income taxes. Consider an alternative: a comprehensive cost-of-living index, which is defined as the amount of income needed before taxes to purchase the standard market basket of goods now used to define the CPI. In my view, this is the index that people should be concerned about in discussing the cost of living and the rate of inflation.

What happens when one of Crandall's reforms is instituted, and subsequently prices fall and the income tax is raised to provide the same amount of subsidy? Note that it is necessary to abstract from a large amount of advocacy of simple government economy that appears in the paper. The introduction of the reform policy would achieve no economy; rather, it would result in a shift from higher prices to higher income taxes. The official CPI would fall, and initially people might think they had higher real incomes. But the comprehensive index would agree with common sense: real incomes would be unaffected by the change, at least to a first approximation. The notion that the policy would be deflationary is no more than an illusion of the CPI. Real incomes can rise only if the policy eliminates deadweight loss. This is the efficiency issue that Crandall does not discuss.

But there is more to the story because the objective of the shift to income taxation was to intervene in the inflationary process, not just to raise real incomes. Suppose, first, that various initiatives that Crandall discussed were adopted and that there were no other responses of monetary and fiscal instruments beyond the increase in income taxes that was part of the initiatives. The public's total dollar income would fall due to the increase in income taxes, and the volume of expenditures would also fall because of the reduction in prices. Money demand would consequently fall, and real output would rise to restore equality of supply and demand in the money market. This is the basic logic of the argument that changes from higher prices to higher income taxes are expansionary, and I find it persuasive. It implies that money demand is not raised by the increase in income tax collections; rather, this demand is lowered by changing the composition of consumers' disbursements.

As I mentioned above, the comprehensive cost-of-living index would not record any significant change as a result of the reform policy. The macroeconomic effect of a policy that reduced prices by 1 percent while holding the comprehensive index constant would be the same as that of an increase in the money supply of 1 percent with prices held constant. If the monetary expansion is undesirable because it eventually would worsen inflation, the policy of reduced prices and increased income taxes is undesirable on the same grounds. The smokescreen of the reduction in the CPI would conceal a move that was actually inflationary.

Advocates of the strategy of lowering prices and raising income taxes are not satisfied with the amount of expansion that naturally accompanies the policy. They propose to take advantage of the temporary lowering of the rate of inflation as recorded by the CPI to expand the economy even more. But, again, this rests on the CPI illusion. The rate of inflation as measured by the comprehensive cost-of-living index would not fall when the policy was introduced, and would rise subsequently in response to the expansion.

I have overstated the case against this kind of policy by neglecting two important points. First, economists still lack a good explanation of why inflation is bad. The inflation I described that would be measured by the comprehensive cost-of-living index would be accompanied by an equal inflation in wage rates, and would leave real incomes unaffected. Because it is not known why any kind of inflation is bad, it is difficult to argue that one index is better than another as a measure of inflation. It is possible that the only costs of inflation are psychological, and those costs will be attached to whatever price index the government decides to publish. In that case, an index like the CPI that admits a "gimmick" for a temporary reduction in reported inflation is actually superior to the comprehensive index that reveals that a policy is no more than a gimmick. Then Crandall's policies become games that the government plays with the populace, although as Arthur Okun constantly reminds us, there are games where the prizes are measured in tens of billions of dollars.

The second point is that the CPI is important despite its conceptual flaws because labor contracts are often indexed to it. Any policy that depresses the CPI limits the wage increases paid to workers with cost-of-living escalators. This kind of policy offers the potential of slowing down the momentum of inflation, but at the cost of some inequity in wage rewards. Those who adopt cost-of-living escalators rely on the CPI as the best available measure of the cost of living, and may feel cheated if the government introduces a new policy that deliberately lowers the CPI without affecting that cost.

Much of Crandall's paper discusses policies that are not mere substitutions of direct taxes for indirect taxes. In fact, many of those policies eliminate deadweight losses now created by the government and so offer genuine reductions in inflation and increases in real incomes. Policies of this kind include deregulation of transportation, reform of national forest management, improved pricing of natural gas, and elimination of the minimum wage. In other cases it is unclear how much of the price reduction represents elimination of deadweight loss. Rolling back regulations of the Occupational Safety and Health Administration, auto safety regulations, and so on would reduce the prices of the products directly affected, but there may be an offsetting loss of the more general benefits of these programs that ought to be considered in any true measure of the cost of living.

Nevertheless, Crandall makes a good case that there is much deadweight loss in these programs as they are now administered. Unhappily, though, the policies whose quantitative potentials are the largest are also those that are almost pure substitutions of one tax for another, and can only be called gimmicks. Examples of these are the replacement of social security payroll taxes with income taxes, and the substitution of direct taxes for state general sales taxes. Besides the distributional argument in favor of the former, all policies are justified only by the desirability of lowering prices without affecting the comprehensive cost of living. The various policies suggested sum to a total reduction of about 4.9 percent in the price level—including deregulation, which would yield a reduction of 0.5 percent, and neglecting the two policies in table 12 that do not carry estimates and incremental costing of natural gas. Of this, 3.3 percent derives from pure tax substitutions, and no claim is made that any increase in real incomes would follow from them.

There is a danger of placing too much weight on the effects of various government programs on the price level—the sort of thinking that goes with an "inflation impact statement." Some desirable moves are highly inflationary—today, any sensible energy policy, either the President's or a more free-market one, is bound to raise the price level, but it is still a good idea. Bad policies like subsidies for the railroad industry may gain support from their depressing effect on the price level. In some countries, the adoption of policies mainly on the strength of their effects on the cost-of-living index has gone to absurd lengths. It would be undesirable for the United States to start in that direction.

Robert Crandall: Both Gramlich and Hall question whether policies directed toward lowering the price level in discrete steps could reduce the rate of inflation, but nothing in my paper suggests that these policies, once promulgated, would necessarily reduce the subsequent upward march of prices and wages. Indeed, I am as agnostic on the issue as Hall and Gramlich. Perry's paper does not rule out a price-wage effect, but whether it is large enough to permit an anti-inflationary dynamic to be introduced by discrete government-induced reductions of the price level remains an open question.

I am somewhat puzzled by Hall's focus on the distinction between a true cost-of-living indicator and the consumer price index. My paper attempted to demonstrate the possibilities for reducing the price level— which could be defined as one or another of the indexes of *market* prices. It did not suggest that reductions in the price level, per se, increase real income. Nor is the exercise in the spirit of promoting deception as a government policy. Any policy that attempts to intervene in the inflationary process will probably affect someone's real income. Whether substituting direct for indirect taxes is more unfair than reducing the rate of growth of the money supply is not a question that I pretend to answer.

It is true, as Gramlich believes, that the efficiency gains for various policies would be a worthwhile basis for advocating them even if they have no lasting anti-inflationary effect. Unfortunately, as Hall notes, the largest efficiency gains exist in those proposals with the more modest price-level effects. However, it should be noted that I have only scratched the surface in detailing initiatives that would undo the misallocative effects of existing government policy. This choice was deliberate because I was interested in focusing on policy choices that are relevant in today's political climate. Thus, for instance, I examined import restrictions on sugar and steel while avoiding the multifiber agreement. Similarly, I analyzed current programs for wheat, cotton, and feed grain while ignoring the myriad of market-order programs that keep the U.S. Department of Agriculture busy.

There seems to be some confusion about my proposals for reform of social regulation. First, Hall sees them as attempts to roll back some regulatory programs that have social value. While I am sure that there are instances in which "rolling back" may be appropriate, this is not my objective. It is only to seek some mechanism by which regulators can be made to realize that they are mandating the use of scarce resources when they pursue their various social goals. Gramlich's questioning of my proposal to reverse property rights in some instances suggests some misunderstanding of my proposal. I would only use this mechanism for existing sources of externalities, and the price paid by the government to these sources for ceasing their damaging activity would become the tax paid by new sources to the government for originating new social changes. While I think that such a proposal is theoretically sound, I am not optimistic that it could be explained to the public.

General Discussion

Part of the discussion focused on the anti-inflationary effectiveness and potential of the general strategy of reducing the cost and price level. Rudiger Dornbusch took issue with Robert Hall's emphasis on the "comprehensive" cost-of-living index. He interpreted Hall's index as a measure of the purchasing power of *income,* but he also saw reasons to measure the purchasing power of *money* as the consumer price index did. He noted that a reduction in the CPI could have important economic effects, even if it were not accompanied by a reduction in Hall's type of index. So long as anti-inflationary monetary policy was influenced by monetary growth targets, a lower inflation rate of the CPI would lead to a greater expansion of real output. Franco Modigliani, however, qualified that conclusion, pointing out that it was true if money demand depended on gross national product, rather than on gross national income—an issue that he considered unsettled. William Brainard supported Dornbusch's general point that the CPI mattered, pointing to its role in labor negotiations and other economic decisions. He saw a case for changing the index used in wage escalator clauses to exclude price increases reflecting payments to foreigners (that is, rising import prices) or higher costs due to increased collective consumption (that is, improved environmental standards). But he noted that such an issue should be clearly distinguished from an analysis of the impact of the CPI on the economy, as wage determination now is conducted.

Donald Nichols thought that much of the controversy between Robert Hall's approach and that of the paper could be resolved by examining the empirical issue of whether nominal wage increases would fall in response to downward shifts in the price level. If, in fact, nominal wages respond to the price level and not to changes in direct taxes, the proposals are not gimmicks. Modigliani commented that the critical empirical issue was whether wages were determined by a wage-wage or by a price-wage mechanism (or some combination of the two). The effectiveness of the proposals discussed by Robert Crandall—unlike the TIP plans—depended on wages following prices, at least to some extent. James Duesenberry elaborated on this in terms of Edward Gramlich's formulation of the inflationary process, noting the critical role played by the coefficients of the lagged price terms. The cost-reducing proposals are more effective, not only if the coefficients are larger, but also if the lags are shorter.

Arthur Okun sought to qualify Gramlich's proposition that one-shot reductions in the price level had a permanent effect on the inflation rate only if the world were accelerationist and if it had a backward-looking price-wage feedback. First, he noted, if the world were not accelerationist, not even a recession would have a permanent effect on the inflation rate. The one-shot reduction in the price level achieved through cost-cutting would still do as much good and have as lasting an effect in slowing inflation as the same reduction achieved through a one-shot dose of extra unemployment. Second, he suggested that a forward-looking process based on rational expectations of future real wages could yield parallel results to those of the backward-looking model.

William Poole was concerned about the pitfall that economists might encounter if they advocated regulatory or tax changes merely because they were anti-inflationary. He thought that a clear distinction should be made between policies that were advocated on the grounds of efficiency and equity and those that were advanced only for anti-inflationary purposes. To him, the efficiency and equity benefits of some of Crandall's proposals were important and deserved emphasis. George Perry and Martin Baily countered that policies have numerous dimensions that economists should be prepared to acknowledge. For example, one might rationally favor policies for energy deregulation because of their allocative efficiency benefits even though they were inflationary. Baily insisted, however, that the inflationary costs should be recognized.

The participants were especially interested in proposals to lower the price level by substituting direct for indirect taxation. Poole saw such a strategy as an attempt to tamper with the workings of price indexes; he thought it might prove counterproductive. People would recognize the increased burden of direct taxes and take steps to preserve their real after-tax incomes by dropping the use of price indexes as a standard. Duesenberry cited experiences in Massachusetts that revealed the suspicions of voters confronted by a suggested shift from sales taxes to income taxes; he inferred that the voters saw the shift as a hidden way to increase government expenditures. To be credibly anti-inflationary, in his view a plan for a shift in the composition of taxes had to be accompanied by a ceiling on state and local spending.

Walter Heller thought that, in developing a social bargain for a wage-restraint program, a payroll tax reduction would probably be more effective than an income tax cut. The payroll tax cut would provide a clearly perceived, readily calculated increase in take-home pay for a given wage, while the benefits of income-tax cuts vary among workers doing the same job, depending on family size, deductions, and the like.

Modigliani cited evidence from studies on the Dutch and British economies that higher direct taxes raised wages and hence the price level. He thought that this issue might deserve further investigation in the United States. Modigliani noted that, to the extent that direct taxes are not significantly shifted forward in higher wages, the proper response of policy to the explosion of oil prices in 1974 would have been a large reduction of indirect taxes that neutralized the price-level impact, together with some offsetting increase in direct taxes.

In the discussion of the regulation issues raised by the paper, Charles Holt enthusiastically supported Crandall's idea of having government regulatory agencies budget the costs they imposed on the private economy. He noted that some regulatory actions had effects similar to tax collections and public expenditures but lacked a comparable technique of control under current procedures. In his judgment, the main payoff from the budgeting proposal would come from greater efficiency rather than reduced inflation. Lloyd Ulman elaborated on Holt's comments, noting that some problems reflected a peculiar antieconomic bias that officials of regulatory agencies develop in focusing solely on their social objectives. Martin Feldstein, however, was skeptical of the feasibility and usefulness of ex ante estimates of regulatory burdens. He doubted the quality and objectivity of such estimates and questioned the ability to detect and control "cost-overruns" ex post.

Arnold Packer saw the need for a survey of the possibilities for reforms to reduce costs and improve efficiency in the private sector. Among the areas of possible inefficiencies in private institutions, he mentioned casualty and malpractice insurance, wildcat strikes, and unnecessarily wide seasonal fluctuation in construction.

Some panel members stated that certain other aspects of government policy deserved more attention than Crandall had given them. Feldstein suspected that Crandall's estimate of the inflationary effects of the increased minimum wage—based on Gramlich's work—was too low and did not fully account for its effects in shifting up the entire wage structure. Gramlich replied that, in fact, half of Crandall's estimated increase in overall wages consisted of indirect effects of the minimum wage on wages above the minimum. Crandall noted that Perry had failed to find any significant effect of minimum wages, and Ulman suggested that, in light of the empirical evidence, perhaps economists devoted too much attention to the inflationary effects of the minimum wage.

Michael Lovell and Baily felt that Crandall had underestimated the potential of more vigorous antitrust policies. Lovell mentioned that some success had been achieved in lowering legal fees, and that antitrust measures might be effective in other service branches, such as real estate and travel agents.

Heller reminded the panel that deregulatory measures took a long time to be implemented. He pointed out that actions now being taken to deregulate airlines were first proposed during the Kennedy administration. He counseled the current advocates of deregulation not to be discouraged if they failed to obtain prompt results.

ALBERT REES
Princeton University

New Policies to Fight Inflation: Sources of Skepticism

A NUMBER of proposals for new methods to fight inflation are being opposed, especially by labor organizations and the business community. Included among the old methods to fight inflation are restrictive monetary and fiscal policies, wage and price controls, and exhortation or "jawboning," all of which have been used in the United States at various times in the past thirty years. Among the new methods are reductions in excise, sales, and payroll taxes; tax-based incomes policies (TIPs); and deregulation, or the elimination of "sacred cows." This paper explores possible reasons for opposition to these more recent proposals, with major attention devoted to TIPs.

The existence of opposition is well known, but little explanation for it has appeared on the record. When considering objections to a proposed policy, it is important to keep in mind that not all objections are consistent with one another. For example, some emphasize reasons why a proposed policy might not work, and others point out possible adverse consequences if it does work. These two kinds of objections cannot be valid simultaneously, but it might not be possible to determine in advance which to take more seriously.

It is far easier to list objections to a proposed policy than it is to advance a better one. For this reason I do not attempt to distinguish be-

Note: I am indebted to Daniel Quinn Mills and participants of the Brookings Panel for helpful comments on an earlier version of this paper.

217

tween two alternative purposes of the objections discussed. They can be viewed either as grounds for rejecting a policy altogether or as points to be considered in trying to improve the proposals under discussion and make them more workable.

Excise and Payroll Tax Reduction

Sales and excise taxes, unlike income taxes, enter directly into the measurement of consumer prices. A reduction in these taxes therefore produces a one-time reduction in the price level.[1] Although this will not offset a continuing source of inflation such as an overly expansive monetary policy, it has an effect opposite to that of the unique events that have helped to raise the price level in recent years, such as the formation of the oil cartel by the Organization of Petroleum Exporting Countries.

Unlike some of the policies discussed below, reductions in excise taxes should be highly acceptable to both business and labor. For example, the reduction in the excise tax on telephone service proposed by President Carter in January 1978 is clearly directly beneficial to the telephone companies, their employees, and the communication workers' union. Even if the reduction were entirely passed on to consumers through lower rates, it would increase the quantity of telephone services demanded and therefore the demand for labor in the telephone industry.

The support of such tax reductions by business and labor should also extend beyond the industries directly affected. The labor movement generally regards income taxes as more equitable than excise taxes because they are progressive rather than regressive. Businessmen often favor cutting taxes whenever possible in the hope that this will eventually result in a corresponding restraint on government expenditures, much of which they may regard as wasteful.

The reduction of excise taxes to lower prices raises a number of prob-

---

1. By one-time changes in prices I do not mean to suggest that the events that give rise to them have no secondary effects. A reduction in excise taxes could have secondary effects through the operation of cost-of-living escalator provisions or through a moderating influence on newly negotiated wage settlements. The term "one-time" is intended to mean that such secondary effects will have a tendency to diminish in amplitude and eventually will die out. For a more precise statement of the effect of a one-time reduction in prices on the subsequent rate of inflation, see the comments on the Crandall paper in this volume by Edward Gramlich.

lems. The federal government has few excise taxes remaining that can be reduced, and the important ones (gasoline, liquor, and tobacco) can all be defended on special grounds. An alternative proposal is to induce states and localities to reduce sales taxes by replacing the lost revenues with federal funds. The problems of this proposal lie in the area of intergovernmental relations rather than in relations between the government and private sectors—an area that will not be explored here.

A reduction in payroll taxes will also tend to produce a one-time reduction in the price level to the extent that the costs of payroll taxes are passed forward in the price of products, and this pass-through is probably substantial. A modest proposal of this sort was made by President Carter in January 1977 when he proposed a small reduction in the federal payroll tax for unemployment insurance. Much more ambitious proposals have been introduced in Congress, which would shift the financing of the Medicare and disability insurance programs from payroll taxes to general revenues. These proposals are favorable to the economic interests of unions and corporations and to most low-income individual taxpayers for whom payroll taxes are more important than personal income taxes. However, unless the cost of the programs being financed is reduced, the proposals will either require an increase in personal income taxes or a smaller decrease than would otherwise be possible. It is difficult to predict the reaction of business leaders to proposals that would benefit their corporations at some possible cost to them as individual taxpayers. The cost may be small, inasmuch as current proposals for reducing individual income taxes do not greatly affect those in high tax brackets.

It is not obvious that it would be possible to lower the price level by reducing payroll taxes and to restore the lost revenue by increasing corporate income taxes or by decreasing them less. Corporate taxes may also be passed forward to consumers to a considerable extent, and not enough is known about tax incidence to predict how much different the pass-through to prices is for the corporate tax and for the payroll tax.

Tax-Based Incomes Policies

Tax-based incomes policies (TIPs) have been discussed for a number of years, but recently have received wider attention and support. The earliest and most prominent among these policies is the Wallich-Weintraub proposal to increase the corporate income tax rate for corporations whose wage increases exceed a specified guideline.[2] More recent proposals differ from Wallich-Weintraub by suggesting tax incentives for compliance with both price and wage guidelines and by suggesting tax reductions to corporations and workers in place of or in addition to tax increases. Some of these proposals were considered by Wallich and Weintraub, who regarded them as less desirable than their own.

The general attitude of business and labor toward the TIP proposals reminds one of the famous *New Yorker* cartoon in which a mother is trying to persuade a small girl to eat her broccoli, and the girl replies, "I say it's spinach and I say to hell with it." Business and labor are now firmly opposed to wage and price controls, and they consider TIP as another form of control. In the sections that follow, I explore some of the similarities and differences between TIPs and controls from the perspective of labor and management.

SCOPE AND COVERAGE

The Wallich-Weintraub proposal would apply to all corporations paying corporate income tax, with a possible exemption for small corporations. This is a far narrower scope than that of the wage controls in effect during the period 1971–74; those controls covered partnerships and proprietorships, state and local governments, and nonprofit institutions. The last two of these have been areas of rapid growth of unionism and collective bargaining in recent years. It is quite possible that in the future strong pressures for wage increases could originate in the unions of the public sector. This appears to have happened in Canada in recent years; the level of wage settlements there has exceeded that in the United States, despite the fact that workers in the private sector in the two countries are largely represented by the same set of unions.

The exemption for small firms and the exclusion of unincorporated business would exclude from coverage many firms in construction and trucking, which are industries with both high wages and strong unions.

2. See Henry C. Wallich and Sidney Weintraub, "A Tax-Based Incomes Policy," *Journal of Economic Issues,* vol. 5 (June 1971), pp. 1–19. Similar proposals previously had been advanced by the two authors separately. See Wallich, "Can We Stop Inflation without a Recession?" *Newsweek,* vol. 68 (September 5, 1966), pp. 72–73, and Weintraub, "An Incomes Policy to Stop Inflation," *Lloyds Bank Review,* no. 99 (January 1971), pp. 1–12.

Wallich has suggested that special policies to restrain wages might be needed for these industries. Unfortunately, he has not stated what these policies would be. The exclusion of trucking would be especially important because the International Brotherhood of Teamsters is the largest and one of the strongest unions in the United States, and its master freight agreement has an important pattern-setting influence beyond trucking, especially in food wholesaling and retailing. More generally, the exemption for small firms could lead to spillovers of wage increases from small firms to larger ones, or could lead to distortions of relative wages.

One supporter of TIP, Laurence Seidman, has proposed an exemption for "very low-paid" workers, without specifying how those workers would be defined.[3] Past experience shows that such an exemption would have strong support in Congress, but could seriously diminish the effectiveness of TIP. For example, the 1973 extension of the Economic Stabilization Act exempted low-wage workers from wage controls effective May 1, 1973, and defined them as those earning less than $3.50 an hour.[4] In May 1973, all production and nonsupervisory workers in private nonagricultural employment were receiving average hourly earnings of $3.85, so that almost half of this group was excluded from wage controls by this exemption.

It should also be recognized that TIP would not apply to those large private corporations that have no tax liability because they are not profitable in a particular year or because they carry forward tax credits. A union such as the retail clerks or the meatcutters negotiating under TIP with several supermarket chains in the same geographical area might choose to make a pattern-setting agreement with an unprofitable chain, which has no tax disincentive applicable to wage increases above the guideline and has the least financial ability to resist a strike. The union could then confront the profitable chains with a newly established wage rate, and it would be difficult for them not to match it.

Some advocates of TIP may feel that the concentration of penalties on profitable firms is desirable because high profits encourage large wage increases. Little solid evidence exists to support this view, however. In such industries as railroads and shipping, unions have bargained for and

3. Laurence S. Seidman, "To Fight Inflation," *New York Times,* December 22, 1976, p. 29.
4. U.S. Department of the Treasury, Office of Economic Stabilization, *Historical Working Papers on the Economic Stabilization Program, August 15, 1971 to April 30, 1974* (Government Printing Office, 1974), pt. 1, p. 347.

won high wages and costly manning requirements not only from unprofitable firms, but even from bankrupt ones.

The scope of the Wallich-Weintraub proposal could be greatly extended by applying the tax penalty to payroll taxes rather than to corporate income taxes. It would then include unincorporated businesses, corporations with no tax liability, nonprofit institutions, and those state and local governments that participate in the social security system.

Wallich and Weintraub argue against the use of payroll taxes for TIP on the ground that those taxes are more likely to be passed forward in prices than are corporate income taxes. It is easier for me to agree that payroll taxes are passed forward than to accept the view that corporate income taxes are not. If one corporation in a competitive industry negotiated a wage increase above the guideline established by TIP and paid the resulting corporate income tax penalty, the firm would have difficulty passing the penalty forward because its competitors would have both lower wage costs and lower taxes. In some cases, however, wage agreements are negotiated with entire industries, such as basic steel. In others, such as automobiles, an agreement reached with one major producer is extended to the others with little or no change. If in such cases one firm reaches a wage agreement that exceeds the guideline and results in tax penalties, it might set higher prices to restore in large part the previous rate of return on capital after taxes. Both the wage increase and the price increase would then probably be followed by other firms in the industry. Indeed, in industries where demand for a product is relatively inelastic, the only major barrier to such an outcome would seem to be foreign competition. For TIP to be effective in industries characterized both by price leadership and by industry-wide bargaining or pattern-following in wages, guidelines and penalties would be required for excessive price increases. Such proposals are discussed below.

Another difference between the use of corporate income taxes and payroll taxes as a base for TIP is that the penalty rates of payroll taxes would augment the effect of higher wages in inducing the substitution of capital for labor. The use of corporate income taxes would presumably not induce factor substitution or, if anything, would cause substitution of labor for capital.

The Wallich-Weintraub proposal is limited to wages because its proponents believe that markups of prices over unit labor costs are historically quite stable. In Weintraub's words, TIP "presupposes that the wage-productivity nexus is crucial in inflation."[5] Thus, in Weintraub's view, postwar inflation has been essentially wage-push inflation. Needless to say, the unions (among others) vigorously disagree with this view; they would point to the rises in prices of raw agricultural commodities and imported petroleum and to the devaluation of the dollar since 1971 as contributors to inflation for which they bear no responsibility. They regard the Wallich-Weintraub proposal as completely one-sided and therefore unfair to labor. Although unions are opposed to any kind of incomes policy, they are most strongly opposed to one that focuses exclusively on wages. They would fight its enactment by the Congress with as much force as an aroused labor movement can muster, which is considerable.

The view that price inflation merely mirrors wage inflation has been somewhat shaken by the events of recent years. From 1973 to 1974 the consumer price index rose 11.0 percent, while average hourly earnings in private nonagricultural industry rose only 8.2 percent, producing a decline of 2.5 percent in real hourly earnings. Although the events of 1974 were highly unusual, the labor movement certainly cannot be blamed for wanting insurance against their repetition (which is not to say that they necessarily should have it).[6]

ESTABLISHING THE GUIDELINE

The problem of establishing an appropriate wage guideline is not much different under TIP than it is under wage controls, but this does not mean that it is unimportant. Perhaps the principal difference is that TIP necessarily involves an explicit guideline, while wage controls do not. The Construction Industry Stabilization Committee, the most successful of the wage-control bodies of the 1971–74 period, operated without an explicit wage guideline throughout its existence.

Labor unions oppose a wage guideline in part because they fear that it might be unfairly set or that it would not be appropriately modified to changing conditions. Both concerns are based on past experience.

Wallich and Weintraub suggest a wage guideline that could be estab-

5. Sidney Weintraub, "Incomes Policy: Completing the Stabilization Triangle," *Journal of Economic Issues*, vol. 6 (December 1972), p. 119.
6. Some analysts would prefer to use compensation per hour of labor in the private sector for this kind of analysis. However, the unions focus on the hourly earnings of production and nonsupervisory workers because they have few members in the private sector who are salaried employees.

lished at some point between a minimum equal to the trend of output per labor hour and a maximum equal to this trend plus the initial rate of inflation.[7] Their minimum is the same as the wage guideline established by the Kennedy administration in 1962, and could be used in a situation in which the initial rate of inflation was zero or close to it. Even under these circumstances, this guideline is not acceptable to the labor movement. It is well known that increasing wages in proportion to output per labor hour will keep constant the labor and nonlabor shares of output and income. In other words, this guideline freezes the functional distribution of income. Historically, however, there has been a tendency for labor's share of income to rise gradually through time, even after adjustment for the decline in self-employment.[8] Understandably, labor does not want this historical trend that is favorable to its constituents brought to a halt, not even temporarily.

A rough check on whether guidelines actually had this effect on labor's share is afforded by computing the compensation of employees as a percentage of national income for selected years. This figure was 71.6 in 1961 before the Kennedy guidelines and 70.6 in 1966; it was 76.3 in 1970 before the Nixon controls and 75.1 in 1973. I would ascribe the declines in labor's share during the periods of guidelines and controls to the business cycle rather than to incomes policy. However, the sharp rise in labor's share during the intervening period when there was no incomes policy is also noteworthy. In any event, the labor movement is not likely to draw favorable conclusions about guidelines from these figures.

The opposite extreme in the range of possible wage guidelines of the Wallich-Weintraub proposal would surely not be acceptable to business. To allow wages to increase by the trend of productivity plus a full allowance for inflation is to allow labor larger gains than it has been able to win in the period since mid-1974, when there have been no guidelines. If we accept 2 percent as a rough estimate of the trend of productivity, *real* hourly earnings of all employees in the private nonagricultural sector have not risen as much as this trend since 1972. A guideline of productivity plus a full allowance for inflation therefore seem more likely to accelerate wage increases than to retard them.

7. "A Tax-Based Incomes Policy," p. 12.
8. See Irving B. Kravis, "Income Distribution: Functional Share," in David L. Sills, ed., *International Encyclopedia of the Social Sciences,* vol. 7 (Macmillan, 1968), pp. 132–45.

Intermediate positions, such as the trend of productivity plus half the rate of inflation, seem superior to the extremes, but even these have substantial difficulties. If the initial rate of inflation were 6 percent and the trend of productivity 2 percent, a wage guideline of 5 percent would result. If such a guideline were enforced, real output per labor hour could rise at a rate of 2 percent a year, and real wages would initially fall 1 percent a year—an outcome totally unacceptable to the unions. Eventually the rate of inflation should decline to 3 percent if the program is successful, but the unions might not be patient enough to wait for this. Moreover, at this point the wage guideline would be reduced to 3.5 percent, again producing a real wage gain much lower than the trend of productivity. Only in some final equilibrium where prices are not rising at all do real wages rise with the productivity trend.

I conclude that if there is to be a wage guideline acceptable to unions, it cannot include a constant allowance for ongoing inflation, but may need to adjust that allowance each year. Formulas based on theoretical considerations may be inferior to more arbitrary ones based on simple deceleration from existing rates of increase in compensation. For the guideline to be acceptable and fair, it must allow for growth in real wages. For the guideline to have any effect in restraining inflation, it must be less than the wage increases that would occur in its absence. It is not clear that a number always exists that meets both of these constraints; indeed, it is not even clear that one exists at present.

Labor's fear that a guideline might become less favorable to the interests of workers over time is supported by the events of both 1962–67 and 1971–74. When the Kennedy administration adopted wage guidelines based on productivity in 1962, the trend of productivity change was substantially above the rise in consumer prices, so that a guideline based solely on productivity provided for considerable growth in real wages. By 1966, the guideline had become a specific number—3.2 percent a year. During 1966, as the Council of Economic Advisers noted in its January 1967 report, consumer prices rose 3.3 percent. Adherence to the guidelines therefore implied a slight fall in real wages. The council nevertheless did not change the guideline number.[9]

9. See *Economic Report of the President, January 1967*, pp. 127–29. Because the position of the council was somewhat ambiguous, a direct quotation may be helpful: "The Council recognizes that the recent rise in living costs makes it unlikely that most collective bargaining settlements in 1967 will fully conform to the trend

A second aspect of the 1966–67 guidelines was also disturbing to the labor movement. The 3.2 percent figure that became the wage guideline was the latest average of the increase in output per labor hour in the private sector for the five-year periods ending in 1963 and in 1964, as measured at the end of those years. For the five years ending in 1965, the corresponding figure was 3.4 percent. In its January 1966 report the council did not accept this higher figure as a basis for revising the guideline on the ground that five consecutive years of economic expansion had created a productivity gain that was above the long-term trend.[10] Although this belated recognition that five years is too short a period to establish a trend was probably correct, the unions were offended because the rules had been changed in the middle of the game. Their sense of grievance, oddly enough, existed although—according to knowledgeable observers of collective bargaining—the guidelines had little or no effect in restraining negotiated wage settlements.[11]

The 1962–66 experience was repeated in 1971–74. In November 1971 the Pay Board set the general pay standard for the new wage control program at 5.5 percent. This was widely interpreted as based on a combination of the long-run productivity trend and a portion of the current increase in consumer prices. The productivity trend was then about 3 percent a year, and the controls program was expected to reduce the rate of inflation to 2.5 percent by the end of 1972. A 5.5 percent wage standard minus a 3.0 percent productivity trend implies a 2.5 percent rate of increase of unit labor costs, which is consistent with an equal increase in prices. By 1973, however, the rate of increase of the consumer price index (December 1972 to December 1973) was 8.8 percent. Nevertheless, the 5.5 percent wage standard was never formally abandoned during the controls programs, though exceptions to it became more and more numerous.

---

increase of productivity. But it sees no useful purpose to be served by suggesting some higher standard for wage increases, even on a temporary basis.

"The only valid and noninflationary standard for wage advances is the productivity principle. If price stability is eventually to be restored and maintained in a high-employment U.S. economy, wage settlements must once again conform to that standard" (p. 128).

10. *Economic Report of the President, January 1966*, p. 92.

11. See John T. Dunlop, "Guideposts, Wages, and Collective Bargaining," in George P. Shultz and Robert Z. Aliber, eds., *Guidelines, Informal Controls, and the Market Place: Policy Choices in a Full Employment Economy* (University of Chicago Press, 1966), p. 84.

Those proponents of TIP who advocate tax penalties or bonuses based on both price increases and wage increases usually select a pair of guidelines that differ by the trend of output per labor hour. If this trend were 2 percent, they might propose a wage guideline of 6 percent and a price guideline of 4 percent.[12] Such a pair of guidelines is consistent, on average across all industries, with unit labor costs rising as fast as the price guidelines.

The problems of establishing a price guideline, however, are much more formidable than those of setting a wage guideline. Okun suggests a "dollar-and-cents pass-through of any increases in costs of materials and supplies."[13] These costs would presumably differ according to the product, which would make departures from the price guideline difficult to detect. Moreover, the term "materials and supplies" may be overly narrow. Are corporations to absorb all increases above 4 percent in the costs of purchased services, such as legal and accounting fees, travel costs, and so on? But even if there were no increases in the costs of materials, supplies, and purchased services, a uniform price guideline would be unfair because the productivity trends of individual industries differ dramatically from that of the economy as a whole. It is reasonable to state that workers doing the same work in different industries should receive roughly the same pay regardless of industry differences in productivity, but it is altogether unreasonable to assume that the prices of the products of industries with different productivity trends should move together.

For the period 1970–75 the average growth in output per production worker hour in the industries for which separate measures are published by the Bureau of Labor Statistics ranged from an increase of 9.2 percent in candy and other confectionery products to a decrease of 4.8 percent in bituminous coal and lignite mining.[14] An industry that experiences no change in productivity and has a 6 percent increase in wages will be forced to raise prices at close to 6 percent unless it uses little labor. An industry whose productivity is rising at 8 percent should be reducing product prices unless its nonlabor costs are rising rapidly. A price-control agency with discretionary authority can take such circumstances into account to

12. See Arthur M. Okun, "The Great Stagflation Swamp," *Challenge*, vol. 20 (November/December 1977), p. 13.
13. Ibid.
14. U.S. Bureau of Labor Statistics, *Productivity Indexes for Selected Industries, 1976 Edition*, bulletin 1938 (Government Printing Office, 1977), table 1.

the extent that available data permit, but it is almost impossible to write them into the Internal Revenue Code.

COLLECTIVE BARGAINING AND INDUSTRIAL DISPUTES

The proposal to tax corporations on excessive wage increases must consider the differences between tax units and collective bargaining units. A corporation might treat all its domestic operations as one entity for corporate tax purposes, but within this entity it might have many different collective bargaining units, often represented by several different unions, as well as a large number of nonunion employees.

Weintraub attempts to convert this problem into an asset, in my opinion unsuccessfully. He writes, "A not inconsiderable virtue [of TIP] is that unions can bargain for sums in excess of the productivity norm and perhaps succeed in redistributing some income from profits and managerial employees."[15] This is a clear statement of why business might oppose TIP.

Even if the goal of policy were to redistribute income by differential changes in compensation to create greater equality, it could not be achieved by the route that Weintraub suggests. Nonunion employees are not all managers. In most firms, the majority of nonunion employees are clerical workers, and they generally receive lower wages than unionized production workers. Suppose that a firm had equal numbers of union and nonunion employees, that the wage norm was 6 percent, and that the union succeeded in obtaining a wage increase of 8 percent. To avoid a tax penalty, the firm would have to hold its nonunion employees to a 4 percent wage increase. If firms chose to do this, there would be an increase in union-nonunion wage differentials, which are already large; many economists might say they are too large. However, in my judgment few employers would risk such a policy. To provide nonunion workers with only half the wage increase of union workers would lower morale and perhaps decrease productivity or invite the unionization of the nonunion group. Most firms would prefer to pay the tax penalty. But if they did, the effectiveness of TIP would be reduced. The unions, however, could and probably would use Weintraub's argument as grounds for not adhering to the wage norm.

The same kind of problem arises when a company bargains with two unions of unequal strength. If the stronger union negotiated first, it might

15. "Incomes Policy: Completing the Stabilization Triangle," p. 119.

insist on a settlement in excess of the guideline, and the employer would have to decide whether to pay the tax penalty or to try to reach a settlement below the guideline with the weaker union. However, the existence of a wage guideline makes it more difficult for a weak union to accept a settlement below the guideline.

The general strategy of the Wallich-Weintraub proposal is to "stiffen the backbone" of employers in wage bargaining—that is, to encourage employers to resist excessive union wage demands. It seems logical that this will increase both the frequency and the duration of strikes, and the Wallich-Weintraub analysis explicitly suggests the latter effect. In the diagram below, which is a slight simplification of a similar one used by Wallich and Weintraub, the horizontal axis measures time, and the vertical axis measures the rate of change of money wages. Point D is the union's original wage demand, and the line labeled U represents the union's modification of its wage demands through time. The line E shows the improvement of the employer's wage offer through time without TIP. The introduction of such a policy, with the wage guideline established at point G, shifts the righthand portion of the employer's offer curve to E^T. Without TIP, settlement is reached at point S_0 at time T_0; after the introduction of TIP, settlement is reached at point S_1 at time T_1. Wallich and Weintraub do not divide their time scale into two segments representing negotiations before and negotiations during a strike. However, if a strike began before T_0, it would be prolonged by the time between T_0 and T_1. Presumably some strikes would also begin in this interval.

Business and labor generally prefer to avoid strikes whenever possible because of the losses they bring to both parties. This aspect of TIP gives them additional reason to oppose the policy. Strikes also impose losses on the general public, and the shortages that result from them can lower productivity and raise prices.

In this respect, TIP is inferior to wage controls, which actually reduce strikes. Days idle resulting from work stoppages were 0.15 percent of total working time in 1972 and 0.14 percent in 1973, the two years in the past decade in which wage controls were in effect throughout the year. These figures are below those for any other years in this decade, including the recession year, 1975. It is easy to understand why controls deter strikes—there is not much point in a union placing economic pressure on an employer to make wage concessions if the government will not permit these concessions to go into effect.

It is crucial to the Wallich-Weintraub analysis that union demands

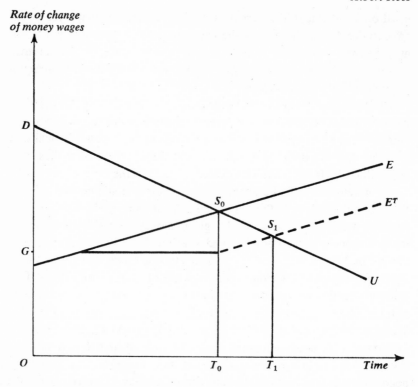

decline consistently through time, although it is by no means obvious that they will. The union may have some minimum demand for which it is prepared to bargain to the point of impasse or even to strike for a protracted period. In the diagram this would be shown by a horizontal segment of U. If this horizontal segment began at or to the left of S_0, TIP would increase the frequency or length of strikes without any reduction in the wage increase at which they were settled. Wallich and Weintraub recognize this possibility, but argue that a union that fails to take account of TIP in its demands is not maximizing benefits for its members.

I know of no evidence that industrial disputes arise from or are settled by maximizing behavior by both parties, any more than are international or religious disputes. It is not unknown for a strike to be settled for more than the union's original demand when a strong union is determined to teach management a lesson and recoup some of the losses suffered during a strike. When the union has the power to win a long strike, it does little good to strengthen management's backbone. There will certainly be some cases in which the TIP guideline would cause the size of the eventual settlement to be smaller. But this would not be true of every settlement, and it is an open question whether the gains would be worth the costs.

One advantage claimed for TIP is that it is automatic and thus easy to administer. The opposite side of this coin is that TIP does not enable its administrators to help in the settlement of actual or potential disputes in collective bargaining or in the improvement of collective bargaining structures. There have been cases in which the administration of wage controls accomplished this in the past, and this has been one of the mitigating aspects of wage-control programs.

If TIP does lead to more strikes, it could also lead to more government intervention to settle those strikes. Such intervention usually brings pressure on management to offer more generous terms because there may be no way in which the government can bring effective pressure on union members. The federal government would then either have to work at cross-purposes with its own TIP or suspend the TIP to help settle emergency disputes.

ADMINISTRATIVE PROBLEMS: WAGES[16]

As I noted earlier, one of the principal claims made for the TIP proposals is that they do not involve substantial administrative costs. Laurence Seidman, in his letter to the *New York Times* of December 22, 1976, lists as TIP's first advantage over controls that "no new bureaucracy is required." Critics of the TIP proposals have been skeptical of this claim. Gardner Ackley has commented, "From my experience in designing and administering price controls during World War II, and again, in a policy role, during the Korean War, I retain keen, and sometimes bitter, memories of great ideas about ways to restrain wage and price increases for which the fine print could never be written—or if it could be written, filled endless volumes of the *Federal Register* with constant revisions, exceptions, and adjustments necessary to cover special situations that could never have been dreamed of in advance by the most imaginative economists, accountants, and lawyers."[17] This section explores the basis for these diverging views.

16. Some of the problems raised in this and the following section are considered in more detail in the paper in this volume by Larry L. Dildine and Emil M. Sunley.

17. Gardner Ackley, "Okun's New Tax-Based Incomes-Policy Proposal," *Economic Outlook, USA*, vol. 5 (Winter 1978), p. 8.

The difficulty of administering wage guidelines depends in part on how increases in compensation are defined. Originally, Wallich and Weintraub proposed four possibilities: (1) total wages, salaries, bonuses, and fringe benefits divided by the number of employees on a given date; (2) total wage and related payments divided by the daily average number of employees; (3) total wage and related payments divided by employee hours worked (that is, compensation per employee hour); and (4) total wage and related payments in each job classification and grade divided by the number of man-hours worked, combined into a weighted index of wage increases.[18]

Wallich and Weintraub recognized that the first three of these proposals were subject to possible manipulation by the employer or could result in windfall gains and losses through changes in the skill mix. For example, an employer could increase wages by more than the guideline in every occupation, yet escape penalty taxes because employment or hours had increased most in the low-paid occupations. By March 1972, Wallich was writing that these proposals "probably will not do at all."[19] Yet Wallich and Weintraub also recognize that the fourth proposal involves substantial difficulties of computation for large firms with many establishments and hundreds of different job titles. Firms do not now ordinarily maintain weighted indexes of wage increases, and even the Bureau of Labor Statistics has only begun such an index in the past decade. Average hourly earnings are easily obtained by accountants from payroll records; weighted indexes of wage changes must be computed by statisticians. Neither the typical corporate employer nor the Internal Revenue Service has the capabilities of the Bureau of Labor Statistics in this area. Specifying the proper computation of a weighted index of compensation increases in TIP is a task that gives rise to the kind of fears that Ackley has expressed.

An area of difficulty in the administration of wage controls that would also be present in TIP is the treatment of fringe benefits. Costs of fringe benefits are easy to compute when employers make contributions of cents per hour to a benefit fund, as they do in the construction industry. They are difficult to estimate, however, when a collective bargaining agreement or an employer benefit plan specifies future pension or health bene-

18. Condensed from "A Tax-Based Incomes Policy," pp. 13–14.

19. Henry C. Wallich, "Phase II and the Proposal for a Tax-Oriented Incomes Policy," *Review of Social Economy,* vol. 30 (March 1972), p. 8.

fits rather than current contributions. Translating such benefits into current costs requires complicated calculations about which competent actuaries can disagree. The Internal Revenue Service already faces these difficulties in auditing employer costs of fringe benefits claimed on tax returns.

Past wage-control programs have controlled benefits more loosely than wages and salaries. This can be justified if fringe benefits are believed to be too low as a proportion of total compensation, which may have been true during World War II and the Korean War. It could also be justified during a demand-pull inflation on the ground that future pensions and health benefits, unlike current wages, do not add to aggregate demand. However, the theory underlying TIP assumes that the problem is cost-push, not demand-pull inflation. To be consistent with this theory, TIP advocates must fully include fringe benefits in their compensation measure.

The costs of fringe benefits can rise not only because benefit levels are improved, but also because inflation raises the cost of maintaining existing benefit levels. Such increased costs have been exempted from previous wage-control programs, but it is not at all clear that this could be permitted in a future incomes policy without seriously weakening the policy.[20]

Another area of administrative difficulty is the implementation of incentive pay programs. In most of these programs, an increase in pay resulting from higher output would nevertheless reduce unit labor costs. Because the main purpose of TIP is to contain the cost of labor per unit, this suggests that increases in amounts received as incentive pay under existing schemes should be excluded from the proposed wage index. However, past wage-control programs have regulated the introduction of new incentive pay schemes on the ground that a large loophole might be created if regulations were absent. Special consideration needs to be given to incentive programs for executives based on corporate and divisional profits rather than on output. None of these problems is by any means insurmountable, but addressing them requires regulations and administrative machinery.

The negotiation of cost-of-living escalator provisions will create an area of increased uncertainty for management under TIP; more than half

20. For an elaboration of this view, see Daniel Quinn Mills, *Government, Labor, and Inflation: Wage Stabilization in the United States* (University of Chicago Press, 1975), pp. 202–05.

of all major collective bargaining agreements now contain such provisions. Any tax penalties arising from escalator provisions can be levied after the fact on the basis of wages actually paid. When negotiating the agreement, management must predict the future rate of inflation, as it does now. However, the possibility of a tax penalty will increase the cost of underprediction. This could restrain the spread of escalator provisions, but those managements already using them will not welcome the added risk.

Attention must also be paid to problems of wage inequities. During the wage-control program of 1971–74, the base date for calculating wage increases was November 14, 1971. Collective bargaining agreements reached before that date were allowed to operate as negotiated unless challenged. Those reached afterward required approval if they exceeded the pay standard, and were often cut back. Situations then arose in which two groups of workers in the same local union who had always received the same wage rate would have different rates because one employer had signed an agreement on November 13 and another had signed an identical agreement on November 15; such differences created great unrest among union members and strong political pressures on union leaders. Some of these inequities were later remedied by awards of retroactive pay to the aggrieved workers. This solution was most distasteful to management, which had not included the originally disallowed wage increases in prices, and viewed retroactive payments as impinging directly on the bottom line of the profit and loss statement.

From a union's viewpoint, TIP is preferable to controls in preventing wage inequities from arising when the program is first instituted. By actual or threatened strikes, unions could compel most managements to follow the traditional patterns established in previously negotiated settlements, even at the cost of tax penalties. However, the inequity is shifted to the firm: the employer who follows patterns pays penalty taxes; the one who sets patterns does not. Again, regulations could be written and administered to address such problems, but not without the usual bureaucratic costs.

Multiyear agreements negotiated before the inauguration of a TIP give rise to a problem even if they do not cause wage inequities. If wage increases in the second and third years of such agreements exceed the guideline, employers could be liable for tax penalties that were unanticipated when they entered into the agreements. To avoid this effect, prior agreements could be exempted from TIP, but this would mean that TIP would need three years to become fully effective.

Not all distortion in wage structure arises from the operation of incomes policies. Some comes from the sequential nature of collective bargaining and wage determination in the private sector. Wage settlements elsewhere and changes in labor market conditions can create situations in which some wages in a firm are inequitably low or are different from prevailing rates in the area or industry. Wage-control programs have always included provisions for dealing with such inequity problems, usually administered by staff with experience in industrial relations. Such exceptions are less necessary under TIP than under wage controls because an employer can remedy inequities and pay the tax penalty without obtaining previous permission and without violating the law. However, if no exceptions were permitted, some employers would probably pay tax penalties resulting from circumstances essentially beyond their control.

The most difficult question for unions in past wage-control programs has been whether or not to participate in the administration of the program. If union leaders did not participate, they feared that the program would be administered in ways that were adverse to the interests of their members. If they did participate, they could be criticized by rivals within the union for holding wages down when they were being paid to raise them. The resulting ambivalence is shown by the several cases in which union leaders have walked out of wage stabilization boards—and sometimes have been persuaded to return by changes in the program. The best option that union leaders have at present is to try to prevent TIP from going into effect.

The threats to incumbent union leaders from rivals within their own unions have increased greatly in both frequency and force since the enactment of the Landrum-Griffin act in 1959. It is public policy, and in my view correct public policy, to encourage democracy in trade unions. However, one disadvantage of the act is that it makes labor leaders less willing to cooperate, in the name of the "public interest," when economic policies are adverse to the interests of their members.

The most difficult union attitude to predict is the reaction to possible tax incentives payable to workers when wage settlements are below guidelines. This carrot approach to the TIP proposal can substitute tax benefits for wage benefits won by a union. Although the individual worker may be unaffected, the benefits are not attributable to the union as an organization and do not win support for union leaders. For this reason, if support of such a plan were voluntary, I would expect that many unions would not participate.

ADMINISTRATIVE PROBLEMS: PRICES

The Okun proposal is less explicit on the price side than is the Wallich-Weintraub proposal. In general, Okun proposes that each firm would have to maintain a price index for its domestic products. Many large firms do so now for internal use, though the methods used must be far from uniform and would have to be prescribed. However, the problems of constructing adequate price indexes are far more difficult than those of constructing adequate wage indexes. Most of these problems are well known, and need only to be mentioned briefly. Regulations would be needed to specify how to handle changes in discounts, delivery charges, extras, and similar components of the final price to the buyer. For some products, such as clothing, problems would arise from changes in style. In other cases, such as computers, there would be problems of measuring quality change. Indeed, computers are currently not included in the wholesale price index.

All the difficulties of devising useful price indexes are now dealt with by the Bureau of Labor Statistics in the computation of the consumer and the wholesale price indexes, which is to say that they are generally not insuperable, although few corporations have the statistical competence and resources of the Bureau of Labor Statistics. Moreover, in the absence of a TIP or a price control program, differences of opinion about how to measure prices will not generally give rise to judicial or administrative proceedings; if TIP were in effect, they undoubtedly would.

The agencies that administered price controls had great discretion to omit some products from control by regulation if they did not seem to be important contributors to price increases. This probably could not be done in a TIP that depends on the average price increase of a corporation's products. If exceptions were not possible, the program would have broader price coverage than that of past control programs.

The Okun proposal also calls for a "dollar-and-cents pass-through" of any increases in costs of materials and supplies. This would again entail additional recordkeeping if firms did not maintain separate aggregate measures of the quantity and price of materials purchased. However, the administrative problems are small compared to the inequities mentioned earlier arising from the application of uniform price guidelines in the face of sharply divergent productivity trends among industries. The answer might be different price guidelines at the industry level, at least where there are adequate industry measures of productivity, but again this could not be done without administrative machinery.

The claim that TIP requires no new bureaucracy may be true in the sense that it would not require a new government agency. However, it might require the Internal Revenue Service to expand its staff and to recruit personnel with the skills of those at such agencies as the former Cost of Living Council.

One important reason for the strong opposition of business to wage and price controls is that the administrative problems they created absorbed much of the time of corporate officers and required large additional expenditures on legal and accounting services, both internal and external. TIP would probably have similar costs. It is entirely legitimate for TIP proponents to argue that the benefits would exceed these costs, but it is unconvincing to pretend that the costs would not exist.

Deregulation

The third nontraditional way in which economists have recently proposed to fight inflation is to repeal or modify some government regulations that raise prices or increase costs without creating corresponding benefits. A modest program to seek such changes in regulation was enacted as part of the Council on Wage and Price Stability Act of 1974 and has been in effect for more than three years. However, the success of these efforts has been limited.

Cost-reducing changes in regulations, like cuts in excise taxes, should have a one-time effect in lowering the price level, with gradually diminishing effects on the subsequent rate of change. Such regulatory reform has wide support among economists: those economists who believe that inflation is largely or entirely a monetary phenomenon support deregulation because it would improve the allocation of resources or reduce unnecessary government intervention in the economy.

The business and labor view of deregulation differs sharply from case to case. Any proposal for deregulation is likely to create both groups that gain and groups that lose among business firms and employees. To identify these gainers and losers it is useful to distinguish two major styles of regulation, which I call old and new.

OLD-STYLE REGULATION

By old-style regulation, I mean the kind of regulation exemplified by the Interstate Commerce Commission, which has broad power to set rates or prices and control the entry of firms in a sharply limited industry or set of industries. Many of the agencies that make and administer such regulations are independent commissions outside the cabinet departments. With a few notable exceptions, the general effect of this regulation has been to set prices or rates higher than they would have been without regulation and to limit entry into the regulated industries. In such cases, relaxing the regulation generally tends to lower prices or rates and to increase the quantity of the service supplied.

Proposals for deregulation can be expected to have a mixed reception by business, depending on how a particular enterprise is affected. A few examples will make the conflict of interests apparent.

Some provisions of the 1936 Robinson-Patman act, administered by the Federal Trade Commission, and certain regulations of the Interstate Commerce Commission prevent private carriers of freight from achieving cost savings by carrying freight on return trips, or backhauls.[21] For example, retailers and wholesalers of food would like to have these restrictions on backhauls removed so that when they make deliveries to food stores they can save freight charges by using their own empty trucks to bring back to the warehouse products manufactured near the destination of the delivery. They understandably complain that empty backhauls waste resources and raise costs. Their efforts are vigorously opposed by the certificated common carriers, who would lose revenue traffic if the restrictions were lifted. These efforts at deregulation are also opposed by some manufacturers of brand-name grocery products who prefer to sell at delivered prices.

In this case, the union representing the affected workers (International Brotherhood of Teamsters) represents drivers for both private carriers

21. Private carriers are truck fleets owned or leased by companies that are not certificated common carriers; these trucks carry goods belonging to the company using the fleet.

and common carriers and thus may not have a large stake in the outcome. However, the union cannot be expected to support a proposal that might reduce the total employment of its members.

Regulated passenger airlines offer another example of a division between firms now protected and those excluded from regulation. For many years all domestic, regulated carriers opposed deregulation, as did the Air Line Pilots Association. Commuter airlines and charter flight operators favored it, presumably because it would give them access to markets from which they are now excluded.[22] Recently some reductions in airline fares have been taking place under regulation. This reflects both the pressures created by proposed changes in legislation and the appointment of two economists to membership on the Civil Aeronautics Board.

Domestic interstate natural gas is a leading case in which industry-specific regulation has kept prices below the level that would exist without regulation. In this case, it is the protected industry that seeks deregulation, and the consumer groups that oppose it. Unions generally view deregulation of natural gas from the standpoint of their members as consumers. Deregulation of natural gas would raise price indexes in the short run, but could lower them eventually if the supply response were sufficient to reduce the need to import natural gas.

The events of the last few years suggest that some improvement can be made in those aspects of old-style regulation that raise prices and costs, but progress will come slowly. Regulation that has substantial effects creates large benefits for some segments of the economy. Those segments that receive benefits will naturally fight harder to preserve regulation than the diffuse losers will fight to reform it.

NEW-STYLE REGULATION

New-style regulation, as exemplified by such agencies as the Environmental Protection Agency, tends to have a narrow focus of concern but a broad coverage of industries. Other examples include the Occupational

22. Among the many anomalies of present airline regulation, I note here that United Airlines is required to serve the eastern Nevada towns of Elko and Ely. In 1970, Elko had a population of 7,621 and Ely 4,176. These locations are served by the smallest plane in the United Airline fleet, a Boeing 737 jet. For a recent discussion of some of the issues raised by air passenger regulation, see Paul W. MacAvoy and John W. Snow, eds., *Regulation of Passenger Fares and Competition among the Airlines* (American Enterprise Institute, 1977).

Safety and Health Administration, the Consumer Product Safety Commission, and (with somewhat narrower industry coverage) the National Highway Traffic Safety Administration. Many such agencies are within cabinet departments.

There are many instances in which the costs of new-style regulation seem to exceed their benefits, or where the benefits are not obtained in the least costly way. Again, the reactions of industry and labor to proposals to reduce the cost of regulation depend largely on the particular regulation in question. The automobile industry and the United Automobile Workers have joined in opposing certain costly motor vehicle emission standards. The automobile industry has opposed the mandatory use of air bags to protect the occupants of automobiles in accidents, while the casualty insurance industry has favored it. Industry frequently criticizes OSHA regulations for being too costly, while labor may criticize the same regulations for being too lax.

There is little general understanding of economists' approach to such questions through benefit-cost analysis. The public and legislators frequently argue that life, health, and safety are priceless, and that no cost is too high to pay for them. This is, of course, nonsense, but appealing nonsense. Decisions are made everyday that implicitly place a less than infinite value on life and health—for example, in permitting the use of cigarettes or in constructing a two-lane rather than a four-lane highway. However, opposition to the excessive cost of some new-style regulation is easily depicted as opposition to its worthy purposes.

Better economic analysis could perhaps reduce the cost of new-style regulation without sacrificing desirable objectives. Nevertheless, the aggregate costs of such regulation and its effects on measured prices will probably continue to rise. Perhaps the most that can be accomplished is a deceleration of the rate of increase.

Concluding Comments

If business and labor oppose some of the new proposals for fighting inflation, particularly the TIP proposals, it is proper to ask whether they would prefer the alternatives. This is not a question they will be eager to answer; it is similar to asking whether one prefers to die by shooting or by hanging. Some guesses about the answer are nevertheless possible.

It seems clear that labor would prefer TIP to wage and price controls, especially if TIP covered prices. Wage controls are a binding constraint on wages, and unions may pay part of the penalties for deliberate violation of them. In contrast, strong unions might feel confident that under TIP they could exert influence through militant strikes, and that management would take the consequences. By the same token, management might choose wage and price controls as the lesser evil because in return for their costs they might effectively restrain strong unions.

Both unions and management might prefer the use of monetary and fiscal policy to either TIP or controls. A probable exception on both sides of the bargaining table is the construction industry and its suppliers, which under present institutional arrangements in financial markets are particularly vulnerable to increases in interest rates.

The labor movement is on record as being opposed to tight money and high interest rates and as favoring an expansionary fiscal policy. But these policies do not impinge as directly as TIP on the central function of the trade union, which is wage determination. Moreover, labor's view is less crucial to the outcome in this area because the use of monetary and fiscal policy does not require new legislation.

Management would clearly favor the use of tighter monetary and fiscal policies. Although management is now generally willing to concede the need for budget deficits in a recession, it would prefer the budget to be balanced over the full business cycle and strongly questions the need for large deficits in the third year of a recovery.

Business support for tight monetary policy rests both on opposition to inflation and on acceptance of monetarist rather than Keynesian macroeconomic theory. An analysis of the reasons for these views is beyond the scope of this paper, but their strength is not open to question. One element of the explanation may be that business believes neither that the economy is far from full employment at present, nor that there are now large gains in output to be achieved from increased monetary and fiscal stimulus. Keynes did not persuade the business community to abandon the old-time religion, and I doubt that Wallich and Weintraub will be any more successful.

Comments
and Discussion

Daniel J. B. Mitchell: The Rees paper reviews a variety of policies that might be used to fight inflation. Although he does not state it explicitly, Rees implies that fighting inflation will have to be done—if it is to be done at all—through traditional demand-restraining measures. In particular, he concludes that tax-based incomes policies are currently unacceptable to either labor or management. Moreover, they are administratively complex and possibly unworkable. Rees does not provide a statement of his views on the efficacy of the traditional demand-restraint approach; that is not the topic of his paper. But I doubt that he would expect miracles in the next year or two from monetary and fiscal policies. So I must take this interesting paper to be essentially pessimistic on the prospect of achieving much on the inflation front.

Rees weighs various pros and cons of the TIPs and other recent proposals. Much of his criticism is on administrative grounds. But the paper does not include an explicit statement of the assumed sources of the current inflation or, at least, the reasons for its perpetuation. At present, a justification for a TIP would probably include some reference to institutional factors or inflationary expectations—especially in the labor market —which maintain the momentum of inflation. George Perry's paper in this volume develops this kind of prognosis of the current inflation. If you do not accept such a diagnosis, you probably do not view TIP as a cure.

If the diagnosis is accepted, however, some of Rees' conclusions might be altered. For example, reductions in excise taxes are characterized as "one-shot" affairs. Rees qualifies this characterization by adding that there might be secondary effects but that these effects diminish and eventually fade. The key issue is whether or not the rate of inflation is lower after the absolute price level effects have worked through the economy.

In some views of the momentum of inflation, it is possible that a permanent reduction in inflation could be made by a coordinated series of seemingly one-shot policies. Much depends on packaging. A cut in an excise tax might be put forward as a minor technical fiscal adjustment. Or, alternatively, such cuts might be presented as part of an overall anti-inflation program. If the latter could be made convincing, the rate of inflation might be permanently lowered, either by affecting expectations or by influencing other aspects of the wage-price setting process that might be responsible for the momentum of inflation.

The same can be said for the type of interventions in the federal regulatory process that the Council on Wage and Price Stability regularly attempts. Taken one at a time, a tilt at the Occupational Safety and Health Administration or at the Civil Aeronautics Board will have little perceptible impact on inflation, although these interventions might be justified on resource allocation grounds. (Such tilting does have the advantage of keeping the council in business when fighting inflation is not in vogue.) But as part of a publicized anti-inflation package, the impact on inflation could be more lasting. Indeed, I had always assumed that the council, under Rees' initial direction, had something like this in mind when it launched its activities in 1974.

Because much of the fault Rees finds with TIP proposals is directed toward administrative considerations rather than the theory of inflation, most of my remarks will focus on the administrative issue. His basic position—one with which I am totally in accord—is that in many ways a TIP would be no simpler to operate than a formal controls program. All the problems of costing, base periods, unforeseen effects, and so on associated with controls arise under TIP. The advocates of TIPs have often underestimated the inherent complexities, and it is useful for Rees to point these out. In effect, Rees tells us that the choice *between* controls (formal or informal) and TIP should not be made on the assumption that TIP will be simple to administer. But there are other grounds for favoring TIP over controls.

TIPs are said to avoid or minimize two important drawbacks of controls. First, in the labor market, controls invite confrontations between unions and government authorities when specific, newly negotiated contracts are reviewed. Such confrontations can discredit a policy if the guidelines are openly flaunted (as in the example of President Johnson and the airline machinists) or the authorities appear to buckle (President Carter's deceleration and coal intervention). Second, controls can create "distortions" of misallocation and shortages, primarily in the product market. TIPs leave collective bargaining to the parties, thus avoiding direct government involvement and reducing the risk of confrontation. And the product-market misallocation that might be created is likely to be less severe under TIP than under rigid pricing rules or ceilings. Rees does not seem impressed by these arguments, but they make sense to me.

Although I agree that controls and TIPs involve similar administrative problems, I believe the Rees paper overestimates the complexity of these problems. Consider the issue of establishing guidelines. Rees takes us over the familiar ground of productivity-based guidelines and the usual arithmetic that wage changes equal productivity plus inflation. Productivity plus inflation has been a convenient rationale for justifying the wage goal of past policies. But the rationale is not that important. Indeed, the goal and the guideline need not be synonymous. Much depends on the nature of the policy. If a controls policy permits few exceptions or a TIP policy imposes stringent penalties, the guideline must be *higher* than the goal. The more liberal the program, the closer the guideline is to the goal.

An explicit productivity guideline, as Rees notes, raises the specter of a "frozen" income distribution. But such fears are exaggerated. The purpose of incomes policies, tax-based or otherwise, is not the redistribution of income—despite the misleading nomenclature—but rather the reduction of cost increases.[1] The goal and guideline should be set high enough to be realistic, but low enough to reduce inflationary expectations. If a productivity rationale confuses the issue, then deceleration or some other rationale can be offered.[2]

1. The term "incomes policy" began to be used in Britain in the early 1960s for several reasons. First, it was more politically appealing than "wages policy," the earlier term. Second, the British were beginning to flirt with economic planning, and the notion of planning incomes seemed enticing. Third, in Britain and elsewhere in Europe, the view that inflation results from deficient saving propensities of the working class relative to capitalists is popular with both left-wing and right-wing observers. Hence, incomes rather than costs are often seen as the target of a controls policy.

2. As long as setting guidelines is viewed as an art rather than as a science, the inflexibility of a numerical guideline cited by Rees need not occur. The 5.5 percent guideline of the 1971–74 program, although rationalized along the lines of productivity plus inflation, was the result of a bargaining process at the Pay Board. It remained inflexible after Phase II simply because the new authorities chose to deemphasize the guideline approach altogether; to change the guideline would have implied recognition of its importance.

Probably the most important arguments Rees raises on the administrative side are in the area of industrial relations. He points out that bargaining units are not the same as tax units. A bargaining unit may be a part of a larger tax unit (for example, unionized blue-collar workers but not white-collar workers) or it may be composed of many tax units (multiemployer bargaining and pattern-following situations). Variations in the occupational and age structure among firms in a multiemployer unit may lead to different cost and tax consequences under TIP.

I think the unit problem is a strong anti-TIP argument. But there is another side that should be noted. Traditional monetary and fiscal policies may also have differential consequences for firms in a multiple-employer bargaining unit or pattern. When faced with economic pressures and technical change, bargaining units sometimes dissolve, as occurred in the glass industry in the 1950s. The differential pressures on members of bargaining units may lead to divergent treatment without destroying industrial relations. (American Motors received concessions from the Autoworkers as did Studebaker before it.) When there are multiple wage-determination units within a firm, the different units are always competing with each other to some extent for their relative shares. A TIP may exacerbate these problems, but it does not create them.

Rees also points to industrial disputes as a potential problem of TIP. Stiffening the backbone of management, he notes, might cause more strikes. In some versions of Arthur Okun's reward TIPs, this would not be an issue. But even under penalty TIPs, whether or not this tendency is thought to be significant depends on the model of the bargaining process that is applied. On the one hand, if strikes are brought about by collisions of inflexible and incompatible demands, anything that widens the spread between labor and management will cause more strikes. On the other hand, if strikes are the results of mistaken judgment about the points of resistance of the other party, the tendency of TIP to increase strikes need not be pronounced. It is likely, however, that whatever the true effect might be, strikes that lead to significant public inconvenience would be blamed on the program.

I am puzzled by Rees' insistence that the proponents of TIPs must inherently believe that unions maximize some specific goal in negotiations.[3] All that is assumed by TIP advocates is that management resis-

3. Rees is critical of the Wallich-Weintraub diagram that shows labor and management positions converging. There have been empirical studies that track the posi-

tance plays a role in bargaining outcomes. If bargaining were simply a process by which unions put forth nonnegotiable demands and management had to accede, wages would be high indeed, and strikes would be nonexistent. Rees states that there will be cases in which the TIP guidelines would cause the size of the eventual settlement to be smaller. Are TIP proponents really assuming anything other than that?

Finally, Rees' overall conclusion that neither labor nor management is likely to favor either controls or a TIP is not surprising given recent history. But neither is it decisive. Both parties have had the recent experience of controls, and found it distasteful. To the extent that the TIP proposal is known outside the narrow world of economic academia and Washington policymakers, it is undoubtedly seen as another form of controls. Yet it is apparent from the 1971–74 experience that such attitudes are not irrevocably fixed. In early 1971, organized business promoted controls, and organized labor was at least unopposed to the notion. Even after the labor walkout from the Pay Board in early 1972, AFL-CIO President Meany said that labor would learn to live with the regulations. In late 1972, when the shift to Phase III was under debate, organized business did not support rapid decontrol. It was during 1973–74, when the authorities persisted in trying to hold back the tide started by the food and oil price increases, that the opposition of business and labor hardened.

Both formal controls and the TIP proposals require congressional action. Congressional debate would have a destabilizing effect on wages and prices. The TIP proposal, in addition, would put an added burden on an already complex tax system. For those reasons, I share Rees' doubts about the various TIP proposals, even apart from the administrative issues he raises. But I am not persuaded, as he seems to be, that attitudes toward all forms of direct intervention cannot be changed. In particular, I am not certain that the prospect of another recession would not be a powerful factor in stimulating a rethinking concerning some sort of social compact on the part of organized labor. The fact that management readily supports demand restraint could well encourage union leaders to reconsider the alternatives.

---

tions of the parties in particular negotiations and come up with curves that look something like that diagram, although they are not as linear. Of course, it is impossible to record the "true" goals of the parties as opposed to the "feelers" they extend. See Roger L. Bowlby and William R. Schriver, "Bluffing and the 'Split-the-Difference' Theory of Wage Bargaining," *Industrial and Labor Relations Review*, vol. 31 (January 1978), pp. 161–71.

Lloyd Ulman: In principle, incomes policies may be divided into two categories: those that restrain wages directly and prices indirectly, and those that restrain prices directly and wages indirectly. (In practice, of course, most policies contain elements of both types.) Each type of policy has often been accompanied in recent years by compensatory modifications of tax policy. Policies of direct wage restraint have been combined with reductions in income or excise taxes to compensate wage earners for gains forgone under collective bargaining; and price controls have been accompanied by reductions in various types of business taxes or by extension of subsidies to protect profits and investment, to minimize industrial strife due to stiffened employer resistance, or both.

Incomes policies of both types have entailed economic or social costs that have limited their effectiveness, either by weakening compliance by the parties at whom they have been directed or by weakening the political will of the community to enforce or even to introduce them. Economic costs involve misallocation and other types of inefficiency and, ultimately, slower growth rates. Social or political costs result from abridged freedom, where the policies are in fact backed by legal sanctions. Across-the-board tax reductions may prove to be inefficient incentives to wage restraint (and hence inadequate substitutes for legal sanctions) because they are not conditioned on compliance in each wage-determining situation. And if direct policies of wage restraint are to be effective, they would remove from the unions a great part of their raison d'être (a greater part than private enterprise would lose from price controls).

The case for tax-oriented incomes policies is that they are free of the defects of other types of incomes policy, and, consequently, that they are inherently more efficient in improving the inflation-unemployment trade-off. They presume an inducement—negative or positive—to restrain at the least centralized levels of wage determination as well as at the most centralized ones. (This minimizes the probability that restraint exercised at formal, centralized negotiations would be neutralized by greater wage drift at the plant level, which is what allegedly occurred in Sweden after a reduction in income taxes in 1975.) The unions would not be stripped of their wage-bargaining function because they and the employers would be legally free to bargain for increases above the norm if it were profitable to incur the tax penalty or forgo the tax benefit for doing so. For the same reason, there is no abridgment of economic freedom. Nor would the operation of TIPs cause serious misallocations or inefficiencies because if compliance would cause them, the employer would have the incentive and the freedom to disregard the wage norm. TIP, in short, would be at once less restrictive and arbitrary and more effective than controls.

"Spinach!" cries Professor Rees, whose task it is to anticipate and evaluate the reactions of unions and of employers. He is led to the view that TIP, in practice, would be no less, and possibly more restrictive and arbitrary than conventional controls, and no more effective than conventional controls. Several points should be mentioned regarding the implementation of TIP. First, the restricted coverage contemplated for penalty TIPs requires a more direct and mandatory wage restraint in such areas as state and local governments, nonprofit institutions, and small firms— where, as Rees points out, the building trades, teamsters, and other strong unions are organized. Wallich and Weintraub recognize that coverage must be restricted, but imply that exemptions can safely be made. However, if relative wages were raised significantly outside the area of coverage, that would threaten the viability of TIP where it is supposed to apply because various traditional wage patterns cut across the boundaries defining the area of coverage.

Second, the implementation of TIP might prove to be less impersonal and automatic than the implementation of controls and, to that extent, no less abridging of freedom. (To identify freedom with legal liberty is to mistake a part for the whole.) Definitional and computational problems, as outlined by Ackley and Rees, might arise in specific situations; and, while they would be neither unique nor insoluble, their resolutions would require interpretation, the exercise of discretion, and, therefore, bureaucracy.

Guidelines would have to be set for TIP; at least in Okun's version of TIP, these would include price guidelines as well as wage guidelines. I agree with Rees that price guideposts would be both a political and an economic necessity. I would go further in one direction than Rees does in his discussion of wage norm issues and not as far in another. In my view, a TIP guidepost should provide full compensation for the prospective rate of inflation. TIP is logically and admittedly designed to cope with only the cost-push component of inflation—which would slow along with wages—and the government should ensure that inflation from other sources does not erode real wages. Aggregate demand policy must avoid excess demand. And government policies in other areas must concern themselves with price stability. Without those additional policies, under a "low" wage norm real wages would fall relative to trend productivity. Such a program would be difficult to achieve; and trying for it could even yield a perversely restrictive effect on aggregate demand as a result of large penalty taxes imposed under TIP. Achieving it would depend on a mixture of persuasion and legal sanctions characteristic of conventional incomes policies, in addition to the tax disincentive. Such a low, downward-ratcheting norm for wage increases could be established and periodically reestablished only under a political process that has come to be known as "big-gun bargaining," which involves the labor movement, some type of management ball team, and the government.

I would not go so far as Rees in holding that TIP requires a norm for wage increases, while an effective system of controls would not. A norm admittedly entails two disadvantages. First, it can act as a red flag for some of the otherwise more resigned or contented bulls in the pasture. Despite this, its net effect might still be to restrain wage behavior, especially if it serves as a signal for moderation to nonunion firms and if it can serve as a scapegoat for some union leaders who might otherwise press for excessively rich settlements against their own better judgment. Second, it is difficult to develop a norm that would allow room for justifiable "exceptions" without sacrificing clarity or signaling efficiency. But these problems also exist for controls. Under controls, the authorities must have some wage or price targets in mind; and these cannot long remain classified information. A system of controls, whether legal or de facto, could operate with a more obscure central guidepost than a TIP system. However, it is not true that TIP needs a guidepost that controls can avoid altogether.

Rees also claims that a TIP would probably "increase both the frequency and the duration of strikes," whereas controls act as an effective deterrent to striking. Wallich and Weintraub question the former proposition. They argue that the prospect of a penalty tax increase could discourage unionists from striking by stiffening the employer's backbone, and thus reducing the prospective gains from a strike. Seidman claims that a TIP with a carrot approach—a payroll tax credit for employees— would reduce the incentive to strike for and obtain wage increases above the norm; to strike, he contends, would deprive employees of the tax credit for marginal increases above the norm and also for all increases up to the norm.

It is useful to distinguish among three components of bargaining power in assessing strike prospects: (1) maximum, or potential, bargaining power, which would maximize the increase in the employer's labor costs, given the market conditions that determine the employer's ability to pay and to resist and given various determinants of the goals and militancy of the union's members; (2) desired bargaining power, which reflects membership attitudes but other things as well and is reflected in the demands by the union's negotiators and leadership; and (3) actual bargaining power, or the actual results of collective bargaining. The question of how TIP would affect bargaining cannot be answered a priori. A TIP penalty tax would increase employer resistance, but if unions were not exploiting their maximum bargaining power, the tax stick would neither discourage unions from striking nor result in reduced settlements. This is consistent with Rees' observation: "When the union has the power to win a long strike, it does little good to strengthen management's backbone." It is indeed possible that a tax penalty would in fact reduce a union's bargaining potential below previously achievable target levels. But if the target levels were maintained, or not reduced in proportion, union dissatisfaction would be increased and so would strike activity, although actual negotiated increases would presumably be reduced. Seidman's tax carrot is designed to reduce bargaining targets, but it will prove tempting only if the wage norm under TIP is sufficiently high relative to the union's target to make the difference between the two less than the probable costs of striking for the target. There is no presumption that a given norm will be consistent with the achievement of the two policy targets of price stability and industrial peace.

These possibilities illustrate another characteristic that TIP shares with other forms of incomes policy, including controls: the levels of performance that can be specified and achieved through enforcement are governed by the public, by political tolerance of industrial disputes, by the more narrowly economic cost of enforcement, as well as by tolerance of unemployment and inflation. But if more strikes and the winning of strikes by unions are to be counted as a cost of TIP, that cost must be weighed against an institutional gain, which helps distinguish TIP from other wage-restraint policies. TIP does preserve a role for union bargaining. In this respect, TIP brings to mind the theoretical basis of the Swedish active labor market policy, which was designed to reduce aggregate money demand relative to output and hence to increase the resistance to union demands by employers who were subject to constrained profit margins.

This method was developed by the chief union economist of the Swedish Federation of Trade Unions in the aftermath of an unsuccessful incomes policy.

Despite the advantage of preserving a role for collective bargaining, the prospect of more or longer strikes under TIP may not enhance its prospects of acceptance by the general public, management, or the unions. But it is worthwhile asking what order of magnitude the cost of additional strikes is likely to be. Since World War II, only a little less than a quarter of 1 percent of working time has been lost due to industrial disputes. Moreover, the economic costs of strikes are often estimated without netting them against any gains that they generate in the form of smaller increases in costs and prices. On the premise that one *New Yorker* cartoon deserves another, I recall one in which the chairman of the board complains to his fellow directors, "We haven't had a strike in ten years. We must have been overpaying them all along." If TIP increases strikes, with the added social and economic costs, it should also increase the associated gains.

The criterion implied in the last statement should be expanded to include other costs associated with TIP, including bureaucratic costs. I concur with the view that TIP is not a "free policy lunch." It is not totally free of the costs attributable to a conventional system of controls; nor is its effectiveness independent of the level of its acceptance in principle by labor and management. One question to be asked is whether a TIP with controls and persuasion is more cost-effective, in the broadest sense, than a system of controls with persuasion but without TIP. This question cannot be answered a priori.

In my opinion, a system with a selective and discriminating tax incentive is preferable to one without it. Given general acceptance, such a tax incentive should prove an effective way to penalize the rogue elephant or to deter others from straying from the herd. For the same reason, the use of discriminating tax reductions may be preferable to across-the-board reductions, unless the latter can be conditioned on restraint by wage (and price) setters. The prospects for contingent tax reductions are limited by two considerations. First, in a system of decentralized wage determination, individual units cannot readily afford to be guided by macroeconomic considerations. Second, some of the most powerful groups of workers are, almost by definition, least likely to suffer the consequences in reduced employment flowing from the exercise of their power. The authorities, representing the general public—including the minority groups that are weakest economically—are unfortunately not in a strong position in this big-gun bargaining encounter. They are not in a position to condition expansionary tax reductions on wage restraint because their desire for high levels of employment may well exceed even that of powerful unions. In this general respect, therefore, TIP is preferable to general tax reductions precisely because it is inherently contingent on prior wage restraint.

General Discussion

Several participants in the discussion differed with Rees' characterization of the bargaining process. Sidney Weintraub said that Rees had assigned union leaders too large a role and that he had neglected the part played by union members and the labor movement in general. Rees replied that union leaders tended to be more restrained than their membership. It was the membership that had broken wage guidelines in the past by rejecting settlements reached by the leadership. He favored union democracy but pointed out that it increased the pressure on union leaders to produce larger gains at the bargaining table. Martin Baily argued that Rees had overemphasized the union sector and a particular model of wage settlements in that sector. Even if a maximization model is not accepted as appropriate, competitive pressures impinged on the bargaining process. The majority of the labor force is not unionized, and wages in the unionized and nonunionized sectors affect one another directly. In addition. there are indirect influences through the product markets and through the option of unionized firms to produce something in-house or to subcontract it to smaller, nonunion firms.

Laurence Seidman observed that a TIP scheme might have a substantial impact on the firms that Rees had said would not be influenced by TIP. Even though an unprofitable firm might not be directly affected by a penalty TIP on profits, the knowledge that TIP would make its profitable competitors resist a high-wage settlement would lead it to be tougher in its own wage negotiations. Even aggressive unions with sufficient market power to ignore TIP would discover that their real or relative wage objectives could be achieved with lower wage increases if wages elsewhere were affected by TIP.

Baily and Seidman both disagreed with Rees' assertion that management's aggressiveness would not be seriously strengthened by TIP. They said that management's resistance would depend on the cost of settlements, and management's opposition to each proposed wage increase would now be greater.

Weintraub suggested that additional features could be added to TIP to meet some of Rees' objections. In particular, some way could be found to encourage wage resistance by firms that were incurring losses and therefore were not subject to profits tax. He also noted that the government could augment TIP effects by contracting only with firms that had adhered to wage rate standards. He noted that the Davis-Bacon act already constituted a form of incomes policy on government construction. Rees added that by changing the administration of the Davis-Bacon act so that the prevailing wage was the median wage in any market, wages mandated by the act would be substantially reduced. But this has never been done because it is too costly politically.

Michael Wachter found both start-up problems and ongoing problems with TIP. Because the wage structure is always in disequilibrium, starting up a TIP program unfairly penalizes those wages coming up for new settlement. Furthermore, the government frequently has a stake in collective bargaining outcomes and becomes involved in such negotiations through the Federal Mediation and Conciliation Service. TIP could place the government in the position of inducing a settlement and then taxing the outcome. But Charles Holt replied that one important benefit of TIP would be to take the government out of the collective bargaining business.

Wachter also noted that TIP differed from controls only in degree, so that it risked the same problems of misallocation on the one hand or of being discredited by excessive settlements on the other. Seidman replied that although a TIP with a prohibitive tax on high settlements would be equivalent to controls, a TIP with a reasonable penalty had the advantage of allowing the necessary relative wage adjustments to take place. However, Lloyd Ulman cautioned that it might not be possible to allow the required relative wage changes and meet a particular inflation objective at the same time.

Seidman reasoned that labor's fears that TIP would be biased against labor's share of income could be allayed by "real wage insurance" rather than treated as an insurmountable obstacle. Baily argued that income shares were an inadequate measure of labor's well-being and that the record showed that controlling inflation was good for labor. From 1950 to 1969, labor's share had declined, but real gross earnings had risen 16 percent. In the 1970s, its share had increased, but real earnings had not risen. George Perry added that labor's resistance to a penalty TIP would almost certainly be greater than its resistance to a reward TIP. Politicians who did not want to vote to penalize wage gains could hardly be equally persuaded not to reward socially desirable wage behavior.

Charles Holt felt that Rees had concentrated too narrowly on the role of a penalty TIP in stiffening the backbone of management and thought most problems with the details of a TIP plan could be solved. He offered his own employee-oriented TIP, with a target range within which wage adjustments would not be affected (to allow room for necessary relative wage changes) and with rewards and penalties for wage changes below and above the range.

ABBA P. LERNER
Florida State University

A Wage-Increase Permit
Plan to Stop Inflation

I WANT TO DISCUSS not the sons of TIP but what is perhaps a grandson toward which the TIP family is developing. It is a wage-increase permit plan (WIPP), about which I have written briefly in *Challenge* and *Social Research*.[1] Although I consider WIPP more logical, manageable, and effective than any of the TIPs, I said in those articles that I would support some form of TIP that seemed more likely to be acceptable and implemented. But the discussion at this conference has convinced me that the objections to the various TIPs are much more serious than I had supposed, that most of them would not apply to WIPP, and that it is not at all clear that a TIP would indeed be more likely to be accepted. I have also been thinking more about WIPP, developing it further, and becoming more fond of it, so I want to restate it.

WIPP is based on a view of the economy such as that suggested by Perry. In my view, inflation in the United States is not caused by excess demand, but by self-fulfilling expectations, with prices rising at about 6 percent to keep up with the cost of production, compensation rising at about 9 percent to keep up with the cost of living and increasing productivity, while the government keeps increasing total spending in the economy to prevent catastrophic unemployment. There is a vicious circle of rising prices, rising wages, and rising total spending in which none of these can stop because the others are going on. And yet there is a new kind of fairly stable, process equilibrium—a 6 percent expectational inflation.

1. "Stagflation—Its Cause and Cure," *Challenge*, vol. 20 (September/October 1977), pp. 14–19; and "From Pre-Keynes to Post-Keynes," *Social Research*, vol. 47 (Fall 1977).

This condition of the economy is the result of a flaw in the market mechanism. Important lessons are to be learned from the natural history of another flaw. During World War II there arose a "shortage" of some essential items that led to intolerable price increases. The poor were deprived of vital necessities that the rich were using wastefully.

The natural history begins with price control. That leads to black markets and to arbitrary and discriminatory informal rationing by shopkeepers. The informal rationing is then replaced by official formal rationing. This is still considered bothersome and wasteful and is greatly improved by point rationing, under which the same ration points can be used for several substitutes. Next there are ration points that are valid for wider ranges of goods and reduce illegal trading of rations and ration tickets. The final stage would take the form of Michal Kalecki's general rationing. This rationing uses a single set of points expressed in money, which essentially serves only as permits to limit the amount of money any individual can spend on the "scarce" essential commodities.

As the scarcity abated after the war, the prices of the scarce items fell so low that the allotted permits (which had drawn large black market prices) almost made possible the purchase of more than people wanted to buy. These permits would have become redundant and quite worthless, but the entire system was scrapped before this happened, which provided a more dramatic (if somewhat synthetic) occasion for celebrating decontrol.

TIP is a similar development of procedures (although not completed) for correcting a flaw in the market mechanism, and most of the objections to TIP raised at this conference owe their validity only to the incompleteness of the correction of the flaw. The flaw in the present instance is a mutation of the flaw responsible for the great depression of the 1930s.

That flaw was diagnosed by Keynes and its cure prescribed in 1936 in the more elementary chapters of *The General Theory of Employment, Interest and Money*. It was the failure of wages to fall far enough and fast enough in response to a deficiency in demand for labor to maintain a satisfactory level of output and employment, given the level of total spending. The cure was easy because of the availability of a free variable—increases in the level of spending. This could be adjusted to take the place of the decrease in wages and prices that was missing. It was costless because of the great scope for continuing government deficits and the growth of intranational debt, and the unlimited scope for costless increases in the quantity of money.

The mutation is that wages do not merely refuse to fall but keep rising, caught in a self-fulfilling expectational inflation. Government and businesses, which seem to have an incurable propensity to treat inflation as if it were due to too much total spending, hold down their spending as long as prices are rising, but desist from this when the resulting unemployment threatens to reach double digits. This is what creates stagflation but does not lead to catastrophic depression.

The simple Keynesian remedy is not effective in dealing with this mutation. The task is now twofold: it is necessary to stabilize the average price (the price level), with average wages rising at the national average rate of productivity increase; and to adjust relative wages and relative prices to the continuing changes in tastes and techniques. To accomplish this task the vicious circle of rising wages, prices, and total spending must be broken. Stopping any one of them could break the spell in which each has to keep rising because the others are rising. But stopping the spending, which the government could bring about, only works through catastrophic depression and severe unemployment. Alternatively, prices or wages could be stabilized. Prices, however, are much more complicated than wages, and price regulation is more easily evaded by quality changes. The best option seems to be to stabilize wages, which are already largely administered by collective bargaining and other large-scale wage decisions.

In the 1940s I developed some rules for wage regulation to achieve the twofold objective and published them in my *Economics of Employment* in 1951. Later this was attempted in practice by wage-price guidelines and guideposts, which included price regulation for political purposes. The first objective was achieved with some success by a freeze of prices and wages, but it was soon eroded by the regulations for adjusting relative wages and prices.

These regulations became an administrative nightmare parallel to the use of price controls against the intolerable price increases caused by scarcities in World War II. The administrators were unable to handle the complexities or deal with the resistances. The bureaucratic, administrative decision mechanism broke down. The task required local decisions by local people who knew the local conditions; thus, something more like a decentralized market mechanism was needed.

Tax-Based Incomes Policy

A great step forward was made by Weintraub and Wallich in proposing such a device in their tax-based incomes policy (TIP). Weintraub used the analogy to laws against speeding, laws that people can break if they are prepared to pay the fine. The analogy is faulty because a speeding law that succeeded in keeping everyone below the speed limit would be regarded as successful. What is needed is a rule—if you could call it that —which would normally and properly be broken half the time.

To fulfill the twofold task of keeping the average price constant while leaving individual prices free, average wages must continue rising at a norm equal to the national average rate of productivity increase while leaving individual wage rates free. For this it is necessary to discourage the granting of wage increases (or to provide an incentive to resist wage increases) in a way that will still permit some wage increases to exceed the norm by as much as other wage increases fail to reach the norm.

If TIP were adjusted to eliminate all subsidies and to provide equal tax incentives at all levels for equal reductions in the amounts of wage increase, with no lower or upper limit (no minimum threshold and no maximum of any kind), it would solve the incentive problem efficiently.[2] (These are indeed the adjustments I suggested in proposing to support TIP rather than WIPP in my *Challenge* article; the second condition, equal tax incentives, is similar to adjustments suggested by Seidman.) But TIP would still be left with much of the "litigation nightmare" of unlimited disputes about the appropriateness or the equity of the charges and the subsidies in different situations, because it does not solve the problem of deciding how strong to make the tax incentive. It would correct only part of the flaw.

TIP would mobilize the essential function of *price* in the market

2. Subsidies are proposed only because of a confusion between the necessity of offsetting the effects of taxes on total spending and the desirability of ameliorating hardships. Hardships apply to people, rather than businesses, and their amelioration calls for income benefits, not changes in prices or wages. Similarly, the word "penalty" is unfortunate because it suggests a punishment imposed for wrongdoing. TIP would impose something like a price, which, as always, discourages people from buying something because they would rather keep the money for other purposes. It is not a punishment for any improprieties. This does not rule out the grants or tax reductions required to increase total demand in order to offset the effect of the incentive tax in reducing total demand.

mechanism, which is to discourage whatever activity calls for a price to be paid and, its mirror image, to encourage whatever enables a price to be received. Still missing would be the other half of the market mechanism, the guide to free decisions in the social interest by the establishment of price at the level that equates supply and demand. WIPP, unlike TIP, uses the market mechanism to provide this guide and to adjust the incentive to the strength required.

Wage-Increase Permit Plan

WIPP works as follows:

(1) The government would grant "wage increase permits" to every employer who qualified by employing more than, say, 100 workers or *any* workers whose wages were fixed by an agreement that covered more than 100 workers—for instance, one permit for each $1,000 of the employer's total costs of employment (called his "wage bill," but including all fringe benefits and so forth).[3] Records would be kept of the employer's wage bill from a base date, including each employee's wages (pay plus the employee's share of the other costs of employment).[4]

(2) Newly hired employees, including all employees of new firms, would enable their qualified employers to obtain additional permits and also a permit for each $1,000 of the new employee's wages. Conversely, on the separation of an employee from a firm, including all the employees of a firm that closes, the corresponding number of permits would have to be returned to the permit authority. This would adjust the total number of permits to changes in the wage bill that were due to changes in employment, rather than to changes in the wage level.[5]

3. "It is now uniformly recognized that payments to common benefit trust funds providing pension welfare, vacation and vocation training and other benefits represent a substantial economic portion of employee wages . . . ." (*Statements and Reports Adopted by the AFL-CIO Executive Council, Bal Harbour, Florida, February 20–27, 1978*, pp. 57–58).

4. Some components of these data are required by the Internal Revenue Service or by the Social Security Administration, with which the permit authority would cooperate. The firm could allocate its total fringe benefits among the employees in any way it chose as long as the total cost of all the fringe benefits was included in the wage bill.

5. Care would have to be taken to prevent evasion by firing and rehiring at higher pay (to obtain free permits for an "employment increase" instead of buying permits for what is really a wage increase) and to avoid related collusions between firms and unions or among firms to exchange employees for this purpose.

(3) Each permit would give the employer who held it the right (by raising wage rates) to raise his adjusted wage bill by, say, $30 per permit (3 percent of the face value of his permits, which is the estimated national average rate of increase in output per employee—"productivity").

(4) The permits would be freely tradable in a perfectly competitive market, like a share of IBM in the stock exchange. Any employer who wished to increase his adjusted wage bill by more than 3 percent by raising wage rates would have to acquire more permits. He could obtain them only through purchase from others who had to reduce the increase in their wage bill by the same amount below 3 percent. Any employer who reduced his wage bill would qualify for a grant of additional permits for the corresponding amount (one permit for each $30 cut from a wage bill), and could sell those permits. The national total wage bill would thereby always be raised just 3 percent a year by the wage bill increases of the different firms. Because the wage bill is adjusted for changes in employment at the level of the firm and at the national level, the national average wage would continue to rise at 3 percent a year. The price of the permit would be set by the market at the level at which supply equals demand; this price would just offset inflationary expectations for raising wages more than productivity.

A year later each 100 old permits would be replaced by 103 new, dated, $1,000 permits. The total number of permits at the national level would therefore keep up with both components of the national total wage bill: the volume of employment and the national average wage.

WIPP would thus indeed "whip inflation now" by achieving the essential twofold objective. It would keep the average wage rising at the same rate as output per worker, eliminating price-level inflation, and leave each particular wage free for determination by individual or collective bargaining. All other prices would be left for free market determination established before WIPP was introduced. The money paid or received for permits would then be just one more of the many considerations that influence wage settlements.

A Comparison of the Two Proposed Policies

Wage bargaining—both individual and collective—could proceed as it did before the adoption of an anti-inflation policy, and the same would be true for setting prices by the market. WIPP, like TIP, does not address other market imperfections, such as restrictive practices, monopoly, monopsony, cartels, and oligopolies. It does not prevent monopsonistic exploitation of workers in company towns or keep strong unions from forcing employers to grant exorbitant wage increases. And it does not stop unions from persuading the government to put pressure on employers when a strike threatens to endanger the economy or the health or safety of the public. For the purposes of WIPP, no individual wage, firm wage average, or wage increase is too much or too little. WIPP is concerned with only the national *average* rate of wage increase.

One important difference between WIPP and TIP is that the former induces employers to buy the required permits *from other employers*. The gains from such inducement are then clearly seen to be made at the expense of other workers whose employers sell these same permits.

This is the elementary lesson that the economics profession has failed to teach effectively. WIPP permits could prevent the pressure groups from recruiting the support of the victims of their extortion. The other workers whose wage increase permits are taken away would be reluctant to support the extortion under the fraudulent slogans of working class solidarity or to honor the picket lines that are picking their own pockets.

TIP, as modified, would simulate price by using the tax as a uniform incentive for resisting the pressure for wage increases, but it would provide no guideline to indicate how large the tax must be to offset this pressure or to monitor the changes in the pressure.

This pressure is nothing but the impact of inflationary expectations. At present these seem to be about 9 percent for average compensation and 6 percent for average prices. If either TIP or WIPP were adopted, these expectations and the consequent pressures would decrease, and the incentives would have to be reduced. Legislative and administrative adjustment of the taxes are much too slow; they would work like decisions required to change the price of IBM in the stock exchange.

In speaking of WIPP as "internalizing the inflation externality," as I sometimes have, I was shortchanging it. The adjusted TIP also internalizes it, but the legislative nightmare, which is diminished by making the TIP tax uniform, can be removed only by WIPP's correction of the flaw in the market mechanism.

"Internalization" is borrowed from pollution theory, where pollution permits are an improvement on earlier antipollution cries such as "prohibit it" or "limit it." But modern economists, prodded by Ronald Coase, understand that the government would be justified in fixing a price for a permit to pollute only if a proper market could not be established.

But if a market were established (which would require definition of a previously undefined, or inadequately defined property right and the settlement of clear ownership), there would no longer be a "pollution problem." There would be merely one more scarce commodity on the market. The externality has not merely been internalized by a charge, tax, or permit and converted into a cost at a level decided by an administrative or a legislative authority. Something more has been done. The externality has been made to reflect the value of the damage as indicated on the market by the damaged party. The market mechanism now serves as a guide to the proper intensity of the incentive. No litigation is required. The market determines the correct price. Clarification of property rights is the euthanasia of litigation.

This completion of the correction of the flaw corresponds to Kalecki's general rationing, which prevents the rich from wasting the necessities of the poor; it completes the process of reestablishing the market by making the general ration points legally tradable.

WIPP thus automatically adjusts the price of a wage-increase permit to the level of the current self-fulfilling inflationary expectations. As it offsets the expectation of inflation, it diminishes the inflationary wage increase, the cost increase, and the price increase. This lowering in actual inflation reduces expectation of further inflation and thereby further decreases actual inflationary wages, costs, and prices. The inflation is automatically deflated. The self-fulfilling expectational inflation becomes self-liquidating.

Because the power of WIPP lies in the price of the permit, and that price is equated in the market to the pressure of the inflationary expectations, and because the inflationary expectations rest on the experience of actual inflation, the price of the permit and the power of WIPP decrease in parallel with the inflation. In making the inflation self-liquidating, WIPP also makes itself automatically self-liquidating.

The decline of the WIPP permit price to zero when the inflationary pressure, the inflation, and WIPP itself are all liquidated corresponds to the eroding of the scarcity and the consequent disappearance of the general rationing permits.

My support of TIP rather than WIPP was partly due to the belief that WIPP would seem to too many people like a wild-eyed revolutionary dream too good to be true. But it is indeed a most conservative device that is operating in our economy countless times each day. It leaves each of the large number of quantities of some item unregulated—for free determination by a large number of people concerned with it—while the average of all these quantities remains fixed. What makes WIPP seem strange is only that the item is a new one and has not been treated in this familiar way in the past.

One example of the familiar miracle will suffice. The number of oranges per consumer is freely chosen by him when he takes the equilibrium price into consideration. This price, reached by the market, automatically makes the average number of oranges demanded per consumer just equal to the average number available per consumer because the total number demanded is equal to the total number supplied.

For this miracle to work, society had to decide to make the ownership of oranges a legal property right of individuals. This undoubtedly was an impious, revolutionary, and antisocial idea when first suggested to the head of a tribe where individual rights were nonexistent.

The new property right that needs to be created unfortunately is quite different from an orange. It is the right of an employer to raise his wage bill and thus his average wage. The property right comes in units of $30; its ownership is registered by the possession of one $1,000 permit. Its (uniform) price and its annual rental are determined by supply and demand in the market in which the permits (rights) are freely exchanged by buyers and sellers and borrowers and lenders. This system of rights could correct the flaw in the market mechanism that has resulted in the present inflation.

Recent Questions Raised

I conclude by touching briefly on a number of questions about WIPP and TIP that have been raised here and elsewhere.

(1) The relatively stable price inflation of 6 percent a year that has been experienced in the last few years has as much right to be called an equilibrium state as the Keynesian unemployment equilibrium of stable wages. This may seem strange to those who have learned from the textbook that a rise in price occurs only when there is excess demand—when demand exceeds supply and there is no equilibrium. But that rule relies

on a hidden, perhaps unnoticed, assumption that stable prices had been expected. It is only a special case of a more general rule. The more general rule says that, if there is excess demand, the previous expectation is raised and the price will rise faster than had been expected. In the special case in which the expectation of increased price is zero, excess demand would cause price to rise faster than zero, and the words "faster than zero" are taken as understood. After all, rising seems to mean rising faster than zero.

If, however, the expectation was not a zero rise in price but a 6 percent price increase, an excess demand, which always makes prices rise more than expected, would now bring about a price rise of more than 6 percent. When demand equals supply, with no disappointed buyers or sellers, no change would occur, but again there would be no change in the expectation—that is, a confirmation of previous expectations and a continuing of the equilibrium 6 percent rate of price inflation. This equilibrium is the vicious circle that TIP and WIPP have to break.

(2) WIPP and TIP share the strategy of placing a price on the granting of wage increases (over and above the actual wage increases) that would make inflationary wage increases more expensive. The use of expressions like "penalty" instead of price or charge is responsible for proposals of progressive punishment for more heinous "crimes" in the form of more than proportional charges for larger wage increases. But price functions properly only if the total paid is proportional to the amount bought, and this also applies to the price paid for granting wage increases.

(3) More recent estimates have reduced the rate of increase in output per worker from 3 to 2 percent. I think this is partly a reflection of the state of depression in our stagflation in which output declines in a larger proportion than employment, so that the figure would return to the previous 3 percent or so if TIP or WIPP succeeded in conquering the stagflation. The reduction may also occur because more resources are used to produce benefits that do not appear in the measure of output—such as improvement of the environment for which only the costs are shown in the figures for output per worker.

However, it will not make much difference whether the figure adopted is 3 percent, 2 percent, or 4 percent. Any one of these will yield a stable rate of inflation between +1 percent and −1 percent and none of the serious inflation or stagflation problems.

There have also been suggestions that instead of setting the wage in-

crease norm at the final goal of 3 percent (or 2 percent or 4 percent), it should be gradually lowered from the current 9 percent to reach the final figure only after a number of years. One reason given for this is that a sudden end to the inflation would give an unfair advantage to those whose compensation had recently been raised at the inflationary rate of about 9 percent, compared to those who had been waiting a year or two for their raise when the imposition of TIP or WIPP reduced theirs to about 3 percent. But other devices are available for correcting such inequities. To soften this effect is much too expensive. It would cost only a tiny fraction of this to provide even the most generous compensation to those who may have been harmed by the sudden and unexpected end to the inflation.

More importantly, a gradual reduction in the rate of inflation is bound to be obscured from time to time by incidental increases and decreases in costs due to changes in circumstances. These would hide the effect of the TIP or WIPP only temporarily, but could easily lead to the criticism that the anti-inflation plan is not working and the program would be dismantled before it had finished the job.

(4) There can be no real distinction between incentives to employers to increase their resistance to wage increases and incentives to workers to reduce their pressure for wage increases. In either case the incentive is the same tax on the same transaction. The remaining issue in all the TIPs is who should pay the tax and who should receive the "grant." This is the source of the litigation nightmare. WIPP solves this problem by its allocation of the property rights. The "tax" is paid by those who buy the permits, and the "revenue" is received by the sellers. A clear title to the property rights eliminates this litigation.

(5) Cutting excise taxes, or any other taxes that enter into cost, would reduce the costs and the price level, and so would reductions of monopolistic restrictions or of restrictions on imports. Such measures do increase economic efficiency, but they do not touch the core of our inflationary process. They lower the level of prices, but only once. They do nothing to prevent the exponential inflationary trend from continuing to rise and soon more than make up for the one-time decline in prices. Such windfalls could affect the inflationary trend only if there were a serendipitous succession of them that would flatten out the actual average price movement for a period long enough to establish expectations of further stability. Although such expectations would have to be based on unwarranted

anticipation of continuing windfalls, they *could* establish a self-fulfilling expectation of stability—a zero rate of self-fulfilling expectational inflation—but such a happy concatenation of windfalls is not likely to occur.

(6) If an efficient TIP were developed—one with the same incentives (tax or grant deduction) to hold down wage increases at all levels, the basic grant (before the deductions) would have to be equal to the sum of the taxes and the deductions, so that the remaining part of the grant would just counterbalance the deflationary effect of the taxes. If the grant were given only to workers who received wage increases less than the norm, we would have a problem (as seems to be implied in Seidman's approach—to induce workers to moderate their wage demands in order to reduce the penalty, the deductions from the grants). The amount of the grants would have to be twice that of the total deductions. Some way would have to be found to prevent workers from doing anything at all to qualify for some of the grant or to prevent themselves from being disqualified. Otherwise, the grant would no longer be "lump sum," that is, independent of the wage increase.

(7) It would not be possible for the government to compete with private industry for permits to raise the wages of their employees. The decision between public and private economic activity is a political one and cannot be left to the free market. However, the same principles are valid *within* the government sector. There would therefore have to be a separate set of government wage increase permits that operates within the government budget. This would check the inflation of government wages while permitting the different departments to compete with one another for employees. It would also yield the same demonstration that wage increases by any government component would have to come at the expense of wages in the other departments from which the government wage increase permits must come.

To have the same permits for government and for private industry would impose great pressure on the government to expand the budget in response to an increased price of permits and would result in a shift from private industry with its limited budgets to the government with its elastic budget.

(8) WIPP does not induce any shift from employing high-paid labor to low-paid labor. I would not consider it a disadvantage if it did. As long as there is greater unemployment among low-wage workers, such a shift would be socially most desirable (although full employment is much

better). With full employment the effect would be to reduce income inequalities; this, too, is socially desirable. It is not even certain that efficiency would be sacrificed to equity in this case. Higher earnings are largely not rewards for investment in training but the result of discriminatory opportunities from one's parents in education, money, connections, and good advice; or just plain luck.

Nevertheless, the complaint is not valid, and any of the benefits mentioned above should be pursued directly. WIPP does not cause such a shift because the permits are proportional to the wages, and the charges for wage increases are proportional to the wage increases. Relative costs are unaffected.

The complaint does hold for TIPs with upper or lower limits to the range of wage increase subject to the incentives or for TIPs with different rates of incentive tax at different levels of the firm's average wage.

(9) WIPP will not add to average cost to be passed on in additional price increases because the increase in cost to those who buy permits is exactly balanced by the decrease in cost to those who sell the permits; and in any balanced TIP the taxes that add to cost are kept equal to the offsetting grants that do the opposite. There remain only the effects of the reduction in the wage increases.

(10) A frequent objection is that the price of the permits would be too high for practical purposes. It is impossible for the price to be "too high." It cannot be higher than what the buyers are willing to pay!

Astronomical figures are obtained by counting the capital value of a *permanent* permit (which would allow wage increases to be paid forever) with the assumption that the inflationary pressure would last forever. But the WIPP permits are *annual* permits.

The permits could also be used to work in the opposite direction if a self-fulfilling expectation of falling average prices and wages, such as that of the 1930s, should ever arise again. An incentive against decreases in wages would then be needed, together with a requirement that permits raise the wage bill less than the 3 percent required for price stability (and a requirement for still more such permits for actually lowering the wage bill). This would have served to cure the self-fulfilling deflation of the 1930s; it could be what was sought in the pre-New Deal attempts of the National Industrial Recovery Act to raise prices, such as "Blue Eagle" appeals to patriotism and ideology or the 1934 increase in the price of gold.

(11) Some concern has been expressed that there would be speculation and hoarding of permits. I can see no harm in speculation, but if it is desirable to prevent fluctuations in the price of the permits to make it easier for firms to plan, it would be possible for the government to engage in "counterspeculation"—that is, buying and selling permits and pegging their price. The problems here are identical with those of fixing the rate of foreign exchange. (The concept of counterspeculation is developed in my books, *The Economics of Control*, 1944, and *Flation*, 1972.) In this case, as in the case of foreign exchanges, I think the argument for a free-market price is the most convincing one.

There is no "hoarding" problem. Any permits purchased for speculative purposes would be loaned out and would still perform their function. The owner of a permit can gain nothing by holding it unused.

(12) There is also the issue of compliance. WIPP requires monitoring to ensure that there is no cheating. This has been considered equivalent to the problem of monitoring compliance with the wage and price regulations of the controls period. However, in that case innumerable prices of different products as well as different wages had to be checked for compliance to see if they were in accordance with the guidelines, and all the problems of checking the quality of products and grades of labor were encountered. None of these applies to WIPP. There is only the problem of ensuring that people do not claim to possess permits that they do not have or provide false wage statements. These situations involve only the detection of fraud. They do not seem to be different in kind or volume from those that are currently being handled by the Internal Revenue Service in connection with auditing the income tax.

(13) WIPP does not require calculations of average wage, classified or unclassified.

(14) It is certain that WIPP and most forms of TIP would be denounced as antilabor because they regulate wages and not prices. Workers might fear that holding down wages would not result in a corresponding constraint on prices so that real wages could fall. The government could alleviate such fears by a guarantee to compensate all employees for the average decline in real wages or for wages failing to increase by a considerable amount. There would be little risk in this for the government. If, in fact, real wages increased by less than the increase in productivity, enormous profits would have been made on which the government could collect high taxes.

It is most inadvisable for the government to attempt to win the support of the workers by giving them an initial tax rebate equal to the wage increase that is prevented by TIP or WIPP. It would give the workers a large increase in real income. The pay raise, based on anticipated inflation, would be used to buy goods at the disinflated prices. It would preempt a major part of the benefits from the possible increase in output generated by the success in combating the depression. Although the pay raise would be worth paying for the sake of obtaining future benefits, there is the danger that it would establish a precedent for workers to expect more than the economy could provide for them in wages; moreover, it could develop into a permanent and economically devastating subsidy to wages that would entail heavy taxation and drastic reductions in government services to prevent demand inflation.

(15) It is frequently implied and occasionally even stated explicitly that workers must want the inflation or else they would not insist on pay increases that are responsible for it. But even if it were conceded that all workers were good economists and understood this, it does not follow that they want the result. No workers decide to attempt to raise wages in general. They decide only to push for the increase in the wages of their particular group. The purpose of TIP and, indeed, the primary purpose of WIPP is to internalize the externality by placing into the particular pay envelope the effects of the wage increase decision on the economy as a whole. To say that workers make individual demands because they want the collective result is similar to saying that, in the case of a fire, people who rush to the exit, knowing that if they individually rush to the exits those exits will block and they will collectively perish, must desire that result!

Implications for Policy: A Symposium

GARDNER ACKLEY
University of Michigan

WE OWE a considerable debt of gratitude to Sidney Weintraub, Henry Wallich, Laurence Seidman, and Arthur Okun for developing the concept of the tax-based incomes policy (TIP), and for keeping it alive in the face of public and professional disinterest. I believe that the papers and discussion of this conference have greatly advanced our understanding of the implications of the proposal, even if they have not answered all questions nor, I am sure, produced general agreement even in this room.

Among economists, just as among other groups, there is and will be opposition to TIP by those who oppose in principle any incomes policy. I am regarded—correctly, I suppose—as one who is skeptical about TIPs.[1] But it surely is not because I am opposed to incomes policies in principle. I first publicly called for such a policy in the 1958 Joint Economic Committee study on the relationship of prices to economic stability and growth.[2] I have supported the use of an incomes policy ever since, and have repeatedly urged that such a policy be established during every subsequent period in which it was not in use. I suppose my participation in administering and defending the guidepost policy of the 1960s equaled or exceeded both in duration and intensity that of any other person; and it reflected an enthusiastic personal commitment. I accept the analysis in George Perry's paper for this conference as fully consistent with a general

1. Gardner Ackley, "Okun's New Tax-Based Incomes-Policy Proposal," *Economic Outlook, USA*, vol. 5 (Winter 1978), pp. 8–9.
2. Gardner Ackley, "A Third Approach to the Analysis and Control of Inflation," in *The Relationship of Prices to Economic Stability and Growth*, Compendium of Papers Submitted by Panelists Appearing before the Joint Economic Committee, March 31, 1958, 85:2 (Government Printing Office, 1958), pp. 619–36.

view of the inflationary process that I have held and promoted for twenty years or more, and I regard the paper as providing a fully adequate theoretical and empirical basis for an economist to support an incomes policy.

Thus, in my view, the question is not whether to use an incomes policy but only what kind to use. There are numerous models, of which I may perhaps usefully delineate three. I eliminate a fourth (compulsory controls) as far too costly in economic, administrative, political, and moral terms.

The first model is that of an incomes policy enforced by "jawboning" and related forms of education, pressure, and persuasion, which centered in the White House during the period 1962–68. From what I know or can assume about the plans of the Carter administration, its present intention regarding an incomes policy conforms essentially to that model. To be sure, the basic standard—"deceleration"—is considerably more vague than the Kennedy-Johnson guideposts; and it is not clear that the policy commands even as much genuine administration commitment as it did in the 1960s. On the other hand, the Council on Wage and Price Stability should supply considerably more and better staff support than we ever had.

I have previously outlined what I regard as the principal weaknesses of the jawboning model.[3] They include (1) the absence of any significant "legitimacy" for the policy in the eyes of those most affected, either through the actual involvement of leaders from the business and labor communities in advisory or policymaking roles, or through any legislative basis for the program;[4] (2) the personal identification of the program with the President, which has disadvantages both to the program and to the presidency that I regard as greatly outweighing the advantages to either; (3) the inevitable highly adversary character of the procedure; (4) the rather hit-or-miss application, primarily to cases that happen to draw government or public attention; and (5) the adherence of a firm or a union to such a policy that rests on the acceptance of a social or political responsibility contrary to economic interest. To be sure, if participation were general, the actual cost to each might be negligible. Even so, the paradox is that the greater the general participation, the greater the individual economic advantage in nonparticipation. I do not consider this as a necessarily fatal defect; but it must be recognized as a weakness.

3. For example, in Gardner Ackley, "An Incomes Policy for the 1970's," *Review of Economics and Statistics,* vol. 54 (August 1972), pp. 218–23.

4. The Council on Wage and Price Stability now at least has a legislative basis.

The TIP model avoids many of these disadvantages. Its necessary congressional mandate gives it political legitimacy; labor and business leaders have the opportunity to become involved at least during the legislative stage; the presidency is not demeaned by brawling confrontation with firms and unions. Rather, each private group makes its own decisions, taking account of costs and benefits, and there is no arbitrary or accidental selection of cases (except through legislative action to exempt areas of the economy from coverage or to provide special treatment).

On the other hand, as the papers and discussions indicate, TIP has its own problems. I am convinced that a price-TIP would be an administrative nightmare. Yet the politics of "wage control without price control" may require that we accept some control on prices if we want to have TIP at all, as Albert Rees and others have pointed out. Moreover, the overwhelming econometric evidence that prices follow wages is demonstrated only at the macro level, not for firms and industries. The public may not understand the benefit of wage restraint, or wish to tolerate it, if the restraint in particular cases is or appears to be appropriated by particular employers. This I believe to be the key to union opposition to incomes policies. I am impressed with several of Rees' points about the difficulties of TIP when an employer deals with several unions or when a union deals with an industry. Indeed, I raised some of these same questions.

I am troubled by the necessary choice between the greater effectiveness of a continuous, penalty-TIP on wages (which Seidman's paper demonstrates) and the far greater administrative costs, public and private, which such a program entails (shown in the paper by Larry Dildine and Emil Sunley and in comments by Richard Slitor). On the basis of previous experience with wage and price legislation, I think we must be prepared to assume that each special interest—and this policy will touch them all—will press for special provisions to protect that interest, either in the initial legislation or in subsequent amendments. Such legislative provisions can destroy the effectiveness of the policy or create an administrative monstrosity, or both, as has happened in the past with price and wage controls. (This is also a well-established characteristic of tax legislation.)

In my view, the chief administrative problem is not tax evasion or even cheating, but rather that, say, one-half of the 1 percent of the firms covered will claim some aspect of the general rules to be unworkable or unfair.[5] Perhaps 10 percent of these complaints cannot be dismissed out of hand. If coverage is substantial—certainly close to universal—this one-twentieth of 1 percent of firms means the administering agency and the Congress must spend millions of man-hours to develop some remedies. And if either the agency or the Congress modifies the regulation or the legislation to handle a case, that almost certainly creates new problems or opportunities for others.

My judgment is that if the TIP model could at least be confined to wages, which may not be politically feasible, it is clearly preferable to the jawboning model of incomes policy. This is with the understanding, as James Duesenberry argued, that TIP is regarded only as a part of a continuing effort to build a consensus in support of mutual restraint.

There is, however, a third possible model, based primarily on voluntarism and persuasion, which might be preferable to TIP. I have described it elsewhere,[6] and will not repeat it here, except to indicate that it includes (1) a *highly selective* coverage of both wages and prices; (2) a legislatively established administrative agency with certain limited powers to require reporting and to delay increases that are above the standard; (3) essential independence from the White House; and (4) fairly elaborate formal arrangements for the advisory involvement of representatives of labor, business, and the public. The administrative (as opposed to the legislative) character of this model more easily permits ad hoc adjustments to avoid the various kinds of efficiency losses our discussion has noted. And it accommodates Rees' observation about the desirability (on occasion) of having incomes policy administrators "help in the settlement of actual or potential disputes in collective bargaining or in the improvement of collective bargaining structures."

My proposal describing this third model has been in the public domain for a considerable period and has attracted little interest, which probably indicates that it is fatally flawed. I refer to it only to point out that the choice is not between jawboning and TIP, or nothing. Social invention has been badly needed in this area and, while TIP is an outstanding candidate, there may be still other possibilities or variants of an incomes policy that would be either economically and administratively more efficient or politically more attractive.

5. By "unfair" I mean that there is an alternative, plausible way to apply the general principle involved that would be more favorable to the complaining firm.

6. See "An Incomes Policy for the 1970's," pp. 222–23.

ALAN S. GREENSPAN
Townsend-Greenspan Company

I HAVE NEVER been persuaded that incomes policies, if that term can be generalized, can work for any protracted period of time or leave any permanent effect on the wage and price structure. Nonetheless, it is clear that the TIP proposals try to confront some of the basic problems of most incomes policies.

Because there is a great deal of incentive—whether carrot or stick— involved in the TIP proposals, they are assumed to simulate market processes in many respects. Thus, if TIP were not employed as a substitute for conventional fiscal and monetary policies, some anti-inflation impact might be achieved. Certainly in the abstract, as the model developed by Laurence Seidman illustrates, it is not difficult to construct fairly general conditions in which TIP would appear to have some marginal advantage.

The difficulty I have had and still have, especially after these meetings, is that, while we can construct a simplified model in which a tax-based incomes policy could work, the abstraction can never fully capture the complexity of a TIP in application. On this point I find myself in agreement with Joseph Pechman. No one questions that we are dealing with a problem in which administration is difficult. But is that difficulty merely something that could be overcome with operational experience, or are we confronted with an issue in which the complexity of administration is its fatal flaw?

I suspect there is no solution to the administrative problem. Larry Dildine and Emil Sunley did an excellent job on their paper. However, it strikes me that they barely scratched the surface of the problems we would confront with a TIP in full-scale operation. Those problems would not be significantly different from the administrative nightmare of our wage-price control experience that occurred after August 1971. What struck me about that period was the inconceivable complexity of what the controllers were attempting to do, firm by firm, product by product, wage by wage, and how the entire process held together, largely because the controllers never really attempted to confront market forces head-on.

There was an accusation at the time that the administrators who ran the control program did not have their heart in it and, therefore, the program could not be successful. In fact, every time they attempted to make the control system work—in the sense of trying to prevent companies and unions from doing what they would ordinarily do—the program ran into extraordinary problems, and the controllers backed away.

One important aspect of Phases II and III of the control program to remember is that although price and cost data were submitted in detail, they were never appropriately audited. There was no effort to actively administer the program. It was de facto a voluntary program characterized by a huge paper flow, frenetic committee meetings, and vague pronouncements. It was fundamentally wheel-spinning. But if TIP were implemented, legislation would require auditing and verification of the elements of the system to the same degree that our tax system is audited. This would create an insurmountable administrative problem. Litigation would quickly swamp the courts and make TIP politically infeasible almost immediately. That does not mean it may not be tried. There is a growing sense of desperation that could easily trigger risk-laden policy initiatives. If the cost of a failure of this type of program were zero, or there were only inconveniences associated with it, there would be no reason not to try. At worst, we would end up with an administrative mess but with no permanent damage. However, there *are* significant costs to every policy failure; and in constructing policy initiatives, it is essential to be aware of what happens if the policy initiative goes wrong. That is certainly true of fiscal and monetary policies.

If a TIP were tried, judging from what has happened during past control programs, the participants would rapidly learn how to beat the system. Because it would be almost physically impossible to maintain an appropriate audit of wages and prices, the extent of avoidance, if not evasion, would become far greater than anything even remotely contemplated in the income tax system. This could be quite disruptive to economic policy.

In the case of TIP, even if it failed, we would still have in place a control-oriented bureaucracy, and I fear the political pressures that would emerge to employ it. When government in effect considers certain price or wage relationships appropriate and a quasi-voluntary program fails to induce them, there is strong political pressure to mandate them.

Obviously, to the extent that a TIP program is narrowed and limited, the problems I outlined above are also narrowed. Thus, a TIP based on a limited form of the stick approach that was restricted to wages and to large companies would only sharply reduce administrative and auditing requirements. Those requirements would still be voluminous and fraught with problems—many of them unforeseeable—but it is unlikely that the system would be swamped by them. However, to the extent that TIP is narrowed, whatever positive benefits are expected in theory would be lost. It is difficult to make an effective judgment a priori on the trade-off between administrative simplicity and anti-inflation benefits. My suspicion is, however, that the impact on wages from a limited program is likely to be much too small to be worth implementing. For even a limited TIP is a large program that would entail administrative burdens. Unless there is a reasonable expectation of a significant anti-inflation payoff, it is difficult to make a case for going ahead with even a limited TIP.

That is not to say I see a simple solution to the current type of chronic inflation. I am not persuaded a 6 or 7 percent inflation rate cannot be changed and that the unwinding that began in 1975 and lasted through late 1976 is necessarily over. If it is, I would be gravely concerned that some form of unsuspected capacity restraint is being created. At this stage, it would seem that it is still possible to continue unwinding the inflationary pressures, provided that reasonable macropolicies are maintained. I think it is much too soon to throw in the sponge on macropolicy, especially if TIP is being considered as the alternative.

This conference has made a great contribution toward airing a number of the problems confronting TIP. But it may be even more complex than those of us who have been involved in similar undertakings suspect and, hence, more analysis is needed. I am most concerned that the administrative problems will be dismissed too easily. If that occurs, some very serious policy difficulties may be the consequence.

FRANCO MODIGLIANI
Massachusetts Institute of Technology

IT IS SOMEWHAT embarrassing to follow two speakers who have had a lot to do with setting up price controls, managing them, and seeing them from the inside. My only claim to being here is that in testimony before Congress in 1971, following an appeal by Kenneth Galbraith for price controls, I strongly urged Congress to avoid price controls and suggested that if it were really serious about controlling inflation it should consider an approach that accomplishes the same objectives but is much simpler.

The approach recommended was basically a variant of the Weintraub-Wallich plan. It relied on the general principle that the law decides which expenses are deductible in the computation of taxes. Wage increases in excess of some established guideposts would not be a deductible expense for the purpose of calculating profits. In effect, wage increases granted over and above the guideposts would come entirely out of the net after-tax profits, instead of 48 percent being paid by the Treasury.

One could also think of a more sophisticated taxation scheme in which an excess profits tax is imposed on the increase of profit margins per dollar of sale above some base period, but without allowing the deduction of wages in excess of the agreed amount in computing the profit margin.

Let me begin by stating that it seems to me that TIP, no matter what form it takes, should be considered only for the purpose of breaking momentum inflation, a theory that Perry has described so well in his paper. He has shown that the source of current inflation is largely momentum. If that momentum could be broken, most people would be better off, and no one would be worse off.

Inflation can be very costly or only moderately costly. But certainly it is costly in practice. At the same time, there is no question in my mind that TIP has distortive effects. The best possible TIP, including that of Lerner, still has some disruptive effects. Accordingly, a transitional TIP might be best.

I agree with Alan Greenspan that inflation is probably still declining in response to high unemployment. Inflation may fluctuate, but it is probably on the expected declining course. Because the effects of unemployment are slow and systematic, the inflation rate could bounce up after a year or two in which unemployment declined fairly fast. But nonetheless, the process via unemployment is extremely costly and painful. If there is another disruption from any source, more restrictive fiscal policies will follow. These issues ought to be faced.

Almost everyone participating in the discussion seems to agree that TIP, although perhaps not the ideal answer, is better than controls. The bleak picture that Alan Greenspan has described in managing price controls is something I have seen on many occasions when I lived through many price-control experiences in Italy. My doctoral dissertation was about Italian price controls in 1935. They were a nightmare.

What we really have to control is wages. But politically it is very difficult to do that without also controlling prices. In fact, it probably cannot be done. That is why I think TIP is really promising—because it can be applied fundamentally to wages, possibly with some reinforcement from an excess profits tax. There are, as we have seen, two basic kinds of TIPs, the carrot TIP and the stick TIP. From the point of view of its appeal, the carrot TIP is far superior. Arthur Okun should be given a great deal of credit for developing a concept that in principle is highly attractive for many reasons. Like the stick, the carrot is easier to apply to wages than to prices. But I have doubts about feasibility because, as most seem to agree, reward must be universal. The government cannot treat a large firm and a small firm differently and provide one with the incentive and not the other. It has to be universal, and if it is going to be universal, it runs into the problems that Joseph Pechman has described quite well.

In my view, the enforcement problems, which may be severe even for large firms, are worse for small firms. Thus, if the employee of a small firm is promoted and receives a higher wage, the firm exceeds the target. Every small firm will have a similar problem. Employees would be changing positions, and there would be no way of forming a base. Think of the new employee at a firm that has already granted large wage increases. He does not receive the benefit of the tax rebate, even though he himself did not have an increase in wages. I think that the horror stories are almost unlimited. The problem of administration would seem nearly impossible.

Then there is the stick TIP. This approach could work through higher corporate tax rates, which is the original Wallich-Weintraub form, or through the nondeductibility of wages, which is the proposal I have made. But I have to modify that claim. After I made that proposal, Senator Proxmire asked me to investigate whether anything like that had ever existed. I then turned to Cary Brown, who pointed out that during World War II there was a provision that allowed the Treasury to disallow deductibility of wages in excess of wage control. So there is a historical precedent, and that is one great advantage.[1]

Of course, there are problems of enforcement with my proposal, too. I would support Okun's suggestion to let firms decide at the beginning of the period how they will classify workers. Let them decide whether they want to report by per capita, by standardized classes, or by any similar system. We do not need to strive for perfection if we rely on TIP as a temporary program, by which we aim to lower inflation by, say, 1 percent a year for three consecutive years, and then call a halt to the program, cutting our losses. And let us be sure that at the time we dismantle the program, we have not reached an unemployment rate that is too low. Otherwise, we immediately re-create a problem. Thus, the enforcement problems do not strike me as totally insoluble, although I agree with Alan Greenspan that once we have settled on one of these methods, we should explore it further.

One problem that would arise is obtaining the cooperation of labor. What we heard from Albert Rees is discouraging; however, his comments focused on the Wallich and Weintraub approach. For the purpose of catching the public's attention, Wallich referred to his approach as backboning rather than jawboning. But that is the wrong way to present the case to the public and to labor—as a plan that would force employers to stand up against labor.

Another way to say it is: here is a program to reduce inflation that uses the guidelines that have been established, and everyone has an interest in sticking to it. We want to put some public disapproval on those who do not stick to it by attaching certain penalties. That places all the emphasis on cooperation, and none at all on backboning. We must minimize the extent of violations. But we could agree that if people want to violate the principle, they may have good reasons, and they may pay the penalty.

Nonetheless, it should be made clear that the intent and purpose is not

1. U.S. Bureau of Internal Revenue, Regulations 111, Subpart B, sec. 29.23(a)-16, published in U.S. Treasury Department, *Regulations 111 Relating to the Income Tax* (Government Printing Office, 1943).

at all to impose the burden of slowing inflation on labor through lower *real* wages. The goal is to benefit everybody. Since the response of prices to wages should be fast, inflation will slow down. There may be a little lag. When wages are rising at only 6 percent, prices may be rising more than 4 percent, but the two variables ought to be declining close together. I think that is the sort of thing that has to be emphasized.

However, there are still other problems. One is that the proposal sounds like an antilabor approach. Second, it is applied only to wages and not to prices. And there is a third aspect: there might be a tendency for the penalty on increases in wages to be transferred into higher prices. Because the excessive wage settlement costs the firm much more, TIP might have this effect. From this point of view, there is much to be said for combining the nondeductibility of excess wage increases with an excess profits tax on the profit margin above some level. In that case, it is highly unlikely that the firm will find it to its advantage to pass on the higher cost in higher prices. That would be a guarantee for labor that they are protected against an expansion of profit margins.

This system should be applied fundamentally to a small number of firms, say, 2,000 as an arbitrary number. That it can be applied to a small number of firms is a helpful point of departure. There is, to be sure, the risk that as we approach full employment, the greatest push may come from the low-wage workers in small firms. That is a problem, and we should not press too hard for full employment. There may be a way to combine coverage of firms employing more than X people with that of unions representing more than Y people. Such unions may deal with many firms, and penalties would be applied at the level of the firm.

Let me conclude by stating some of the main problems of a TIP. One area of concern is the administration problems that we have heard about from the experts, particularly the legal and management aspects. It seems to me another serious problem is starting out. In the beginning, some people will have had a recent increase in wages, and others will not have had one for three years; that raises the issue of equity.

That is a tough problem, and I have learned a great deal about this from Gardner Ackley on a recent occasion when he talked about the efforts to maintain equity in a program of this kind. The problem would probably be alleviated if the average wage of the three years preceding the program were used as a base from which to compute allowable wage increases. Limited duration of the program would also help.

I have already mentioned the distortive effects. I believe that any TIP will have such effects beside the desired effect of slowing inflation. It is important to be aware of this, and try to dismantle any such program as fast as possible.

I am inclined to disagree with Alan Greenspan's pessimism about the possible effect of failure of this policy. I do not understand why there should be pressure on the political system. The experience we had at the end of Phase IV was that everybody was fed up with it, even those who had been in favor of it. Only four years later those failures seem to be forgotten!

I am not impressed with the argument that TIP would create evasion pressure. Evasion pressure assumes that firms are eager to pay higher wages. It seems to me that pressure to evade is questionable, because it provides a basis on which the firm can stand. It supplies an "objective" figure for the firm, at which it can say, "That is the point at which we stop."

In the end, I think a TIP design based on a stick approach with a limited number of firms—possibly my proposal or something similar—deserves further consideration. Certainly this conference has persuaded me that all forms of TIP, including my own version, are not as alluring as they once seemed. But reliance on unemployment still appears to me to be even less alluring.

Comments
and Discussion

Henry C. Wallich: Of course, nobody likes TIP per se. It is really a question of the alternatives. We are running out of good options and have to look at choices among unattractive ones. The discussion of this conference has brought up a number of important points, some of which have caused me to change my mind about various issues.

For instance, I am no longer persuaded that the income tax is necessarily the best tax through which to levy a penalty. Perhaps disallowance of excess wage increases, despite the possible adverse shifting effects, is a more meaningful and manageable procedure. There is a precedent for it in the tax code.

In addition, I am no longer convinced that TIP must be widespread in its coverage. Perhaps the top 2,000 firms would be the appropriate universe with which to deal in order to simplify the administrative problems.

I have also acquired some doubts as to the fixity of the link between prices and wages. If a plan is to be at all acceptable to labor, that relationship needs to be demonstrated more firmly both at the empirical and the theoretical level. But there are ways of overcoming the doubts and reassuring labor against the danger of runaway profits. If those profits should tend to go above some benchmark level, one could impose a surcharge on the corporate profits tax that would stabilize the share of profits in the GNP. Such a surcharge would not be an excess profits tax on any single company but one on the entire corporate sector, including high earners and low earners.

At one time I thought TIP should be terminated as quickly as possible. But the possibility of reducing the natural rate of unemployment strikes me as an important point in favor of a TIP of longer duration. I feel that Laurence Seidman's argument on this matter is fairly clear and persuasive.

If TIP could lower inflation, that benefit could be used to lower inflation at the existing natural rate of unemployment, hold inflation constant at a lower natural rate, or something in between, as long as TIP remained in force and its guideline were lowered year by year.

Finally, I am gratified that the discussion here has been largely between those who would favor some form of TIP and those who are generally skeptical about it. It is important that the various proponents of the different schemes have not argued against each other, but rather have tried to develop the implications of the alternative approaches to see how something viable could be best constructed. Nothing is ever enacted the way it is first proposed. The need at this point is to keep the discussion going. If I could push a button to make a proposed TIP go into effect now, I would not push that button; but I would urge strongly that we continue to examine this type of proposal.

Arthur M. Okun: I see an urgent need to develop new strategies against inflation because the outlook on the present scenario is extremely bleak. I believe that inflation has already accelerated a little above the 6 percent plateau of recent years. That movement stems, not from excess demand, but from an inevitable catch-up in nonunion wage rates, a gradual adaptation of private decisionmaking to the higher secular inflation rate, and an addictive attachment by the government to cost-raising measures—just the opposite of the constructive course that Robert Crandall outlined in his paper. I wish I could share Franco Modigliani's and Alan Greenspan's brighter view of the economic outlook. In my judgment, inflation will next decelerate only when unemployment rises and, in light of the current stance of monetary policy, probably during a recession. Of course, as George Perry highlighted in his paper, recession will slow inflation, but only at the absurd cost in production of roughly $200 billion per point.

Faced by costs of that magnitude from recession, our society is challenged to find some mechanism for a mutual deescalation of wages and prices in prosperity. When our common interests so clearly outweigh the conflicting interests of various groups, the ability of the nation to lick stagflation is a serious test of our democratic political process, and not merely a question of our ability to find the right unemployment rate. TIP and the cost-reducing strategy, focusing on reductions of payroll and excise taxes, are a route to mutual deescalation without recession.

I have no deep substantive convictions about the relative merits of a reward TIP and a penalty TIP. I first tried to promote interest in the Wallich-Weintraub plan in 1973; many people who were sympathetic to its objectives regarded it as inequitable and hence politically unacceptable. Because of that reaction, I sought to convert the stick to a carrot. To be fair to workers *in fact,* a penalty TIP on wages needs some indemnification for the first year, when, according to the empirical evidence, the slowdown in prices would be likely to lag behind a slowdown of wages. To be fair to workers *in image,* however, a penalty TIP needs further modifications; I believe that some of the suggestions made at this conference may point the way.

If a penalty TIP were incorporated into proposed legislation, I would support it enthusiastically. Nonetheless, I am convinced that a reward TIP belongs on our list of promising options. Unquestionably, rewards must be offered *universally* to employees of small firms as well as large ones. Undoubtedly, universal coverage adds to administrative burdens, but, I would insist, to only a limited degree. The same set of rules must be prepared on how to evaluate compensation whether the program applies to a handful or a myriad of firms. In this connection, as Richard Slitor suggested, the present rules developed for the income tax—on such issues as pension funding, stock options, and health insurance—are entirely adequate for a TIP, whether its coverage is narrow or universal. If they are good enough for a universal tax under which corporations pay 48 cents per dollar, they are good enough to handle a marginal increment or decrement in the tax rate. The only enforcement of any penalty or reward TIP would operate by auditing tax returns, rather than by monitoring behavior or requiring advance approval of action. If the low-probability threat of audit is a reasonably effective way to make all firms comply with the provisions for depreciation, the investment tax credit, expense allowances, and all the other complex features of our income tax, then it should be good enough for a reward TIP. Obviously, a universal program would raise more inquiries from taxpayers, necessitate more mailing, and hence require a larger staff at the Internal Revenue Service to provide those services. But surely that is a small set of added costs.

Nor is the record keeping required of firms in a reward TIP inherently any more onerous than that imposed by the employment tax credit or the deductibility rules for entertainment and travel expenses. But suppose that the Congress shared Joseph Pechman's view that it is an onerous burden on small firms. In that event, if Congress insisted that tiny businesses with, say, less than 20 workers could qualify their employees for the reward with a mere pledge of good faith to restrain wages, the program would lose little of its effectiveness.

The basic advantage of a reward TIP is that, when businessmen have the opportunity to qualify their employees for a tax cut, they have a strong incentive to translate that tax cut into a slowdown of wages. Because of the rational self-interest of employers, a reward TIP should have a significant marginal effect on the actual wages paid by firms. After hearing the criticisms made at this conference, I remain convinced that a reward TIP on wages is an entirely feasible and manageable program.

On the other hand, I am convinced by criticism, particularly from Gardner Ackley, that a price reward raises severe administrative problems. I was searching for symmetry in proposing that, but the measurement of prices is not symmetrical with that of wages. Because price measurement is so complex, a feature that was intended to assure workers of evenhandedness might turn out to bestow arbitrary and unmerited tax cuts on some business firms.

Any TIP must be built on the foundations of a social consensus in favor of mutual deescalation. It will take a lot of education and more bitter experience to convince a majority of citizens that TIP may be the option that is the least bad. The polls tell us that the American people— union members, as much as any group—detest inflation. Albert Rees has not told us how labor leaders will react when they realize that the realistic alternative to TIP is a series of recurrent recessions brought about through monetary restraint. The U.S. inflation rate will be lowered over the next decade; the serious question is whether that is going to be accomplished by inefficient and inhumane recessions, by stifling price-wage controls, or by some innovative, sensible method like TIP.

General Discussion

Charles Holt pointed to a new rich body of data that might be useful for simulating the administrative problems of a TIP. The information, constructed largely for research purposes by the unemployment compensation system, is based on quarterly reports from employers in thirty-seven states on the earnings and hours of individual workers and is being assembled into a longitudinal sample.

Joseph Pechman cautioned Franco Modigliani against coupling an excess profits tax with a penalty TIP on wages, noting the adverse experience with that tax during wartime periods and its deservedly bad reputation.

Alan Greenspan felt that the conference had produced something approaching a consensus that the penalty TIP on wages is the form most likely to have a reasonable chance of effectiveness and administrative feasibility. Yet it was clearly the scheme that was most difficult to sell politically. George Perry agreed that the administrative advantages of a penalty TIP had been emphasized by many at the conference; but he did not find the arguments convincing. He thought firms were much less likely to cheat in claiming rewards for their workers than in minimizing liabilities for penalties on themselves. Because of its universality, a reward TIP could afford more leakages and still have a larger total impact in slowing inflation. Finally, he was not convinced that random audits from the Internal Revenue Service were an ineffective technique of enforcement because they seemed to work reasonably for the income tax as a whole.

William Brainard thought that Modigliani's remarks about the distortions of a TIP raised many broader issues. To the extent that TIP alters relative prices, the consequences depend on whether (and if so, how) inflation itself distorts relative prices, as is frequently asserted. Brainard shared Laurence Seidman's view that TIP would work in part by changing expectations. The resulting deceleration of inflation need not have any adverse allocational costs.

Index

DATE DUE

GAYLORD

PRINTED IN U.S.A.